20/20 MONEY

FISHER INVESTMENTS PRESS

Fisher Investments Press brings the research, analysis, and market intelligence of Fisher Investments' research team, headed by CEO and *New York Times* best-selling author Ken Fisher, to all investors. The Press covers a range of investing and market-related topics for a wide audience—from novices to enthusiasts to professionals.

Books by Ken Fisher
The Ten Roads to Riches
The Only Three Questions That Count
100 Minds That Made the Market
The Wall Street Waltz
Super Stocks

Fisher Investments Series
Own the World
Aaron Anderson

20/20 Money
Michael J. Hanson

Fisher Investments On Series
Fisher Investments on Energy
Fisher Investments on Materials
Fisher Investments on Consumer Staples

FISHER
INVESTMENTS
PRESS

20/20 MONEY

See the Markets
Clearly and Invest Better
than the Pros

MICHAEL J. HANSON

WILEY

John Wiley & Sons, Inc.

Published by John Wiley & Sons, Inc., Hoboken, New Jersey.
Published simultaneously in Canada.
Photo credits: Corbis Digital Stock.

For general information on our other products and services or for technical support, please contact our Customer Care Department within the United States at (800) 762-2974, outside the United States at (317) 572-3993 or fax (317) 572-4002.

Wiley also publishes its books in a variety of electronic formats. Some content that appears in print may not be available in electronic books. For more information about Wiley products, visit our web site at www.wiley.com.

Library of Congress Cataloging-in-Publication Data:

Hanson, Michael J., 1979-
    20/20 money : see the markets clearly and invest better than the pros / Michael Hanson.
        p.   cm.— (Fisher Investments Press)
    Includes bibliographical references and index.
    ISBN 978-0-470-28539-8 (cloth)
        1. Investments.   2. Investment analysis.   3. Portfolio management.   4. Speculation.
    I. Title.   II. Title: Twenty, twenty money.
  HG4521.H2384   2009
  332.6—dc22   2009000841

Printed in the United States of America

10   9   8   7   6   5   4   3   2   1

Then, they were Mom and Dad, and they taught me everything I needed to know by example of their own principled lives. Today, they are Loree and Cary, two of my best friends. That is wondrous good fortune.

CONTENTS

ACKNOWLEDGMENTS

Of all the professional gifts I have been given, learning how to think—how to see the world and make one's way in it—is the best one I can imagine. It's been my great privilege to serve and learn under Ken Fisher, Andrew Teufel, and Jeff Silk—the three members of Fisher Investments' Investment Policy Committee. From them, I have obtained skills and lessons that will remain with me the rest of my days. In some sense, I owe everyone at Fisher Investments a debt of gratitude, for if it's true that we are only as good as those we choose to work with, I am humbled by the thought.

It's also true that hard work and desire mean nothing without opportunity, and in that spirit I owe a great deal of thanks to Andrew Teufel and Fabrizio Ornani—two who gave me more chances than I probably deserved and believed in me to achieve when there was often little reason to.

Then there is Lara Hoffmans. Good writing, even investment writing, is about clarity, intelligence, daring, freedom, and energy. None of that exists without her presence and influence on Fisher Investments Press. And that is especially true of this book and the daily work we do at Fisher Investments' MarketMinder.com website.

Anyone who's ever written anything knows first drafts are always terrible. It's in the editing process a manuscript goes from dreadful to serviceable, eventually becoming something worthwhile. I owe Dina Ezzat, Ashley Muth, and Evelyn Chea much thanks in that effort, and also Jason Dorrier and Carolyn Feng for their honest opinions when I needed them. The same goes for the team at Wiley, especially David Pugh and Kelly O'Connor—their expertise and guidance, on issues large and small, always made a big difference. And Marc Haberman and Molly Lienesch deserve enormous credit for making Fisher Investments Press a reality.

Last, investing books aren't much without data. So the help I received from the Fisher Investments Research Department was invaluable throughout the process, and the same is true for the folks at Thomson Datastream, MSCI Inc., and Global Financial Data for providing the data for our research.

INTRODUCTION

We need a new investing lens. Most investor mistakes come from blindness about the basic ways markets work and the best strategies to invest. This book is designed to be a set of glasses to help you see the markets more clearly. Having 20/20 investing vision means making more money, and that's my ultimate goal for you.

Sight is by far the most important human sense—life as we know it is more or less impossible without it. But the notion of sight is also one of life's most important metaphors. We often talk about sight when we really mean understanding. We have "visions" about the future, we "see things clearly," we have "points of view," and so on. To see, in other words, is to understand.

Too many investors are blinded by conventional investing ideas that don't work. This book is about seeing the stock investing landscape clearly—investigating new ideas and challenging widely held conventions. I wrote this book to tell investors the things I wish they knew about investing, to give them a clearer view and thus make better decisions.

I'm no investing guru, but I work for one. For years, I've been an analyst working under Ken Fisher. In that time, I've learned his methods and have also studied the methods of many others. One day, just a few weeks into my career at Fisher Investments, Ken addressed a group of employees. He said, *"If you want to be any good at investing, you have to go out and learn about the whole world and how it works."* That will stick with me forever.

"Learning how the world works" is a tricky thing. Most investors will attack the problem by seeking "the rules." People crave conventions, laws, systems . . . predictable order. The fact is, there is no "black box" or rule set you can follow for successful investing. If there were, we'd all just do so and be trillionaires by now. If there's one thing I'm sure of, it's that there is never "enough" learning about the world because the world is always changing. Investing successfully is closer to "being along for the ride" than coming to some grand conclusion or final wisdom.

So this book is not a manifesto. Often, it will raise more questions than it answers—and that's a good thing. It's designed to make you think better about your investing choices, not give you some set of rules to blindly follow. I want you to see clearer. This is a series of observations and thoughts about markets and investors in my time as an analyst. If you want rules, go somewhere else. My aim is to allow you to see things in a different way than the consensus—to help you think differently. Often, a mere shift in perspective is all it takes. The world is a changing, dynamic, evolving thing. So to learn how the world (and specifically, investments) works, it's vastly more important to learn how to *think* about them.

Often, investors believe it's impractical to spend time on flighty or abstract issues like how to think or to understand a concept more fully. In my view, it's the most practical thing possible for investors to pursue—getting that part right underlies all else, saving time, angst, and, importantly, money. Amazingly, few ever learn how to think! Not in college, high school . . . not in exams . . . nowhere! So a lot of this book is going to seem unorthodox simply because similar content is relatively sparse.

Chess players understand this intuitively: There are tactics and there are strategies. Tactics are what players do on a move-by-move basis, but *strategy* is what drives the logic of those moves and the shape of the game—and, ultimately, success. No standard set of moves can always win because eventually your opponent catches on. But a well-defined strategy will help you make real-time decisions to beat your opponent in a constantly changing environment (the composition of the chess board).

Similarly, investors (and I'm talking about professionals, too) overwhelmingly focus on details like economic data, valuations, trading techniques, tax efficiencies, and so on (all important things, no doubt), without ever really having a fully developed, well-tested, and appropriate philosophy to help drive their decisions. Mounds of data and tactics, but no real comprehension or strategy! Instead, they use a hodgepodge of theories and methods that often unwittingly conflict and contradict . . . and then later wonder why their portfolio results are subpar. It's like using reading glasses to gaze at the stars or a telescope to read a book! The lenses are distorting the views.

The way I see it, successful stock investing over the long term is about two things:

1. Thinking about investing problems the right way to make the right choices in an always-evolving market environment.
2. Discipline and self-knowledge.

I'll be blunt: Neither of those is easy to achieve. Learning to see the world correctly and finding self-discipline are not short paths—they're long roads requiring time and experience and hard work to master. (Well, no one ever truly masters them—you just keep learning.)

I'll refrain from evoking that old cliché about giving a man a fish and you've fed him for a day, but teach a man to fish and you've fed him for a lifetime. (Ok, I just did it.) But that's how it works in investing. Wall Street is full of data and ideas and perspectives, and you could spend your life reading every analysis you get your hands on and never sift through even a fraction of what's out there! No one can know everything, so learning successful investing means learning to focus your limited time and attention on what matters and interpret those issues correctly.

ASKING THE RIGHT QUESTIONS

I have a question for you: *Why are you an investor?*

I think you should know that about yourself before we get started. Otherwise, a lot of this book may not make much sense to you. I can't answer for anyone but myself: I think investing is one of the noblest things to be done with money. This is often not a popular view. I can understand why the professional investing community is often seen as greedy and evil. There are charlatans and crooks in every industry, always. On the whole, I believe allocating capital from where it's plentiful to where it's needed is good for the world and its development; that wealth is created and not just divided; that it's a virtue to use money in a way that helps others grow while also enriching the investor.

I believe deeply in those ideas. Frankly, I think it's difficult to be an investor otherwise. Economist Johan Norberg says it well: "Believing in capitalism does not mean believing in growth, the economy, or efficiency. Desirable as these may be, those are only the results. At its core, belief in capitalism is belief in mankind." Stock investing is one of the primary mechanisms of capitalism and, in my mind, a very worthy endeavor. But also one where folks make a lot of mistakes.

Ever noticed how investors clamor for the methods of legendary investors, yet few ever bother to learn how legendary investors' minds actually tick? People seek answers without ever knowing what the right questions were! I've spent my years as an analyst focusing on learning how to ask the right questions and letting the answers ensue.

Where does the learning come from? Everywhere! That means much of the wisdom of this book comes from places and minds far outside the narrow realm of investing. Most of the great investors loved to learn—they were extremely (often obsessively) curious about the world and saw new ways to understand investing in just about everything they did. They sought the *why* as well as the *how.*

Second, and maybe this is obvious, *investors are humans.* Humans are jumbled amalgams of experience, emotion, instinct, reason, and perspective. At any given time they're blinded by biases and foibles, often leading to regrettable decisions. And it's not just "they;" it's *you* and me, too. All of us. I've fallen prey to most all the mistakes outlined in this book at one time or another many times.

We simply cannot be successful investors without gaining an explicit understanding about how our minds and the minds of others work. It will tell you a lot about how markets function and will also help you personally. This is part of the discipline of investing: Train yourself to self-assess and understand when your natural thoughts are leading you astray.

It's going to be a strange trip. In this book, you'll learn to:

- Study the investment world like a scientist, yet also avoid the pitfalls many scientists fall into.
- Discover the power of self-awareness and self-observation to build discipline and avoid common investing pitfalls.
- Use current discoveries in neuroscience to understand how our perceptions and natural emotions are often contradictory to our best financial interests.
- Learn how to navigate the media and gauge investor sentiment—not only to get the information you need, but also to ignore the daily noise.
- Understand the stock market and economy as a complex, emergent, adaptive system (CEAS for short). The CEASs reflect all well-known information via the mechanism of prices. We'll explore this seldom cited but powerful way of understanding markets at length by looking at other natural systems—everything from ant farms to how a simple strand of DNA becomes a person!
- Forecast stock markets in terms of probability. We'll see how the only way to reasonably predict the future must be via probabilities.
- Explore stock market forecasting using pattern recognition. Experts call them a million things—drivers, indicators, valuations, and so on—but in the end all attempts to use past data to predict the future are forms of pattern recognition.
- Use all these observations and ideas to create a framework (or set of heuristics) to approach stock portfolio management in a practical way that can achieve long-term goals.
- Study the nature of risk in its many forms (from psychological to mathematical) and discuss how to avoid common mistakes during turbulent times like bear market panics.

Along the way, we'll also dive into some basic strategies for thinking and learning and how those can be applied to better investing. For example, what are the benefits and pitfalls in using logic and theory versus historical market observations? Or how does associative learning help achieve a better perspective?

I come from a firm that believes in teaching people. That probably sounds mundane, but it's a pretty radical idea in my industry—that an analyst would go out and deliberately use his time to teach clients. Aside from being a stock market analyst, each year I have the privilege of speaking to folks around the country about investing—how forecasting works, how to understand global economics, proper portfolio management, and so on.

Helping people learn to make better investing decisions has been one of the most fulfilling parts of my job. Most in the financial community won't do it. In a roundabout way, that attitude presupposes wealth cannot be made—only divided. Maybe the only reason you'd need investing secrets is if you believe your slice of the pie can be diminished by giving knowledge away.

That's wrong. I believe wealth is created, not divided—and the more investors can gain the vision needed to make good investments, the more they gain for themselves and also help markets and economies become more efficient . . . ultimately enriching everyone.

20/20 MONEY

1

INVESTING IS A SCIENCE

Seek simplicity, and distrust it.
                    —Alfred North Whitehead

*. . . but somebody said, "I don't believe it," and we had an
interesting conversation because I said, "You don't have the option
not to believe. Believing is not optional. If you accept that this is
replicated science, then belief is obligatory."*
                    —Daniel Kahneman[1]

If we want to see investing clearly, one of the first things we must do is view its foundations—the ideas investing is supposedly built upon. This first chapter is going to be a doozy. In it, we're going to take a careful look at science and mathematics—two subjects that serve as the foundations of modern knowledge, especially for investing—and debunk them. Well, not fully debunk, really. More like cast serious doubts on them both as panaceas for investing knowledge.

Math and science are, at their core, philosophies. They are ways of seeing the world; they are not some rules about the world we've

1

discovered. I realize that will sound blasphemous to many. But as we uncover the inherent limitations—and benefits—of math and science, much will be uncovered about how exactly stock markets and investing work.

APOLLO'S ARROW SHOT CROOKED

In the Greek Pantheon, Apollo was the god of reason. He represents light and the sun, truth and prophecy. He carries a bow and arrow—a master archer—and shot straight and true. He is an oracular god—the bringer of truths and clear vision.

And Apollo lives today! His spirit pervades the western world, dominating our way of thought through math and science—our religions of the twentieth and twenty-first centuries. Science and math are great things. But we put far too much faith in them. Like all methods, philosophies, and theories, there are flaws. Math isn't perfect; science can skew us. The limitations of both are prevalent in investing.

I call science and math "religions" because they tend to conjure a kind of faith in us. We "believe" they give us truths about the world as if they are an eternal set of rules we've discovered. Today's hyperrational faith has led many to believe in a deterministic, predictable, clock-like universe that always moves in a straight line according to set rules. We only need to discover them. As a culture, we tend to bow at the altar of science the same as Greeks bowed to the Oracle at Delphi or prayed to Apollo thousands of years ago.

Math and science are great things, but they're not worth our undying faith. That's the Apollonian impulse. Instead, it may be better to think of them as excellent methods of describing what happens in the world.

Most investment knowledge is predicated on math and science. This chapter won't dismiss either, but it will provide a different perspective to help us see both in a way that helps us invest better. They are not religions, but useful ways of seeing the world sometimes by breaking down or

Math and science are great things, but they're not worth our undying faith.

contradicting reality. Good science holds skepticism as its highest value—that is what we wish to cultivate. Even to be skeptical about science itself! Often enough, mathematical theories contradict or compute results that simply do not translate into reality. As neuroscientist Jonah Lehrer said, "No truth is perfect, that doesn't mean all truths are equally imperfect." The findings of science are the best we have at objective knowing, but that doesn't mean they are a panacea.

Sometimes, Apollo's arrow of knowledge is shot crooked.

DIONYSUS—MORE THAN JUST A GOOD VINTNER

Somewhat in opposition to Apollo, there was always Dionysus. He is the god of wine, the inspirer of ritual madness and ecstasy, the messiness of life and its sometimes chaotic nature. Dionysus represents that which we cannot compute or rationalize but nevertheless is. He is the "liberator" from pure reason.

Dionysus was a popular Greek deity, but in today's world he's pushed to the fringe—the god of wine and frivolity, fun and spirits. (Many know him best by his Roman name, Bacchus, the root of "bacchanalia.") We dare not let him into the fray of our work or allow him to dwell in the investment world—he might disrupt this rational and ordered territory we believe in so deeply!

If we cut the brain down the center into two hemispheres (right and left), we'd find that differing sides serve different functions—reason on one side and creativity on another. (This is, of course, a gross generalization and both hemispheres hold parts of each, but nonetheless is generally true.)

The left brain is traditionally logical, sequential, rational, analytical, objective, and tends to break things apart to look at the constituents instead of the whole. The right brain is more intuitive and holistic (it sees things as a whole instead of parts, synthesizing and subjective). The right brain is where we think abstractly, where the imagination resides. The right's flighty creativity can be disruptive to the left's desire for rationality. Today, most believe Dionysus—the messiness of creativity—is a figure to be *overcome*, not embraced. But this is wrong—both the creative and the logical are valid and important modes of thought for investing.

We tend to favor one side over another, but most everyone has the capacity to utilize both. Thinking with both sides of the brain can readily create paradoxes—we can see things as a whole, or just the parts; we can see something rationally, or colored with imagination. We can see things from many perspectives. So the brain itself is capable of these different ways of thinking and can create its own paradoxes.

The distinction between the right and left brains is something like the problems between Apollo and Dionysus. Taking in as many viewpoints as possible and assimilating them all is the way to better thinking and investing—it is the heart of true inquiry. Throughout this book, we will attempt to shift perspectives and see things in ways many fail to.

We ultimately cannot reason very well without Dionysus. Abstract thinking, imagination, and creativity are not paltry things—they are essential for good investing. We cannot, nor would we wish to, be computers. There is no advancing of thought or discovery of new things without the imaginative component and the ability to change perspective. No inspiration for new investing paradigms ever came without a dose of imagination.

Investors tend to have a near dogmatic belief that purely left-brain thinking is the optimal way to approach investments—check the data, run the analysis, and so on. This is true enough insofar as it goes. Market analysts are usually hyper-developed in the logical modes of linear thinking. But it's very much worth noting those usually thrown into the "genius" category were highly developed creative thinkers too. And we're not talking about artists—it's true for the sciences as well.

No inspiration for new investing paradigms ever came without a dose of imagination.

My favorite examples are physicists: Carl Sagan, Richard Feynman, Albert Einstein. In particular, I have read Richard Feynman's autobiography, *Surely You're Joking, Mr. Feynman!*, many times—whenever

I need to remember the importance of developing many types of intelligence to be good at what I do. Mr. Feynman, along with being a Nobel-winning physicist, also was a painter and noted player of the bongo drums. Carl Sagan was well known for the almost child-like wonder and glee he got from contemplating the possibilities and mysteries of the cosmos.

In any case, what separated the great physicists from the pack wasn't the mathematics they knew (they all at least had a few peers in that), but their creativity. Each had an uncanny ability to imagine and associate their knowledge, to put ideas together in ways no one had before and create new insight. Einstein himself often regarded his imagination as tantamount or superior to his rote math skills. (Of the many biographies of Einstein out there, I prefer to read the quirky but fascinating writings from the man himself: *The World As I See It* and *Ideas and Opinions* are two good options.)

Einstein was a terrible investor, but his method of thinking holds true for investing. A dirty little secret about great investors is that they're all tremendously creative thinkers. It rarely looks that way to the public because most put on airs of being rigid, starched, disciplined, linear thinkers. After all, most folks want nothing but the most "computer-like" minds to manage their money! But the fact is, the only way to get an insight—to know something others don't know—is to have huge and deep creative thinking about the world that must—by definition—defy convention.

The fruits of creativity (new ideas) come less often from some sudden insight (as we tend to romanticize it), but rather from many small insights building upon one another after many thousands of hours of labor and thinking.

USE THE METHOD, NOT THE DOGMA

That said, if the behavioral sciences have taught us anything, it's that our natural brain wiring can cause biases and distorted views of the world. This is sometimes referred to as the issue of *grounding*, which means if we know our senses can deceive us, how do we know where deception ends and truth begins? How can we "ground" ourselves to a clear perspective? Do our brains deceive us about everything? Or just a few things? If we could just get some foothold on reality, perhaps we could be grounded enough to be both rational and objective in their due course.

Here is where science comes in. The best answer we have to the problem of grounding is science. Science can provide us that "foundation" of knowledge, revealing to us through experiment and objective results, verified over and again, how something works in the world. It's the method of science that we are after to become better investors, not its dogmatic claims to truth.

I THINK, THEREFORE I INVEST

Most have heard of Descartes and his famous proclamation "I think therefore I am." Philosophers call this turn of phrase the *cogito*. Either way, it's an important statement for how scientific thought is done. Particularly for investing methodology, the cogito is the foundational statement of *objective thought*.

Objectivity is the opposite of subjectivity. Subjectivity is the idea you can only see things from your point of view, with your own personal biases and ego. We are stuck inside ourselves—there's no other way to see things except through our own eyes. That's a problem because we know biases and emotions can sabotage our thinking and lead us to act wrongly. Neuroscientists have known for years we can't think without emotion—all thinking has emotion wrapped up in it in some way. This means we cannot surmount subjectivity since we cannot escape our brains. So how can we go outside ourselves and surmount our inherent subjectivity?

Descartes was among the first to make a formal statement attempting to separate oneself from the world and acknowledge the world inside our heads and the world outside our heads is different. This is *objectivity*.

Why is objectivity important for investing? It forces us to acknowledge a framework outside our biased and subjective selves—the point of the scientific method. Science helps us systemically and objectively (as possible) attack problems.

I know of no investing success story—ever—that achieved riches by trusting intuition and emotion over the long run. But I do know the world is chock full of many who got poorer that way. Your brain needs a system or framework that disallows personal biases and intuitions to interfere. We should strive to be as objective as we can be about how we observe the world. The framework you set for yourself will influence all your conclusions. Academics sometimes call it heuristics (more on this in Chapter 8). I just call it clarity.

THE SCIENTIFIC METHOD

Descartes may have brought us a long way in articulating objectivity, but just what is it exactly in the real world? Is it following the right procedures? Is it an attribute of the person—like emotional detachment? Luckily, Francis Bacon had an answer.

Bacon wrote the *Novum Organum* (Latin for "New Instrument") in 1620. Many considered Bacon a philosopher, but he didn't propose a new philosophy—rather, a new method of thinking and gaining knowledge. He deemphasized human intuition and feelings, asserting that one should proceed through inductive reasoning from facts. He wrote, "The cause and root of nearly all evils in the sciences is this— that while we falsely admire and extol the powers of the human mind we neglect to seek for its true helps."

Bacon declared that the thinker must free the mind from certain false notions or tendencies that distort the truth. Bacon called these "idols." He named four types of idols, or biases, a person can have:

- **Idols of the Tribe**: These are biases all people have—natural, inborn instincts. For example, fear is an emotion, arising in everyone in the presence of danger.
- **Idols of the Den**: These are beliefs a person comes to believe on their own through subjective experience. People often mistake their personal experiences for the larger whole.

- **Idols of the Marketplace**: These are biases that stem from the misuse and misunderstanding of language and other forms of communication. (Think about it, we misunderstand each other through e-mail and speech daily!)
- **Idols of the Theatre**: These result from an abuse of authority where people are led to believe dictums of the state by virtue of authority, not facts. Very often, we believe something simply because it is the law or is widely accepted.

Perhaps you think you're immune to these, but you'd be wrong. We all suffer from such biases and many others—this is really only a partial list. But in Bacon's day it was wildly innovative. From these ideas came the *scientific method*, emphasizing objective observation and outside corroboration of ideas.

The scientific method is, by far, the best human technique for acquiring new knowledge, as well as for correcting and integrating previous knowledge. It is based on gathering observable, empirical, measurable evidence. Here's the method:

- **Observation**: All data must be based on verifiable and observed facts. No assumptions.
- **Prediction and Hypothesis**: Information used must be valid and consistent for observations past, present, and future. That is, anomalies in data need to be identified and everything should be "apples to apples" so that it is comparable.
- **Control**: Actively and fairly sampling the range of possible occurrences, whenever possible and proper, as opposed to the passive acceptance of "opportunistic data," is the best way to counterbalance the risk of empirical bias.
- **Falsifiability**: This is the key to identifying much popular pseudo-science. This is a gradual process requiring repeated experiments. One must be able to replicate results in order to corroborate them. This means all hypotheses and theories are, in principle, subject to disproof. A theory must be falsifiable, otherwise it is not scientific. Many investment studies wrongly

assume answers and then seek to corroborate that notion with data—very dangerous because there are many ways to make data bend to your will.

- **Identification of Causes**: Identification of the causes of a particular phenomenon to the best achievable extent. The causes must correlate directly with observed effects. It's not enough to just observe something; one must be able to explain it. No correlation without causation—many things are related by coincidence.

This may seem simple, even trite. But folks succumb to their "idols" more often than we care to admit. That's because our idols are close to our natural proclivities, but science requires discipline and isn't natural to us.

Sadly, few think to apply the scientific method to investing. From this simple framework, an investor can obliterate false notions and see through common fears and widely held (but wrong) beliefs. To be a successful investor, one must be a scientist, not an idol worshiper. Bacon says it best:

The scientific method is, by far, the best human technique for acquiring new knowledge, as well as for correcting and integrating previous knowledge.

> Men have sought to make a world from their own conception and to draw from their own minds all the material which they employed, but if, instead of doing so, they had consulted experience and observation, they would have the facts and not opinions to reason about, and might have ultimately arrived at the knowledge of the laws which govern the material world.[2]

THEORY AND REALITY

Generally, investors shouldn't make a trade unless they can observe a phenomenon in reality and also understand why it's happening. Without both corroboration of the data and a reasonable explanation (AKA a theory), big trouble can ensue.

Trading on theory alone is fraught with danger. Many defunct investing ideas make perfect logical sense in theory, but never worked in real life. Conversely, an observed pattern without an understanding of why it's happening is also problematic.

It's best to never act on an idea without both correlation and causation. A correlation is just a mathematical way to describe the degree of association between two variables—not a way to explain *why* the relationship is happening. There are many random correlations that are simply coincidences. A coincidence doesn't have predictive power and can lead to *false positives*, or thinking there is a meaningful relationship between two things when really there is not.

dating

A classic investing example is the way many compare today's price-to-earnings (P/E) ratios to some past period and try to predict where stocks will go. It makes intuitive sense that relatively "high" P/E ratios should predict lower stock returns in the future, and vice versa for "low" P/Es. But reality has shown over and again this isn't true.[3] P/E levels have never been predictive of stock market direction.

?

Additionally, one could run thousands of correlations between P/E ratios and other economic factors like interest rate movements, changes in accounting rules, capital structure ratios, economic cycles, future earnings expectations, and so on. The sky's the limit! Heck, you could run a correlation between divorce rates and P/E ratios if you want. Many will produce a positive correlation. But that doesn't mean we ought to use them to invest with.

Even the seemingly objective process of experimentation and testing can create biases in our thinking. Just the act of focusing on something influences how we perceive it—spending a lot of time on something can unconsciously make us believe it's more significant than it might really be. You can take anything, however small, and amplify it by focusing on it—precisely what experiments do.

Let reality be your baseline. If your theory doesn't work in the world, it's useless as an investment tool. Likewise, if you can't explain something observed, it's similarly ineffective.

Let reality be your baseline. If your theory doesn't work in the world, it's useless as an investment tool. Likewise, if you can't explain something observed, it's similarly ineffective.

The Only Worthwhile Philosophy Is a Pragmatic One. One time I asked my boss Ken about "other intellectuals like himself." He didn't answer the question. Instead he said, "I am not an intellectual." And that was that. I was incredulous. I smiled a little, thinking he had to be joking. He was not smiling back.

That was an important lesson for me. Ken's stance wasn't some far flung personal bias—it was an important professional attitude. Intellectuals entertain all sorts of flights of fancy, existing in worlds where reality doesn't necessarily ever need to come into the picture. Believe it or not, most all mathematical research is done explicitly in a reality that does not exist—it may only "hypothetically" exist. There is nothing wrong with that—living and thinking in a world of abstraction can produce important advancements in knowledge.

But Ken, as a money manager, is explicitly in the business of reality—focusing on how the world demonstrably really worked—not how he (or anyone else) thought it worked or believed it should work. That is an attitude, I've come to learn, successful investors share.

Thus, philosophical systems don't usually have a very strong place in a good investing strategy simply because they're so, well, airy. But there is at least one I think is worth consideration. William James—known as a pioneer of psychology—was also a leader in a philosophical idea called Pragmatism in the late nineteenth century. Its founder was Charles Peirce, who created the *pragmatic maxim*:

> In order to ascertain the meaning of an intellectual conception one should consider what practical consequences might conceivably result by necessity from the truth of that conception; and the sum of these consequences will constitute the entire meaning of the conception.[4]

Pragmatism says a theory is only worth the effort if it helps us understand reality and the world better. Now that's a philosophy I can get into!

For example, Irving Fisher's theory for the quantity of money is stated mathematically as $MV = PQ$. This powerful equation describes

Reverse Engineering for Better Investing

Scientists regularly solve problems with the principle of reverse engineering (RE). This is the process of figuring out how something works by analyzing its structure, function, and operation. That is, you figure something out by seeing how it works and then work backward to find the principle causes of why it works that way. Scientists often use RE to analyze mechanical devices—using RE as a method of reducing a problem to smaller parts.

I don't think this kind of reasoning is advisable or even possible for investing, but I do have my own alternative types of RE to use.

Type 1: If something is true one way, the reverse usually ought to be true.

For example, many folks believe a weak dollar is bad for the stock market. If it's true, then the reverse ought to also be true—a strong non-dollar should be good for stocks. Right? Well, hopefully just by framing the question in this way you can see how ridiculous it is. There's no good reason a strong non-dollar should be good for stocks any more than a weak dollar would be bad. The simple act of reversing a problem in this way often reveals—almost immediately—how flawed investor logic can be. In fact, the data bear this out—neither a strong nor weak dollar has much correlation with performance of the global stock market over time.

Type 2: Observe how the system works, not the parts.

Stock markets and economies don't often work in simple cause-and-effect relationships. Moreover, the micro, or local, behavior of an economy doesn't necessarily add up to how the whole system might function. So instead of watching an economy's smaller parts and trying to glean how the system works, observe the system itself. The patterns of the larger economy and market are often different than the behavior of individuals acting in that system. That may sound a bit obtuse. In Chapter 5 we'll cover this idea in greater detail.

In both cases, reversing the process and/or viewing the system itself are effective tactics for investors. Or, as Sherlock Holmes (that is, Sir Conan Doyle) says in "A Study in Scarlet":

In solving a problem of this sort, the grand thing is to be able to reason backward. That is a very useful accomplishment, and a very easy one, but people do not practise it much. In the everyday affairs of life it is more useful to reason forward, and so the other comes to be neglected. There are fifty who can reason synthetically for one who can reason analytically.

the relationship between inflation, prices, and the money supply, and offers us better understanding and insight about the process. But the big error is people want to use it to describe reality. Yes, Fisher's equation helps us think through how—in an isolated and abstract way—money flows. But to actually try and calculate it is a nightmare. There are too many assumptions and other potential affecting factors in the real world to ever come up with a reliable calculation. That's the pragmatic part—separating the theory from the reality. Most theories are there to help us understand a perspective, not perfectly predict a very messy and noisy world. Be pragmatic!

CAREFUL WITH CATEGORIES

How do you categorize things? Most never think much about it save for organizing their file cabinets once a year, but our categories say a lot about how we see the world and it's a fundamental activity of the sciences.

All sight is done through a lens of some kind. That's literally true (eyes, electronic or organic, all have lenses), and it's also figuratively true. Brains have a natural tendency to create lenses to bring the world into focus by making *categories*. We are categorization machines, constantly looking for similarities and patterns to lump things together. The kind of lens (or category) used, then, can make all the difference in how we see things. This gets treacherous because our minds want to create categories unconsciously—without our knowing. Bad categorizations cause big biases in investing and life generally.

Here's a fact: There is no such thing as a category in the natural world—humans make them up. A category is a not a thing, but a way of seeing things. That makes your choice of categories all the more imperative because *categories are really more about interpreting the world than they are about seeing reality.*

Sound strange? Let's take an example.

There is no such thing as a "species" of animal. Think of a bear. What is a bear? What makes it "bearish" (bad market pun intended)? Is it the claws? Nope—bears of the world have many different types of claws and some not at all. Many other animals have claws, too. Fur? No—just as various. Muzzle? Hibernation? Bone structure? No! There is no one characteristic of a bear that actually makes it a bear—every single trait (or *phenotype*, in science speak) varies among regional types of bears. Heck, big brown bears are in many respects closer to other warm-blooded animals than they are to pandas.

There is little real consistency across various types of bears. To call them all bears was our choice. In truth, every animal is a completely singular cluster of DNA that will never be exactly repeated. There are only similarities. As a result of genes mixing over time, what we call a species today won't last for more than a few million years anyway and eventually evolve into something slightly different. We simply use "species" as helpful categories to see and delineate life's different forms at this specific moment. "Bear" is just our way of describing similar animals in the world. So, categories are really useful to help us make sense of the world—but they are perspectives on how we view the world, not an appraisal of reality.

The same is true for markets. There are many long-held categories in markets—ways of slicing and dicing stocks to see them clearer—that are simply wrong and lead to investing mistakes.

An example is the division between small and large cap stocks. There are industry "standard" ways of computing what is "big" and what is "small" that most folks adhere to without thinking twice about it. Most portfolio managers consider small cap stocks something below $10 billion in market cap or thereabouts. Sometimes $5 billion or less. In any case, it's almost always an arbitrary distinction.

In certain parts of a market cycle, it's believed small caps will outperform large caps, and vice versa. But there's no way to get that right if the categories are wrong in the first place.

What seems "big" usually isn't. Instead of the arbitrary $10 billion or $5 billion distinction for small caps, a better way is to take the weighted average market cap of the whole market. Anything bigger than the weighted average should be big, and the rest should be small. Those are better categories for viewing the investing landscape because they are "grounded" (recall the problem of grounding and the scientific method a few pages ago) in reality and also in the context of their peers (other stocks), not an arbitrary distinction that seems "big" to us.

It turns out a very small number of companies are truly "big"— that is, actually bigger than the weighted average. The vast majority are smaller—and guess what, they tend to act "small," too! In market cycles, it's only the mega-big stocks that act "big."

As of this writing, the weighted average market cap of the S&P 500 is $78.8 billion. That means many stocks we'd traditionally consider "big," like eBay, Gap, or Nike, actually act rather small.

The point? Before we can do any cogent analysis, we ought to check our categories first and make sure they aren't biasing us in ways we hadn't before imagined. It can make all the difference between a right and wrong conclusion.

COULD MATH BE WRONG?

There are two kinds of people in this world: Those who believe math is the discovered law of the universe, and those who think math is a human way of describing the world. I fall into the latter category. I think all investors should.

Math is maybe the greatest of all human inventions. Yes—invention. It is an invention with near countless possible uses, but it also has problems and limitations. My aim isn't to say math is bad. It's great! I just hope to show you a good investor won't trust numerical equations as religion—there is much more to markets than math is capable of describing. George Lakoff and Rafael Nunez, in their fascinating and often brilliant study of how human minds understand math, *Where Mathematics Comes From*, argue persuasively math is a feature of the mind, not reality.

> Mathematics is seen as the epitome of precision, manifested in the use of symbols in calculation and in formal proofs. Symbols are, of course, just symbols, not ideas. The intellectual content of mathematics lies in its ideas, not in the symbols themselves.[5]

What strikes me most about that passage is the archetypal way Apollo and Dionysus are clashing—this is the classic "imagination versus reason" conflict renewed.

Part of the dogma of science is a tacit but widely held belief math is something we humans "discovered" about the world. That math is in everything, and all we need to do is "find" the right equations and we can explain and know everything about how the world works. Many believe observing the Fibonacci series in flowers and logarithmic spirals in snails proves math is reality. Even most formal logic is structured around math! To learn math is to learn how nature works, and it would be shared by any intelligent life in the cosmos—the universal truth!

So the story goes.

Maybe, but I think mathematics for investors is better used as a kind of philosophical, descriptive system than a rule book. Math is a way to comprehend the world around us in ways our brains can handle—a way to describe the world. Math often mirrors nature, yes, but very often it falls short or is contradictory to reality as well. Talk to any student studying for a math PhD (and, believe it or not, I've conversed with a few), and they'll immediately tell you math is not reality, but a "rough approximation of reality."

What's the point for investing? Our aim is to find the right perspective to invest successfully. Dethroning math from its godlike perch will make you more dubious of statistics and "verified" results. That's a good thing. No matter how often "science" might corroborate something, the fact is we can only corroborate things in ways intelligible to us. Good scientists know asking the right questions is more important than having the answers. Often, we don't even know how to ask the questions because there are many features of markets and economies outside our ability to comprehend.

No amount of math as it exists today is able to predict or even successfully describe how markets work. At best, some of the parts have loose theoretical calculations that often break down. Today's math:

BEWARE OF NORMATIVE AND POSITIVE

One thing to be aware of whenever scanning investing news or thinking about investing decisions is the difference between a normative and a positive statement.

Normative: How something ought to be.

Positive: How something truly is.

For example, to say, "A weaker dollar should affect stocks negatively," is a normative statement about what someone thinks ought to happen. But a positive statement is, "Stocks moved higher in 2007 even though the dollar weakened." That is a falsifiable, verifiable fact.

exception to norm does not disprove norm

The point? It's fine to think in normative terms—much of abstract thinking calls for it, and we often need it to think creatively and hypothetically. But when you're dealing with real money in the real world, normative statements can get you into big trouble. Essentially, it's the difference between what could happen theoretically or hypothetically and what really is.

Another example: Many folks believe in the "wealth effect"—the idea that if housing prices go down (or the value of any other personal asset), people will feel poorer, thus they will spend less, which will lead to smaller economic growth and less jobs for producing goods and services, which then leads to further falling home prices and lower income, and the cycle continues in a downward spiral on and on.

In theory (normatively), the logic of the wealth effect makes sense. But in reality, this cannot possibly be true. How to know? If it were true, any time asset prices fell they would cause a downward spiral we'd never recover from. But every time things like stock markets or housing prices have fallen, they've eventually recovered, as has the economy. This has always been true through time. The reality destroys the theory.

Normative thinking is fine and good, but always seek reality before making a decision or believing an analysis.

norm is cyclical

- Is reductive (more on this in a moment)
- Can generally only accurately deal with a few variables at a time and has difficulty with rising complexity
- Tries to achieve exactitude where none may exist in reality

For example, much of how we look at stock markets is done via charts and graphs. What's wrong with that? For starters, a line graph can only account for *two variables at a time*. Just two! Stock markets and economies have millions of variables interacting constantly.

Even when correctly used, math can distort reality. Darrell Huff's *How to Lie with Statistics* was written in 1954, but to this day is one of the best studies of how statistics can cause intentional and unintentional problems. I won't recount its content here, but I highly recommend it.

If you're not yet convinced math is a philosophy, consider this: Numbers are unnecessary to do math. Numbers are an afterthought, a kind of symbol that can be plugged into equations. Most math PhDs never even use numbers, they just use symbols. Math, at heart, is a self-contained system of logic, not a depiction of reality.

As a brief, real-world example where math failed, let's look at the infamous casualty (and oft thought catalyst) of the 1998 financial crisis—Long-Term Capital Management.

WHERE MATH FAILED: LONG-TERM CAPITAL MANAGEMENT

Long-Term Capital Management (LTCM) was a prominent hedge fund founded by a handful of financial bigwigs, including John Meriwether (former vice-chairman and head of bond trading at Salomon Brothers), Nobel Prize winner Myron Scholes (the economist credited with developing the "Black Scholes" options model), and Robert C. Merton, also a Nobel Prize winner in Economics.

The fund used complex mathematical models to take advantage of fixed-income arbitrage opportunities and employed huge leverage to make profits. Sometimes called *convergence trades*, profits on individual trades were small, so the fund took big leverage positions to grow profits. At one point in 1998, LTCM had borrowed over $124.5 billion and carried a debt-to-equity ratio of about 25 to 1.

For a time, the fund reaped huge profits based on its purely mathematical investing techniques, with over 40 percent returns after fees in its first few years. But in 1998, LTCM lost nearly $4.6 billion in the span of just a few months as the financial crisis in Asia took hold—a so-called *exogenous* event.

The failure was so huge, the Federal Reserve was forced to initiate a bailout of LTCM by other major banks—all because the mathematics behind LTCM's strategy couldn't ultimately account for certain unpredicted events. In other words, <u>math failed to account for reality.</u> 1% risk

If you want to learn more about LTCM, read *When Genius Failed: The Rise and Fall of Long-Term Capital Management* by Roger Lowenstein. Later, in Chapter 9, we'll explore other failed mathematical attempts to understand risk and discuss the infamous "Value at Risk" (VaR) equation partially responsible for the 2008 financial crisis.

REDUCTION: WHY YOU CAN'T QUANTIFY EVERYTHING

Equations and models can predict how a machine will work, but living things have properties that cannot be quantified.

Math describes much of the physical world quite easily—objects (usually inanimate) that are governed solely by physical laws. If you throw a football, all you have to know is a few variables like velocity and acceleration and gravity and you can pretty easily figure out where the ball will land. You can do the whole thing by using an equation and plugging in a few variables. Like a miracle, it will work every single time! Totally universal.

Another familiar mathematical dictum: If you solve each step, or part of the larger problem, eventually all those small solutions add up to the bigger solution. Think about a car as an example. A car is a big machine made up of a bunch of smaller systems—engine, air conditioner, power steering, and so on. When you put all the little systems together, you get a car. Same with the human body: Scientists commonly understand our bodies by reducing the problem to the smaller parts—systems like circulatory, nervous, skeletal, and so on. Or we can go even further and think about individual cells. If we can understand first how our cells work, then we can simply put all the cells together and then get to a solution about how the body works.

But <u>complex systems</u> like stock markets, which involve humans, don't behave like physical systems. Intentionality isn't the territory of physics. Minds, feelings, urges, thoughts—there is no set of mathematical rules (we know of) to explain them. But that doesn't stop folks from perpetually trying to impose the logic of physical systems on complex systems like stock markets.

This typifies the scientific problem of *reductionism*. Part of the mission of the scientific method is to "reduce" big problems—separate them into manageable parts, small problems—that can be easily solved.

A bit of scrutiny reveals how damaging reductionism can be for understanding economies and markets, which very obviously do not behave in the same ways basic physical systems do.

REDUCTION IS GOOD!

Most science is predicated on the idea reduction is a valid way to solve problems. Math problems routinely try to break a problem down into discrete variables and individual parts. It's near ubiquitous dogma that the methods of reductionism can go hand in hand with investing. Most of today's economic and market models rely on sets of equations based on definable (that is, quantifiable and identifiable) variables. Just check out any economic textbook—you'll immediately see it's a field mostly based on mathematics and reductionism.

As we'll see in future chapters, some systems are too complex, dynamic, and interconnected for simple math—literally, the sum is greater than the parts. Stock markets and economies are such systems. There is no way to quantify many things in an economy. Math can indeed help explain and compute some of the parts, but never the behavior of the whole, and can almost never help in predicting what will happen.

But in some sense, reduction is the only reliable way we know to solve problems and is wonderful for many reasons. Our brains are limited, so taking small problems one at a time is a great thing. We tend to do very well with "steps," or taking problems in sequential order to achieve some larger goal. For instance, buy a tricycle for your kid and the instruction booklet will have "step-by-step" instructions on how to build it. That's reduction. One thing at a time and build to a solution. We naturally think this way. That science is accommodating to our natural thought processes is great. But there are plenty of pit-falls with reduction, too. . . .

REDUCTION IS BAD!

The scientific principle of reduction is fine for many things, but leads to pitfalls in others—especially investments. Markets cannot be *reduced* to purely mathematical rules. There are no accurate math-based models to forecast how stocks will perform, and likely never will be. If you think about it, that's pretty intuitive: The value of things (especially for stocks, or anything economic) is ultimately based on the idea of "utility," or the perception of value. Perception of value is always and everywhere an arbitrary and contextual thing—a psychological thing. Which means a mathematical value assigned to it is fuzzy at best.

To see this, think about a human brain, which is a classic complex system. Reductionism says we ought to be able to understand how brains work simply by studying and understanding what brains are made up of—neurons, synapses, dendrites, and so on. Many

> There are no accurate math-based models to forecast how stocks will perform, and likely never will be.

neuroscientists have tried it, but all have failed! Understanding how neurons work may tell us much about the mechanics of brains, but it doesn't explain how the larger system creates consciousness, emotions, or thoughts in general. We have to study how the larger system works for that.

Here are some additional problems with reduction and market analysis:

Linear Relationships: Much of science sees life as moving from point A to B, then to C, and so on. Linear, direct, straight. Cause and effect. Markets do not follow such patterns. They zig and zag and often circle around. For instance, economic outcomes seldom translate into stock prices exactly, or sometimes at all. Positive earnings releases don't always lead to an up stock; GDP growth doesn't necessarily lead to an up market. Why? Because if anything were that predictable, we'd all be trillionares—investing would be too darn easy! Any possible real direct relationship gets priced in very quickly.

Correlation and Causation: This is related to the idea of linear relationships. There's a deep human need to see all things in terms of a clear cause and effect, leading often to "false positives." Brains are wired to seek relationships even if one isn't really there. A simple correlation—even if apparently hugely significant—on its own doesn't really hold much information. Markets are complex systems where millions of variables are dependent upon each other, so it's nearly impossible to analyze two factors discretely. You may observe an incredible correlation between, say, growth in US beer sales and times just before Eddie Van Halen enters rehab, but that doesn't necessarily tell you they are significantly connected. There could be an unforeseen third factor actually driving that relationship, or a number of outside factors. Maybe Eddie entered rehab during the Super Bowl—one of the biggest US beer consumption days of the year. Or it could just be a casual coincidence they happened at the same time. In markets, again, there are so many factors working upon each other at once, gleaning a true correlation that's consistently useful over time for predicting stock moves is quite rare.

The Simplest Possible Terms: Human brains love binary; that is, simple yes/no propositions. Gray areas mean ambiguity, and brains don't naturally like ambiguity. Yes/no is better to us. Reductionists often try to get to yes/no equations—to find a "trigger" for when someone should buy or sell stocks, for instance. (Entire firms are founded on so-called "quant" funds that specifically design mathematical models to generate such triggers. None have ever worked in the long run.) Indeed, science is often described as a way of seeking simplicity. For example, Isaac Newton's third law of motion—for every action, there is an equal and opposite reaction—is elegant and simple. But it doesn't necessarily hold for markets (as we'll see in Chapter 5).

Reduction means getting rid of "gray" areas. It should be fairly obvious, however, that markets are not matters of yes/no, on/off. Subtlety and magnitude matter a great deal. Gray areas are actually more common than absolutes. Most financial math as it exists today cannot account for such subtlety.

The Desire for Elegance: Many scientists believe a simple, "elegant" solution to how the cosmos works must exist—it's just a matter of us discovering it. That tantalizing idea has driven scientific minds through all time and is part of the fetish of reductionism. This dates all the way back to Plato—who saw all things in the world as crude representations of a more perfect abstract "form"—and goes all the way forward to Einstein, who believed it was possible to find a single equation to describe the whole cosmos. There is no law or rule saying any investing solution must be neat and tidy or simple or beautiful—nor is there any rule that even says there must be a solution we can understand at all! Aesthetics don't count in investing.

Smaller Problems: Reduction wants to divide big problems into smaller problems that can be handled discretely from each other. If you want to fix a broken clock, you don't really have to think holistically about the whole clock. All you have to do is identify the part that's broken, fix that part, and integrate it back into the system. Clock fixed. But markets and economies don't work that way—most variables cannot be separated from one another or observed in a vacuum. The moving parts of a market have real-time effects on all the other parts. As one changes, the dynamics of the whole system change. So how all the variables interact matters a lot. Open up the *Wall Street Journal* on any day, though, and you'll see experts talking about "single" issues like interest rates or the money supply as if they were discrete from everything else. In fact, many factors both affect and are affected by interest rates—they simply cannot be understood on their own. This simple observation destroys the validity of most reductionist economic models.

REDUCING THE TRUTH AWAY

Now we've seen a bit of the good and the bad about reduction. Let's take an example of how this might translate into the real world of investing.

With any cutting-edge field of study, new ideas get thrown around wildly, and most conclusions are at best preliminary, but often wrong. Scientific theories take years or decades to vet—requiring testing and retesting before they're canon.

The mainstream media moves too fast for all that. Once the intellectual paparazzi gets a hold of a new theory, things tend to spiral out of control, ideas are often distorted and misconstrued, and scads of irrational conclusions are consecrated as scientific truths. This is often referred to as pseudo-science, or science-ism.

The investing community is not immune. Below is a quote from the book *Mobs, Messiahs, and Markets* by William Bonner and Lila Rajiva. It's a study using behavioral economics to analyze market behavior.

> What if all animals [and humans included] simply act according to various prefigured survival strategies, the purpose of which—as far as we know—is nothing more than genetic replication?

Seems reasonable. It's a riff on Richard Dawkins' theory of the Selfish Gene. Hearkening back to the mid-1970s, the idea posits that organisms act principally to replicate their own genes and enable survival of the species. Classic reductionist thought—a single principle to explain all animal behavior and ultimate motivation.

Bonner and Rajiva's book is full of useful and thought-provoking ideas, but there's a big problem lurking in their prose: Their representation of the Selfish Gene is vastly over-simplified and too rigid to reflect reality. It's a classic case of misused reductionism.

By operating on the premise gene replication is the only rationale for animal behavior, science is sent backward, not forward. Representing humans as pure automatons of genome willpower is essentially a re-visioning of BF Skinner's theories on instinct and Pavlov's dogs. It isn't cutting-edge neuroscience; it's a cognitive U-turn back to the twentieth century!

Many new books and articles on economics and human behavior take a reductionist approach, and it's something to be wary of. Reductionism can thwart your investment analysis as fast as any basic miscalculation.

Just 10 years ago, scientists believed once the human genome was mapped, we'd hold the key to countless medical breakthroughs, which would occur in rapid succession and revolutionize all medicine. We accomplished that goal only to find things weren't so simple. No, the real keys to understanding human life had to do with the proteins those amino acid strings produced by DNA—in what measure, at what time, and in what combinations. So they did a bunch of work on proteins (and continue to). And we found it's not just protein synthesis, but protein interaction with the surrounding environment that's probably responsible for expression of traits. Put another way, understanding the most basic keys to human life turned out to be vastly more complicated and nuanced than just mapping DNA strands.

And so it is with understanding brains, too. The more work done in neuroscience, the more complicated things become. Every neuron is interconnected and dependent upon other neurons—interconnections so vast and intricate that simply understanding how the brain "sees" an image captured by the eye is enormously difficult.

Simply, understanding humans—from the molecular to the behavioral—is trending away from simple dictums toward greater complexity and intricacy. Just so, stock markets are too vast and complex to be reduced to rules everyone can follow. If it were so easy, we'd all be rich.

Again, this isn't to say all reductionist thinking is bad. The true test of any theory, however, is its predictive power. A theory can be wholly logical but still not work in practice (more on this in Chapter 7). If a theory can't repeatedly forecast an outcome, it's of little value. A bit of skepticism pointed toward the grandiose claims of behavioral scientists and market gurus, and it'll be apparent how flimsy and unscientific most theories really are.

Apollo's arrow shot crooked yet again.

CHAPTER INSIGHTS

Because of innate human limitations and biases, we need a system that helps us be more objective about solving investing problems. Science is such a method. However, like any approach, science has its pitfalls and is no panacea.

- We need both reason and imagination to invest well—pure calculation alone cannot produce new insights.
- Science provides "grounding" for us to glean insight and gain knowledge.
- The scientific method is just that—a method. Not a dogma. It allows us to test ideas and see if they pair with reality and are repeatable.
- The difference between reality and theory is an important distinction. Theories are descriptions of the world in terms we can understand, not necessarily direct representations of reality.
  - Theories are only as good as their ability to *predict* and *describe* reality.
- The way we categorize the world says a lot about how we see the world.
  - Categories are human things, not observations about reality.
  - Often, the categories we create will influence the outcome of our experiments.
- Mathematics is not necessarily a "discovery," but one way for humans to understand the world around them.
  - Often math cannot explain much of the real world.
  - Some mathematic models, such as the VaR, have caused undue faith and contributed to financial catastrophes.
- Reduction is a feature of math and the scientific method.
  - Reduction helps us separate big problems into simple parts and jibes with the human propensity to find cause-and-effect relationships.
  - However, reductionist methods are often contrary to how complex systems, like markets and economies, work.

2

INVESTING IS A DISCIPLINE

Discipline is the bridge between goals and accomplishment.
—Jim Rohn

With self-discipline almost anything is possible.
—Theodore Roosevelt

*When man learns to understand and control his own behavior
as well as he is learning to understand and control the behavior
of crop plants and domestic animals, he may be justified in
believing that he has become civilized.*
—Ayn Rand

I don't care what they say, most investing theories (not all, but most) are versions of gambling. Personally, I'm terrified of gambling. Casinos set up games where the odds are explicitly and deliberately stacked against the players—yet folks come from all over to play! That's beyond perverse, but commonplace and old as time.

Maybe this will freak you out a little: The bright, blinking lights at a Chuck E. Cheese's game arcade for kids are pretty much the same shiny lights Vegas uses to get you to play craps and slots. We seem to be drawn—even in adulthood—to bright, shiny things and willing to give up our cash for the thrill of playing the game. It's not much of a stretch to make another comparison and see the blinking lights of the big board at the New York Stock Exchange (NYSE) as similar.

Discipline is the only way to ensure your investing habits aren't gambling habits. Most of the dangerous things about gambling are also pitfalls of investing. If you want training in how to invest, just go to a casino and observe the habits of chronic gamblers. Scrutinize their psychology, the way they rationalize losses and wins, and all the strange ways they behave. Then do the opposite. When they win, they think they're geniuses and want to keep playing, believing they can keep winning. When they lose, it was just "a run of bad luck." Same with investors.

Most of the advice I see in financial publications and on cable TV is based more on the fundamentals of bad gambling than good investing discipline—momentum, technical trading, short-term valuation plays, and so on. All gambling. The key difference: In casinos, the odds are stacked against you. In stock market investing, the odds are in your favor—only you can screw it up; the house can't take it from you. (We'll cover probability and stock markets in much more detail in Chapter 6.)

How? Stock markets go up over time—just being in the market forever produces a winning result! That tells us most of the time investors fail simply because they aren't being disciplined—they squander the natural advantage they have. Our emotions get the better of us; we lose track of our long-term goals; we trade too much; we think we're geniuses; we swing for the fences—all things that forfeit the inherent advantage we have over the house.

Need proof? Witness the stock market panic of late 2008 or any long-in-the-tooth bear market. Suddenly, otherwise rational people become short-term focused and panic-sell along with the masses. A disciplined investor knows to stay put or even buy in such times. We all know it and have heard that advice over and over—yet somehow, few are able to heed it. Why? Lack of discipline or self-control.

The way to save yourself from yourself is self-awareness. There is no antidote for irrationality. We are all emotional and subjective. Our best hope is to recognize it and gain some chance of surmounting our natural tendency to foil ourselves. That is the subject of this chapter.

DISCIPLINE, DISCIPLINE, DISCIPLINE

A single quote from Warren Buffett will guide us through much of this chapter:

> Success in investing doesn't correlate with IQ once you're above the level of 125. Once you have ordinary intelligence, what you need is the temperament to control the urges that get other people into trouble in investing.[1]

Every investing book I've encountered pushes a method, telling us how to get rich with some strategy. Some are good, others aren't. But no investing book I've encountered spends significant time on what Mr. Buffett alludes to. A cursory glance at the newspaper, TV, or magazine rack tells the same story—experts are selling methods but ignoring temperament.

Mr. Buffett understands the genius mentality won't get you far. The overwhelming majority of investing success comes from temperament. It's something so obvious, few recognize it.

In other chapters, we'll talk about tactical ways to be disciplined in investing, but here we're going to do something few investing studies are willing to do: explore the issue of discipline itself—how to get it and keep it. Some of these methods and perspectives won't appear to have much to do with investing. But make no mistake—they do and are worth the time in cultivating.

My definition of discipline? *Self-control and self-awareness.*

This doesn't mean rising at sunrise every day, practicing austere mediations, and eating only rice and water. Good investing is not tantamount to being a monk. A common investing myth—or path to wealth generally—is the notion that one must be austere, a miser, to save enough to get rich. Nope. Plenty of rich investors spend a lot of dough. True, being a saver can only help you—often significantly. And saving is a discipline-based endeavor. But this book isn't about saving—it's about investing. Self-control for our purposes is the part of investing where what's saved is used to compound wealth.

A secret of discipline is *self-knowledge.* Self-knowledge is important in just about every walk of life, but it's especially true for great investors—they are almost agonizingly self-aware. They know their strengths and weaknesses; they've (mostly) figured out their personal biases. Often, when we hear "self-consciousness," it usually has a connotation of embarrassment or timidity. "Jimmy will come out of his shell one day, but he's so self-conscious right now." True enough, but that's not what we intend here. Self-understanding in investing means being able to step back and assess oneself—recognize when we're emotional or are wrong about something and change course.

Most have trouble acting contrary to a strongly felt emotion. The daily turbulence, fear, and euphoria of market moves loosens whatever grip we had on reality in favor of purer sensation. This is true across every facet of investing. All investors are humans—even the professionals. Everyone is susceptible to making emotional decisions and then rationalizing them by convincing themselves reason was used. Thus, no investing training is worth anything unless we can first learn to control our emotions.

> A secret of discipline is *self-knowledge.* Self-knowledge is important in just about every walk of life, but it's especially true for great investors—they are almost agonizingly self-aware.

> Everyone is susceptible to making emotional decisions and then rationalizing them by convincing themselves reason was used. Thus, no investing training is worth anything unless we can first learn to control our emotions.

Strangely, investing professionals don't receive any formal training on how to control or even recognize emotional responses—they usually only have developed skills in math or various methods of analysis. That makes the pros generally no better at investing than most anyone else. Find investors who've achieved long-term success and it becomes clear that, yes, those are some pretty smart folks, but they're also severe market ascetics. They're not moved by sentiment or emotion or panic or euphoria. They're consistent, prudent, level-headed, and understand their own foibles and biases. They do not act when they feel pressure or when the whole world is telling them they're wrong.

Yet, they are constantly aware they may in fact be wrong. Humility is a huge factor in investing discipline. It's not only knowing you could be wrong, but also having the humility to acknowledge it and change course where appropriate. Today's fast-moving world requires versatility as a key part of intelligence—that is, the ability to learn, un-learn, and re-learn as necessary. To constantly adjust.

In practice, this is extremely difficult for a variety of reasons. Our brains love routine and form powerful networks to reinforce familiar behavior and corroborate existing beliefs, even in the face of contrary evidence. But just as importantly, changing one's mind is often regarded as a sign of weakness, of "waffling." Yet, to

Humility is a huge factor in investing discipline. It's not only knowing you could be wrong, but also having the humility to acknowledge it and change course where appropriate.

see the folly of one's way and change course, leaving behind all we once believed, is to my view among the most courageous and heroic actions possible. Funnily and perversely, we do not typically see it as such.

Discipline is also about understanding personal limitations. Overconfidence is one of the great investing sins—and most overconfidence errors stem from believing we understand more than we really do. We understand little; we are aware of little; we can remember little. Yet we often think we understand how the whole world works. Great investors rarely claim to know much more than what they themselves are up to. Disciplined folks understand they can't know everything, so they focus on achieving what they are capable of and usually in the simplest way possible.

To see the principle of self-awareness more readily, it's worth first delving into the subject of consciousness.

PUT YOURSELF IN SOMEONE ELSE'S SHOES

Dr. Howard Gardner, in his book, *Frames of Mind: The Theory of Multiple Intelligences*, claims intelligence isn't a yes/no kind of thing—it varies by category. There are different kinds of intelligence, and different people are gifted in different ways of thinking. For instance, some may be good at mathematics but terrible at writing and languages. That is, there is more than one way to be smart, and most of us are developed in just a few ways and underdeveloped in others. Here are a few of the categories Gardner identified:

- Verbal-Linguistic
- Logical-Mathematical
- Intrapersonal
- Musical
- Visual-Spatial
- Bodily-Kinesthetic

Daniel Goleman, in his now classic book, *Emotional Intelligence*, expanded on the theory of multiple intelligences and introduced the emotional kind of thinking to the public, arguing smarts aren't just about hard, cold, logic—they're also about understanding oneself, controlling emotion, and intuiting the emotions of others.

Emotional intelligence has become the basis for much of leadership and management theory and is clearly important for investing, too. This may seem obvious, but it's interesting to note most formal education ignores emotional intelligence completely. The methods for gauging intelligence today (especially standardized testing in schools) are based on logical thinking only.

The conclusion is simple: To be truly smart in a broad sense, one needs to develop many different types of intelligence, not just one. This is an imperative for investors, who need to be learned in many disciplines—statistics, history, psychology, math, and logic, to name a few.

One of the ultimate intelligences is the ability to empathize and think like someone else—to "put yourself in someone else's shoes."

Our brains come packed with a specific kind of cell called *mirror neurons*. Mirror neurons allow mimicking behavior. This is how we learn when we're very young—we watch others speak or do things, then we mimic them and learn to do it, too. Our brains are made to imitate.

Empathy is somewhat similar. Some experts believe women are wired to empathize more than men. Maybe. It's impossible to say definitively. One thing we do know, however, is empathy often takes work and thought—it requires development. We naturally operate from our own point of view. We use our perspective as the only one. But if you desire to know how others think, you have to actually think about how others think. In crafting his literary masterpieces, Anton Chekhov said about the process of creating characters, "Everything I learned about human nature I learned from myself." He studied and created his characters through self-observation.

CONSCIOUSNESS: BEING HUMAN IS GREAT! HERE'S WHY . . .

When it comes to investing, most behavioral scientists will say "we're our own worst enemies," "our brains trick us," and so on. That's one way to think about it (and true enough), but it seems pretty bleak. Instead, look at the bright side: Self-awareness (AKA consciousness) allows us to observe bad behavior and correct it! Even better? We can observe it in others, too! The ability to be hyper self-aware is perhaps the greatest gift humanity ever got, but we rarely see it for what it is. It's quite sad so relatively few utilize that tool effectively or even realize how special it is and try to actually cultivate awareness as a skill.

Instead of just feeling and acting on emotions, we humans have the ability to step back and observe what we feel and then decide to act or not. That is extraordinarily powerful and a key to investing success. The first step toward greater awareness is asking some questions about consciousness proper.

What are you conscious of right now? What were you conscious of a minute ago? What is "in" your consciousness, and what is "out" of it? And most importantly, is any of that truly your decision? Are you really directing your consciousness? Do you get to decide on your thoughts at all?

These are difficult and strange questions usually reserved for philosophers. Even today the problems of consciousness baffle our best minds. There are two main problems to be solved for the riddle of consciousness. According to David Chalmers, professor of philosophy at the Australian National University, these are the "easy" and "hard" problems. The easy problem is, well, pretty easy. Science has effectively demonstrated the mind and body are linked. If we want to know how we react to stimuli, we simply observe the brain and its chemical reactions. An emotion can literally be seen as it's happening in the brain during fMRI scans; we can observe the electrical and chemical responses to fear, and so on. A brain can even be observed thinking and where certain types of thoughts happen under fMRIs.

When we alter brain chemistry with drugs, our state of consciousness is also changed (ask any pothead or alcoholic); when neuroscientists tinker with the brain or cut out whole sections (like a frontal lobotomy or brain tumors), whole parts of a person's memory or conscious awareness can be destroyed—even certain kinds of emotions might be eradicated!

The two brain hemispheres have two (generally) separate functions and create two different realities, or modes of thinking. The right side experiences and processes stimuli through feelings. It sees the world in holistic terms and looks for general patterns, while the left side processes language and focuses on the specific, taking note of differentiations. (These are generalizations, of course.)

But that's why the easy problem of consciousness is easy—we know how to solve it. We just look at the brain and what it does whenever we have thoughts. It's really just a question of biology.

Unfortunately, simply observing where thoughts happen isn't even half the battle. The results of the "easy" problem don't really tell us what consciousness is or how it works. The "hard" problem of consciousness is all about accounting for our uniqueness—our subjective experience of the world and awareness. We have a sense of self; we have individual, subjective experiences—we are not zombies who just react to stimuli. Philosophers call these experiences *qualia*, or the subjective qualities of experience that can't be quantified.

Most "reason" or rational thinking happens in the neocortex, but that doesn't say anything about how we feel about our thoughts. The hard problem is all about the way we see things—our specific perspective as opposed to objective reality.

Here's the interesting part: *There's no place in the body or brain where consciousness "lives."* Nowhere in the detectable body is there a locale for the "self." There is no center in the brain, and no electrical or biological signature that says, "This is conscious thought."

It's difficult for scientists to pin consciousness down because it's not a single thing; it appears to be the result of many things happening at once in the brain. This is often referred to as *bundle theory*, or the idea that conscious awareness arises as a result of many things going on at once in the brain. It could very well be that self-awareness simply arises from the sheer complexity of our brains. In fact, many experts believe consciousness to be a complex, adaptive, emergent system (more on this in Chapter 5)—the result of trillions of neural connections, acting together to create something more than the sum of the individual parts. In this way, consciousness might best be thought of as a *technology*, or feature, of evolution because self-awareness is such a clear and powerful advantage over other animals. But no matter where you believe consciousness comes from, its implications are vast for how we perceive and make decisions.

Real, or Imagined?   One important feature of consciousness is that our experience of the world is mostly imagination. Sound strange? It's true: Our sensory organs (eyes, ears, skin, nose, and so on) are in many ways crude instruments, taking in information about the outside world in haphazard, disjointed ways. Our brains take those crude readings from our senses and recapitulate them into images, memories, thoughts, emotions, and so on. But what's reconstructed inside our heads is not reality as such; it's an approximation of reality based on how our brains interpreted the data. Even worse? Our sense of continuity about the world is wholly constructed in our brains. Think about it: Ears can only hear, eyes can only see, yet when we watch a movie the whole thing *feels* like a unified experience—our brain does the work of putting the images and sound together to create the perception of continuity. Thus, no one knows what reality looks like; we only know what reality looks like to *us*. Andy Newberg, in his book *Why We Believe What We Believe*, says,

By the time perceptual information reaches consciousness, each individual has transformed it into something new and unique. The reconstruction of reality is the foundation from which we construct all our beliefs about the world.[2]

The important thing for investors is to simply be aware of it. It's vital to realize how limiting and often contorting consciousness can be because it suddenly makes discipline the most important feature of investing when we recognize our perception of the world may not be reality—our brains are making the story based on limited information from our senses. Our senses are too dim to detect radio waves, the individual molecules around us, what your neighbor is doing right now, whether your intestines are digesting your spaghetti dinner, what some stock trader in Tokyo is currently up to, and so on. Thus, reality as it exists in the world is probably very unlike how we perceive it. Our view of the world is so myopic and dim it almost undoubtedly hinders us from understanding much of what we think we do.

Can you picture 10 one-dollar bills laid out on a table? Most people can. But can you conceptualize what a million one-dollar bills laid out in a row looks like? No! Humans cannot—our brains weren't made to be able to conceptualize a number that large. When we think about a million, it becomes an abstraction. The whole world is made up of things and events we can only comprehend by abstraction or not at all. That is, very quickly we must begin employing imagination in order to understand many issues in today's very complex and large world.

The whole world is made up of things and events we can only comprehend by abstraction or not at all. That is, very quickly we must begin employing imagination in order to understand many issues in today's very complex and large world.

Knowing all this, we can't help but think: Which is the truer reality—the one out there or the one in our heads? Understanding consciousness reveals the importance of studying our emotions and practicing discipline with our investments. The more we know about ourselves, the less we can trust! Which is why the scientific method (or the attempt to achieve greater objectivity) is vital.

Free Will or Free Won't?   Some philosophers and neuroscientists refer to our ability to choose not as "free will," but instead they call it *free won't*.[3] Like any animal, when we are prompted by a stimulus, our nervous system responds. If a threat arises, particular hormones are secreted, the eyes dilate—our bodies get ready for action automatically. That's an *emotional* response. Such experiences are innate—wired into our being—and thus very similar, if not near identical, within our species. If someone brandishes a knife, it's fight or flight and the adrenaline starts pumping; when we took our first driving test at the DMV, we all felt at least a little nervous; when a guy sees a beautiful woman . . . well, you know. These are *reactions*, not conscious acts of choice.

So we have universal emotional reactions to things. Our reactions to stock markets are no different. When stocks go up a lot, we become overconfident and feel euphoric. When they're down a lot, we become panicky and worried. We can't much control that. The real gift of consciousness is that we have the ability to observe those things in ourselves and *decide* whether to act on them. That's why it's "free won't." Most folks tend to feel similarly in similar situations (like grief when a loved one dies or fear and anger when stocks sink), but it's up to you if you're going to act on those emotions. You have a choice. Choice is something other animals don't have—they generally act automatically relative to conditioning or stimulus. That's the great advantage of being human. In my view, the majority of great investors through history have mastered this ability to at least recognize when emotion seizes them and manage some control.

When stocks go up a lot, we become overconfident and feel euphoric. When they're down a lot, we become panicky and worried. We can't much control that. The real gift of consciousness is that we have the ability to observe those things in ourselves and *decide* whether to act on them. That's why it's "free won't."

Rewire Yourself?

Some folks seem more naturally skilled at choosing to control their emotions than others. Most of us mortals have to cultivate such a talent. Rewiring your brain isn't easy and many can't do it at all.

No matter your religious inclination, a good clue-in is Buddhism. The story of the Buddha is, essentially, a hero's long quest to find the secret methods of gaining self-awareness and self-mastery, and then to communicate those secrets to the world. Buddha tried everything to find enlightenment, from severe ascetic disciplines like nearly starving himself, to meditation sessions that could last for days. He wandered for years, looking for clues about enlightenment—studying himself, nature, and those teachers that he could find. It is an amazing story of perseverance and highlights the difficulty in overcoming our natural biases. There are countless accounts of the life of the Buddha, but my favorite is Thich Nhat Hanh's *Old Path White Clouds: Walking in the Steps of the Buddha*, which is an epic story but told in lighthearted prose.

Do you have to become a Buddhist to be a good investor? Of course not. But its system provides interesting clues into the study of self-mastery. Aside from their beliefs, the process of meditation is, essentially, a rigorous program to quiet the mind, exert some control over it, and become as self-aware as possible. Techniques for this are as old as time—an ancient kind of deliberate brain rewiring. But if you want to learn about it, there are several great studies out there to educate you on the principal of neural plasticity and the strategies involved in going about it. (See the Selected Bibliography and Further Reading.)

But maybe delving into Eastern philosophy isn't your bag. No problem. For my money, there is no better treatise ever written on the virtues of self-investigation and really getting to know and master oneself than the writings of Ralph Waldo Emerson. Emerson was a nineteenth century Unitarian minister. After his wife Ellen died of tuberculosis, he took to living in the wilderness for long stretches—simply to investigate nature and, principally, himself. In this period, he produced some of the most famous essays in US history, and he is often credited as a founder of the American spirit of "rugged individualism," otherwise known as *Transcendentalism*. Perhaps his most apt work for the purposes of investing is his essay, *Self Reliance*, which is ubiquitous in any published compilation of Emerson's work. Emerson believed deeply in developing oneself to the fullest—realizing total potential and doing what one must to know oneself in total. He is widely and often quoted. Here are a few of my favorites:

> *Trust thyself: every heart vibrates to that iron string. Accept the place the divine providence has found for you, the society of your contemporaries, the connexion of events. Great men have always done so.*

> *A man should learn to detect and watch that gleam of light which flashes across his mind from within, more than the lustre of the firmament of bards and sages. Yet he dismisses without notice his thought, because it is his. In every work of genius we recognize our own rejected thoughts: they come back to us with a certain alienated majesty.*

Tips for Boosting Self-Knowledge and Self-Awareness. Here are a few tips for boosting your self-awareness when investing.

- *Step back.* Do so as often as possible, and try to observe yourself as if you were an onlooker to your own life. Just see what you're doing. "Every day I brush my teeth before I shower. Why do I do that? I never realized it—never even thought about it before!" Our lives are filled with a million little things we do in routine but seldom think about. Take a step back and just observe and learn about yourself.
- *Put yourself in someone else's shoes.* Try to think like another person. If you want to know how Warren Buffett thinks, try to actually put yourself in his shoes. This is difficult to do at first—may even seem impossible—but it gets easier with practice. Of course, we can't actually think like someone else

exactly. But what is possible is achieving a similar perspective, which can be very useful.

- *Talk to yourself!* Before you act on any investment decision, just ask yourself questions. Folks think I'm crazy, but I do it all the time. I'm no schizophrenic—I'm just helping myself see all sides of an issue.
- *Be deliberate.* Unless you work on the floor of a stock exchange, almost nothing in investing has to be done quickly. Ever. Just allow time to ruminate. That doesn't mean think yourself into inaction—it means giving yourself time to shield against emotional decisions, which tend to happen under duress. Emotions are designed for short-term responses. If you give yourself time, reason has a better chance of winning.
- *Seek outside opinion.* We're usually worst at judging ourselves, so ask for another's opinion. It doesn't mean you have to do what they say, but it will clue you in on whether you're making the choice you actually want to make, or whether some other factor you're blind to is influencing your thoughts. At the very least, it forces you out of your biases and to see a different angle.
- *Assess your strategy in relation to your goals.* Ask yourself if what you're doing is part of your long-term goals. Most emotional decisions will act to counter someone's long-term investing or saving goals. If it's not aligned with your goals, you don't have any business doing it. (Chapter 8 covers goal-setting in more depth.)
- *If it feels bad . . . good!* If something feels counterintuitive or wrong, you may actually be on to something. Keep going down that line of thought and see where it takes you. At the very least, explore all the options you can fathom and, if nothing else, disprove them.

All these little tactics are easily implemented for investors. Just stepping back every once in a while and questioning your standard investing and research routine will yield interesting results.

SIMPLE IS SUPERIOR

Wall Street analysts seem to have a genius mentality. We work ourselves into all manner of labyrinthine logic trying to sound more sophisticated than we really are. Don't be impressed by financial jargon just because it sounds good. Stick with stuff you understand. Most of the investing mistakes I've made were about trying to tackle something too complicated. The successes have all been simple and well within my understanding.

The more jerry-rigging and qualification an analysis needs, the more likely it's forcing results to support a hypothesis. If you can't understand and explain something in simple terms, you don't understand it, and you certainly can't rely on it.

I wish it weren't so. But we know how limited our brains are, how limited perception is, and how many strange biases we have (and some we're not even aware of!). In the investing world, you need ideas you can trust and rely on. By definition, those must be relatively simple and clean because we probably can't understand them otherwise or are making some mistake in understanding we haven't thought of. Always look for this feature when considering another theory or analysis. Does it need a lot of qualification? Are there tons of exceptions to it? Is the data very clean and straightforward? If so, it's a great clue there's a problem.

SAGACITY: SEEING ISN'T BELIEVING

Here is a big word worth knowing: *Sagacity.* It means being judicious and forming opinions by distinguishing, evaluating, and discriminating. We could say investors should have a high degree of sagacity about themselves. Always exercise your "free won't" and check your perceptions and experiences with the wider reality.

You know the old saying "seeing is believing." Seems true enough, right? Wrong! Hopefully, what comes next will scare you out of that habit forever.

Humans are visual animals. We tend to think and understand in a visual way. It's not a coincidence that in order to

If something feels counterintuitive or wrong, you may actually be on to something. Keep going down that line of thought and see where it takes you.

understand something, we use visual cues or allude to what we can "visualize." Symbols are images; we have "visions" of things; we imagine in images. Even words usually describe what we wish to "see." But the problem with all that is our *eyes aren't windows, they're interpreters.*[4]

Our eyes don't see reality as such. We have a perspective on the world around us and not an objective view. The "true" reality of things would be impossible for us to even fathom—perception is subjective and based on how our brains construe information received from the eyes. Eyes don't take in everything we think we see; they aren't sophisticated or powerful enough for that. At any given moment, our eyes take in an opaque and an un-detailed photo of what we think we see. The brain uses that incomplete image and fills in the missing parts of a scene by *assumption, experience,* and *memory.* This is true not just for vision but for all senses and interactions. Thus, "seeing" is an act of imagination as much as anything objective. According to Steven Pinker:

> People cannot reconstruct an entire visual image or scene. It's fragmentary. Images are "slaves" to the organization of memory. Visual thinking is often driven more strongly by the conceptual knowledge we use to organize our images than by the contents of the images themselves.[5]

And neuroscientist Andy Newberg:

> Everything we see is an illusion in the sense that our eyes, memories, and consciousness can envision only a symbolic representation of the world.[6]

For instance, color is a purely subjective experience. In "reality," colors are just differing wavelengths of light. The brain takes that information and creates the experience of what we see. In fact, we don't even see anything in 3-D—our brains create the depth. Stereoscopic vision between our two eyes renders a high-definition 3-D image of the world in our minds, when in fact the eyes themselves are taking in a 2-D image. Depth perception only happens in the brain.

The eyes and their associated components within the brain are perhaps the most wondrous and complex systems in the body. A great deal of the brain's power, energy, and geography are used to process images. Everything we see, tangible as it seems, isn't. There are no solids in the universe. There's not even a suggestion of a solid, and not a surface or even a straight line. We just see things reduced to these forms from the human perspective. Weird but true! Again from Mr. Pinker:

> At best, we have an abstract appreciation of the stable structure of the world around us; the immediate, resplendent sense of color and form that fills our awareness when our eyes are open is completely different. Vision is not a theatre in the round. We vividly experience only what is in front of our eyes; the world beyond the perimeter of the visual field and behind the head is known only in a vague, almost intellectual way.[7]

Notice that a picture or painting is nothing more than a convenient way of arranging images in a certain pattern to appear as real objects. It's not our eyes that create the "reality" of the art, but our brains that do the work. When we view a photograph, our brains do the heavy lifting in imagining a depiction of reality.

Now, I want you to think the same thoughts the next time you read a stock chart. Look at Figure 2.1. It's a standard chart. What do

Figure 2.1 Generic Stock Chart

you notice about it? First, it's two dimensional, which means it can only relate to us two variables in relationship to each other. Just two! But we know there are millions of variables out there, interacting with each other in strange ways. Yet our basic visual minds can really only think in this model of two dimensions. This tells us our natural way of seeing the world is extremely limited—what we see or are capable of seeing isn't the whole story but merely a fraction of it.

What's the point of all this vision talk? Experiential learning is very important, but it isn't everything and often our interpretation of events is just wrong. Sagacity means penetrating through, or at least recognizing, these inherent problems. It's an important lesson that the conduits of our perception can actually skew our thinking. It was Obi-Wan Kenobi who said "Your eyes can deceive you, don't trust them." (Laugh if you want! But *Star Wars* is chock full of investing wisdom.)

 Investing discipline means questioning what we see, challenging our preconceptions, and never allowing ourselves to sway from an appropriate strategy, even when our emotions are crying out for us to do so . . . even when our eyes betray us.

Learning from experience is essential in life—it's the primary way our brains learn about the world around us. But the key is to be reflexive and realize much of what you perceive is our interpretation of the world. Investing discipline means questioning what we see, challenging our preconceptions, and never allowing ourselves to sway from an appropriate strategy, even when our emotions are crying out for us to do so . . . even when our eyes betray us.

DATA DRUNK

Here's a real-world investing example of vision and sagacity (or lack thereof). Most market analysts I read just regurgitate a lot of information and frame it as insight. That's a kind of *anti*-sagacity. Here are two statements, both with big problems. Can you *see* what they are?

"You're seeing a backup in iron ore prices lately."
"You're seeing interest rates climb after the Fed's speech today."

GET SOME PERSPECTIVE: ALTITUDE MATTERS

If you were going to study traffic patterns, how would you set about it? All else aside, the first thing to do is decide how you'd observe traffic. Will you watch it from the street level or maybe go up to the top of a skyscraper? Better yet, maybe you could commandeer a helicopter and watch from thousands of feet up!

Whichever option you choose, it will make a difference in how you observe things. Too low (street level), and you can only see a few cars at a time in one spot; too high, and you can't see any of the action at a local level at all! The perspective you choose will influence the results of the study.

Seldom do investors consider their perspective. Looking at day-to-day news is like watching traffic whiz by with your cheek on the pavement—ultra close-up and without any visibility of the wider patterns. The technical term is *myopia*, where a narrow perspective creates a lack of foresight and the ability to discern wider patterns. With the wrong perspective, it's impossible to get the right outlook.

Pull yourself up from the concrete and get a better perspective. Most patterns aren't detectable when looking at day-to-day price moves. Data tend to be erratic— bouncing around by the week and even month. In most cases, the best thing to do is ignore the short-term stuff and look at data from a quarterly or annual perspective.

Let's take an example. Figure 2.2 shows basic stock market price returns. That one looks pretty scary. But now look at Figure 2.3. That one looks mostly like a straight line. Guess what, they're both the same data! Both are graphs of the S&P 500 Total Return Index since 1926. Why the big difference between the two? It has to do with the scale of the graphs themselves, not the data.

Figure 2.2 shows the index on a linear scale, so every point move in the index takes up the same amount of vertical space. An increase from 100 to 200 looks the same as a move from 1,000 to 1,100. But that's not a great way to look at market growth over time. After all, going from 100 to 200 represents a 100% increase in stock prices, whereas a move from 1,000 to 1,100 is only a 10% rise. As a result, looking at the data on a linear scale makes gains since about 1990 seem stratospheric simply because the index level is higher. But average annualized market returns from 1990–2007 weren't markedly different than those from 1926–1989 (11.0% versus 10.2%, respectively).

Looking at market growth over time is much better suited to a logarithmic scale as shown in Figure 2.3. On a logarithmic scale, percent changes in the index look the same even if the point changes are vastly different. So an increase in the index from 100 to 200 (a 100% change) looks the same as a rise from 1,000 to 2,000 (also 100%).

(Continued)

(Continued)

Don't be scared away from stocks because gains seem unsustainable when presented on a linear scale. In reality, market growth has been pretty steady over time. Proper perspective matters. Without it, it doesn't make a difference how great your data is—you can still come to the wrong conclusions.

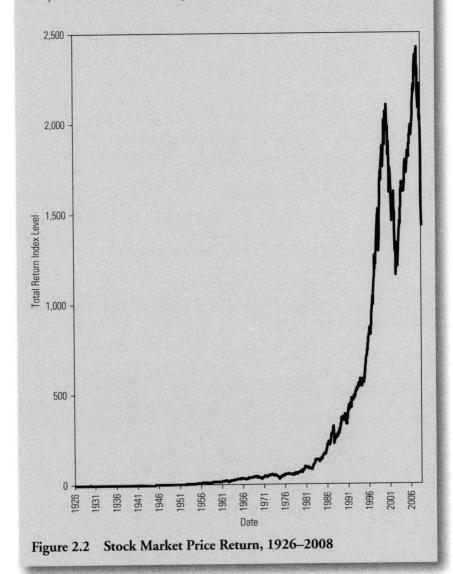

Figure 2.2   Stock Market Price Return, 1926–2008

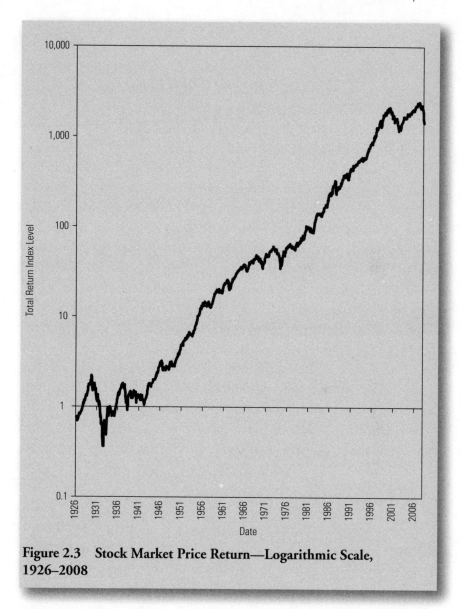

Figure 2.3   Stock Market Price Return—Logarithmic Scale, 1926–2008

Whoever said that sure sounds smart! But they're probably not. How do I know? (Caution: What I'm about to tell you will drive you batty the next time you turn on CNBC.) Data regurgitators always begin sentences with "you're seeing." Listen for it. This might sound trivial, but little turns of phrase like that reveal a lot about what folks are really up to. "You're seeing" is another way of saying, "Here's what happened." That's not analysis, that's just data reporting. There is a giant difference between clear thought and data regurgitation. If you listen closely to most financial analysts and pundits, most only spew back at you things they've read or numbers they've crunched. It's no less ironic that they use the metaphor "seeing," given what we know now about the pitfalls of vision and perception.

Why is data reporting and analysis such an important distinction? Because most investors don't differentiate between *data* and *information*. A key to disciplined investing is knowing the difference and only acting on useful information. In a world where data and analysis are increasingly available (much more is produced in a day than you could ever probably read in your life!), folks become what I call "data drunk." We gorge ourselves on information, feast on numbers—it's a dizzying act of daily gluttony. Instead of the quantity of data, focus on better understanding.

Of course we all want scarce information to help us as investors. But there is a difference between something merely esoteric and truly meaningful, scarce knowledge. No information is better than wrong information. It's not about genius or some special knowledge only "pros" have—it's about interpreting information correctly. More information has little to do with forecasting. If it were true, then the data houses and media outlets would always beat the market. They never do.

UNDERSTANDING AND BEING CURIOUS

Call me a flighty intellectual if you want, but I'm big on understanding stuff. I don't believe anything of value is achievable in investing over the long term unless you understand what you're doing through and through. Otherwise, it's just luck. Understanding is one of the truest ways to be practical about investing.

 I don't believe anything of value is achievable in investing over the long term unless you understand what you're doing through and through. Otherwise, it's just luck. Understanding is one of the truest ways to be practical about investing.

No one is born a natural investor. There isn't a single legendary investor who didn't put in much back-breaking work to become what they are. They learn from experience, theories, their elders, history, and peers. They look for answers in places others don't; they're eternally inquisitive and thoughtful about their job. Most love what they do.

It's hard work, requiring eternal vigilance. Good investors have a spirit of humility (knowing they could be wrong); they know perpetual learning is what makes their success. To me, humility and discipline are shades of the same concept.

Find any portfolio manager with a track record of long-term success and you'll see a few universals: continual learning, continual studying, perpetually trying to see what the market can teach them. They do not impose themselves on the markets—they go with it, they learn from it.

We're not talking about punk analysts fresh out of business school. Observe the salty dogs, with decades of experience. There's little arrogance about them and their approach. Yet they're simultaneously convicted and indefatigable. Garry Kasparov, perhaps the greatest chess player of all time, called this the "champion's paradox"—to at once be humble and respectful of your opponent and also believe in yourself to the fullest. Good investors are constantly aware the market is smarter than any individual, and they pay requisite respect to it. Great portfolio managers simply never feel they've learned it all and always ask how they might be wrong.

Stock markets are changing and evolving things—that means you have to evolve over time, too. It takes <u>observation</u>, <u>critical thinking</u>, <u>self-knowledge</u>, and a good dose of <u>courage</u> to get it <u>consistently right over time</u>.

How to understand? Or perhaps a better question: In a world where we know information and knowledge is incomplete and our brains limited and myopic, how do we know if we understand something? Understanding is a slippery thing. The more you investigate something as big and complex as stock markets—or any field of study for that matter—you'll come to realize quickly there is sometimes a <u>consensus</u>, always <u>dissenting</u> opinions, and rarely <u>absolute fact</u>.

Stock markets are changing and evolving things—that means you have to evolve over time, too. It takes observation, critical thinking, self-knowledge, and a good dose of courage to get it consistently right over time.

So, when I say understanding, I really mean carefully vetting conflicting views (preferably in a scientific way, but logic and thought experiments can work, too) and coming to some conclusion in the most informed, objective way possible. If you want definitive conclusions—particularly about the future—you're dipping your toes in the wrong waters. Stock markets are too slippery for that. We just have to live with ambiguity sometimes.

The way to come to the best understanding, in my view, is to be a fox instead of a hedgehog. That is, study many topics—don't myopically focus on one. If we know most "knowledge" is contextual and relational, then seeing things from as many views as possible is key. So it's using experience, study, theory, history, learning from peers, learning from fields completely outside the norms of markets, and so on. Look for answers in places others don't.

Here's the discipline part: Recognize when you're "in over your head" and don't act on it. You don't have to know everything. Often, the best investing choice is realizing you aren't qualified to make a certain judgment and leaving it alone.

CHAPTER INSIGHTS

One of the most important parts of long-term investing success has to do with the discipline of self-awareness and self-control. No strategy can work unless we are able to execute it properly—meaning we must be able to control our emotions and keep a proper perspective.

- Discipline is:
  - Self-awareness.
  - Self-control.
  - Not necessarily ascetic or severely miser-like behavior.

- Understanding the nature of consciousness helps cultivate self-awareness.
  - We are often aware and in control of much less than we think.
  - Controlling oneself has more to do with "free won't" than "free will."

- Sagacity is being judicious by being distinguishing, evaluating, and discriminating.
  - The limitations of human vision are great examples of the problems regarding our awareness and the importance of striving for the right perspective.
  - Most great investors through time are curious and seek understanding rather than piling on more data.

3

HUMAN BEHAVIOR

Behavior is a mirror in which everyone displays his own image.
—Johann Wolfgang von Goethe

*People's behavior makes sense if you think about it in terms of
their goals, needs, and motives.*
—Thomas Mann

These days it's vogue to say humans are irrational—scores of new books from respected behavioral economists tell us how dumb we all are and how we continuously act in ways contrary to our best interests.

I disagree. We're a very rational species—just not in the ways classical economics wants us to be. Humans—in both hardware (brains) and software (the mind)—are the finest machines ever built, but we weren't built for the civilization we've got. Our cultures, economies, and markets are something bigger than we are—and expanding at an accelerating pace. We "irrational" humans gave rise to systems far beyond our individual capacity to understand. We simply weren't made for dealing with markets—our minds and bodies were evolved over many eons to survive in the wild, pre-civilization. Toward that end, we're quite an impressive species! Humans evolved so well, we dominate the planet and utilize resources far better than any life form ever has.

But while markets evolve at breakneck speed, the mind doesn't. Human brains—their instincts and natural emotions—simply do not change as quickly as markets or societies do. Economies and capital markets move faster than our brains can keep up with. It takes (even by the quickest estimates) hundreds or thousands of years for any meaningful evolutionary change to take hold—and usually a lot longer. Well, we've got a little over 80 years of meaningful stock market data (at best). Thus, our primal reactions are fairly consistent over time because we simply can't evolve much or at all within a few generations. The brain hasn't changed much in that time—therefore, as Thomas Mann said, the "goals, needs, and motives" of human behavior won't have changed much, either.

Human brains—their instincts and natural emotions—simply do not change as quickly as markets or societies do. Economies and capital markets move faster than our brains can keep up with.

Fear and joy and overconfidence and all sorts of other typical human biases aren't going anywhere anytime soon—they're wired in our brains. Even better, across time and culture, a lot of human emotional behavior is *fungible*. That is, you can roughly apply what you know of pure human instinct to anybody, no matter the culture or place in the world.

Unfortunately, many of the features that helped us conquer the pre-civilization wild aren't useful—often they're problematic!—for navigating investments and understanding the economy. Markets are made of humans, so a better understanding of who we are as a group will help us make better, more informed decisions about how markets move. In Chapter 2, we discussed the importance of discipline and self-knowledge in investing success. A study of wider human behavior is another big step toward that goal. Macro thinking helps us understand markets and forecast more easily.

Important note: When we talk about human behavior, we're talking in general terms. Not all humans are the same—we aren't automatons. On average, these are features of human behavior. Specific cases will always vary.

Sometimes, psychology is the only thing that really matters in judging markets. Often, a crisis in confidence can be as potent as anything fundamental (as we well know from living through 2008's financial panic). Markets don't really work without a measure of belief, which is entirely psychological. If we do not *believe* in money as a store of value, for instance, it simply becomes paper with green ink on it. The same with property laws—if for some reason the collective decided to stop obeying them, they would simply cease to exist. It is a fascinating characteristic of humanity that we adhere to laws and communal norms so readily and automatically.

So far, this book has been about understanding ourselves and the processes we sometimes use to understand markets. We've discovered a reasonable goal is to become more aware of our limited personal perceptions and to use discipline and the right perspective on science to help overcome them.

In later chapters, we'll move on to the ways big, complex systems like stock markets and economies function. But first we need to dig deeper in observing ourselves (humans) and, specifically, how we tend to act in marketplaces.

BRAIN BASICS

There are four big ideas you should know when thinking about how brains work:

1. The *triune brain*—reptilian, limbic, and the neocortex.
2. Brains are hierarchical and most neural activity is unconscious.
3. Modular instinct.
4. Neural plasticity.

The Triune Brain

In the 1950s, Dr. Paul D. MacLean theorized brains have three main systems that evolved over time. Human brains as we know them today aren't "new"—they evolved over many eons, and a lot of that change happened in different species altogether. Much of the neural system we have is a leftover from the neural systems of our evolutionary lineage. In other words, brains didn't "reinvent" themselves each time a new species arrived. Instead, new brains built upon the old system or made some minor modifications. The new is based on the old.

MacLean's theory is somewhat crude and outdated as a formal scientific model, but remains a useful framework for understanding brain basics and development.

- **The Reptilian Brain.** Sometimes called the R-complex, this usually includes the brain stem and cerebellum. MacLean called it "reptilian" because these are the brain parts reptiles have, meaning it's the "oldest" part of the brain in evolutionary terms. The reptilian brain cannot consciously think, but simply reacts to stimuli. It also controls instinctual mechanisms and many of the body's self-regulating systems like heartbeat and breathing.
- **The Limbic System.** As species evolved, the brain grew, adding parts and features. The limbic system is the part humans share with other mammals. Here is where emotions and most instincts come in—everything from fear to hunger to (some believe) maternal instincts. We might say this is the "emotional center" of the brain. We should be careful, however. Evolution doesn't just add parts to the brain—it also alters the old parts. Brains don't operate like a car engine, where separate areas only perform one function—the whole thing is interconnected and there is much overlap and redundancy. For instance, memory is something that goes on in different forms in all three parts of the triune brain.
- **The Neocortex.** This is the "outer layer" of the brain—the wrinkled tissue surrounding the rest of the gray matter. The neocortex

is found only in highly developed mammals. This is the place—predominantly—where we are self-aware, where speech happens, and reasoning. Our highly developed neocortex is a major part of what makes us human.

All three systems are highly interactive. In fact, emotions and reactions to stimuli coming from the reptilian and limbic parts can often be overwhelmingly powerful relative to any rational self-aware thoughts we have. Those two "older" parts of the brain are generally geared toward survival, and many scientists believe they carry an over-riding mechanism to our thoughts when danger or hunger or some other immediate need arises.

The limbic system and reptilian brain are usually bad things for smart investing—they will shout "fight or flight" at inopportune times, make us overconfident at others, and generally cloud our best judgment. Remember, these were made for survival in the wild, not in markets.

HIERARCHY AND THE UNCONSCIOUS

Jeff Hawkins, founder of Palm (maker of "PDA" handheld devices popular in the 1990s), in 2005 published *On Intelligence*, an excellent account of an important neural theory: the hierarchy.

Brains have over 100 billion neurons, each with up to 10 thousand interconnecting dendrites—allowing for an astronomical number of unique associations and possibilities in every single brain. The circuitry of brains is a great deal slower than today's sophisticated computer circuitry, yet in practice they (at least so far) can process information far faster because they work *in parallel.* That is, they can do all sorts of things at the same time. You can read this book while your brain is busy with other activities like digesting food, regulating temperature and heartbeat, and so on. Even when sleeping, your brain's doing a lot of things!

Brains can do all that because they have a hierarchical function. Essentially, most of our neural lives are unconscious, and very little actually makes it "up" the hierarchy to our actual awareness. Very few things demand our conscious attention. Hawkins calls it the "cortical algorithm." It's a good thing our brains don't tell us every little thing they're going to do. The unconscious parts of brain activity are constantly registering information and making decisions for us without our explicit permission. You don't need to tell your eyes to focus when you shift your gaze from a book to the horizon; they just do it. Your stomach doesn't ask if it should start digesting that burger you ate; it just does it. That's a good thing.

This means most of our brain activity is unconscious—and very little ever makes it up all the way to our attention. This is extremely important. Our unconscious makes most of the decisions. How often do you actually think about things like your digestion, heartbeat, or hair growth? Seldom, and when you're thinking about it, you're really only observing it, not actually directing it. Parts of your brain (or nervous system generally) are doing this for you without you ever needing to make a decision about it. It's true for many complex functions as well. When you lift a fork to your mouth to eat something, do you actively think about all the tiny muscles involved? Do you ask each muscle in your jaw to contract and release? Do you call upon your throat and tongue to close the windpipe and open the esophagus? Do you tell your stomach to start producing the acids necessary to begin digestion? Of course not. Those decisions are automatic and your brain does them without your conscious involvement.

Hawkins' idea is very important for investing. It tells us we automatically make assumptions, become habituated, and often make decisions on things we never really thought about. This is so easy to see in investing, where we assume so much and rarely think many decisions through properly. Why? *It costs a great deal of energy and effort to push things into our consciousness*—our brains would rather take the easy path and just assume things. This is a bad idea for investing,

Investors unconsciously tend to believe some things to be true simply because their brains never brought the issues to their full awareness. We have unconscious biases and behaviors we don't even know about! All because most of our thinking is done without our consent.

where we must continually question everything we think we perceive. Investors unconsciously tend to believe some things to be true simply because their brains never brought the issues to their full awareness. We have unconscious biases and behaviors we don't even know about! All because most of our thinking is done without our consent.

Modules and Instinct

Harvard Professor Steven Pinker studies brain functions almost purely from the standpoint of evolutionary thought. He thinks of the brain as a computer and the mind as the software that runs the computer— both are shaped by eons of evolution.

Evolution is the implicit (and often random) logic of nature. The implicit logic of the body is in some sense the logic of all nature, for they are crafted by the same forces, governed by the same laws, and find their origins in the same place. We emerged from what's around us. The mind is made from instincts, built and reinforced hundreds of thousands of years ago, often stronger and more powerful than any conscious thought we could have.

Evolutionary theory can be an effective tool to describe much of our neural makeup. We are far more alike in the ways we appear and the emotions we have than we are different. But universality in itself doesn't mean exact sameness. Just as there are variations in height, skin color, eye color, muscle size, and gender, there are differences in the brain's software, too. But that doesn't change what it is to be human, and it also doesn't mean we are automatons or slaves to instinct.

Evolution is not a tidy process. Over millions of years of adaptation, all sorts of processes are jumbled together into our DNA, and the environment we live in helps give rise to gene expression (AKA phenotype). This is especially true in the brain. Some neural processes are optimized only for certain kinds of situations, while others don't work as well as they could. There's some duplication of effort throughout regions of the brain, and even some conflicting processes. Evolution didn't set out to optimize us for living; it only gave us facility to survive relative to the dangerous world around us.

Humans and their brains are essentially the same as they were at least five thousand years ago—only the situations we deal with (civilization and technology, for instance) have changed substantially. For decades, scientists believed the brain was a "blank slate" at birth, free to absorb and learn from culture and outside influence. That is, many believed the mind, or software of the brain, was free of instinct. But this cannot be so. Heartbeat, breathing, crying—we're capable of these at birth. The mind must come pre-wired with many kinds of instructions. But there's interplay between instinct and outside environment. The combination of the two is what makes us and our natural reactions.

Evolutionary science refers to instincts as "modules." Consider the emotion of fear. Why would evolution want us to fear things? Why would we be wired to feel fear? Fear is probably an emotion we'd like to be rid of if we could help it, but thousands of years ago, when humans lived in the wild and were prey to fierce predators, fear kept us alive by forcing us to stay away from danger.

One could say fear is a "module." The fear module will have all sorts of features—instinctual recognition from the visual areas of the brain on *what* to fear, hormonal responses when fear arises, and so on. Thus, most instinctual modules use many areas of the brain. Fear was great for helping us be mindful and avoid a lion hunting us for dinner, but might not be so great for us today—perhaps by inhibiting us from things we'd otherwise like to do.

Again, because emotions are instincts, they *happen* to us; we do not get to decide to feel them—they arise mostly from parts of our brains we do not control, based on stimuli we receive from the outside world. We can only experience emotions as they happen to us and attempt to inhibit, liberate, or alter them with our conscious thought.

Emotions are not ethereal little specters floating around in our heads; they have a specific biological signature, which is one reason scientists like Pinker refer to them as modules. Emotions are tangible in the body; they're visceral, real things. All thoughts, emotional and reasoned, are in some way grounded in the body. Hatred, fear, love, and joy all look similar and happen in similar parts of the brain under an fMRI scan, no matter the person, and produce mostly the same hormonal responses. Our similar emotions emit the same analogous chemical and hormonal reactions. What we love or hate might be unique, but the way the brain processes those emotions is near universal. Pinker says,

> What we should appreciate and fear are the cunning designs of the emotions themselves. Many of their specs are not for gladness and understanding. . . . But self-deception is perhaps the cruelest motive of all, for it makes us feel right when we are wrong and emboldens us to fight when we ought to surrender.[1]

Emotions, in an evolutionary sense, are the drivers propelling you toward goals; they are the blood of mental life and motivation. Some might think we're better off without emotions, but this is ridiculous. Without emotions, there cannot be intelligence because feelings give us goals and desires and reasons to do anything at all. Anyway, reason and emotion do not appear to be separable—emotion is an inextricable part of the mind, forever linked to all thought. Just like the mind and body. As noted neural scientist Marvin Minsky says in his book, *The Emotion Machine*:

> Emotional states are not especially different from the processes we call "thinking"; instead, emotions are certain ways to think that we use to increase our resourcefulness—that is, when our passions don't grow till they handicap us.[2]

Emotions like love, hatred, jealousy, and fear are universal, and they drive our destiny. Too often do we believe our emotions separate us from the world—that no one could possibly understand what we feel. But deeply felt emotion does not separate us. It puts us in touch—when we feel love, our brains react in the same way. Our subjective experience colors our emotions, and our reactions to those emotions make us unique, but the human brain and its instincts are largely the same.

Investors should take note—if emotion cannot be separated from reason, indeed, if emotion and reason are essentially the same but only feel different, we know we must be skeptical when we believe we're being objective. Too often, we find reasons to rationalize our emotions and not reality. Too often, we find ways to deceive ourselves.

NEURAL PLASTICITY AND NEURAL NETWORKS

Instincts, or modules—those "automatic" parts of the mind—are only one half of the equation. Our brains aren't just reactive machines; they can also take in and process information, remember, learn skills, and alter behavior. In short, our brains can *change* themselves. This is called the principle of *neural plasticity*.

Neuroscientists often refer to brains as "general problem solvers." When we have an experience, our brains make all sorts of new connections between neurons, forming networks. These networks are reinforced over time and added to. The first time you learned algebra, your brain made all kinds of new connections over and above the simple arithmetic you knew before. Those new connections created associative knowledge in your head. Some of it stuck; some you forgot over time.

Our experiences, thoughts, and actions are always changing the composition of our brains. Think of the brain like the Internet. Each website on the Internet is like a neuron. Websites link to each other and self-organize spontaneously with all sorts of connections and functions as content is added and amended through hyperlinks. The Internet is always the Internet, but it grows and modifies as we add to it—a giant, incredible, functioning digital brain of sorts.

The ability to learn and form neural networks is perhaps the greatest of all evolutionary adaptations—it's the ability to think and not just be a slave to instinct. New neural networks can be formed as information and experiences are transformed into chemical, physical presences.

The crux of all this is memory. Learning is not something only humans do—many animals have the ability to learn. In fact, learning is largely the same thing as memory. By retaining experiences as information in the brain, we can compute and use that knowledge in the future. No one could possibly learn without memory, and memory has a specific biological signature based on protein synthesis and neural connections in our heads.

As children, our brains are in hyper-development mode, creating basic neural pathways by the millions as we encounter the world for the first time. Only the most latent instincts are truly present in the beginning of our lives. The neural networks we create in childhood and reinforce as we develop are likely to stay with us throughout our lives. Little tendencies, traits, and idiosyncrasies we pick up from our siblings and parents are embedded within our brains—we act and reenact them far into adulthood usually without knowing we're doing it. There are even neurons made especially for learning by mimicking. These are called *mirror neurons.* The act of human mimicry is one of the most important ways knowledge is passed on.

If instinct and emotion are modes of human universality (what's common between us), then the brain's plasticity—its ability to learn— is a source of difference and uniqueness among us. The older you get, the less capacity your brain has to change itself. Neural networks—reinforced through behavior and experience through the years of your life—become rigid and calcified. This is crucial for understanding how we react to market events—we tend to get set in our ways over time while markets constantly evolve. A good way

The older you get, the less capacity your brain has to change itself. Neural networks—reinforced through behavior and experience through the years of your life—become rigid and calcified. This is crucial for understanding how we react to market events—we tend to get set in our ways over time while markets constantly evolve.

to combat that tendency is to continually learn new things in entirely new fields. It's important to simply be aware of the problem that our brains get set in their ways over time, but markets won't ever do that. In fact, the rate of change and evolution of markets, if anything, is likely to accelerate. So we have to keep a careful vigil—the stuff that worked in the past may not work tomorrow. Always question the things you thought you knew. *Question what you think is new.*

The more things change the more they stay the same.

FOXES ARE BETTER THAN HEDGEHOGS

The world is moving toward greater specialization—doctors increasingly specialize in one part of the body or another, and dentists too. Colleges start narrowing a person's field of study earlier and earlier. Heck, even liberal arts colleges are getting rarer.

Thinkers can be divided into two categories: Those who view the world through the lens of a single defining idea, and those who use many ideas and draw upon experiences to form a worldview. The Greek poet Archilochus is usually credited with saying "the fox knows many things, while the hedgehog knows one big thing." But the dichotomy was truly explored in Isaiah Berlin's 1953 book, *The Hedgehog and the Fox: An Essay on Tolstoy's View of History*. In it, Berlin analyzes Leo Tolstoy's (the great Russian writer) view of great thinkers through history and their uncanny tendency to be either foxes or hedgehogs in their approach.

It's a fact: Human knowledge is expanding so rapidly most folks have to specialize in something narrow in order to become an expert. These are traditionally called "hedgehogs" because they burrow in one place—never milling around in other fields, just concentrating in one area. That's fine and good, but there are huge limitations to it.

I think a good investor must be the opposite—a fox. Foxes dabble in everything, ambling around the forest, seeing and testing many things—getting a sense of the complete territory. Hedgehogs don't have any concept of the wider world around them—they just burrow deeper and deeper into their little corner of the world.

The investing world, like the rest of the scientific community, is moving toward greater specialization—more hedgehogs. We don't just have, say, Energy analysts today, but Energy analysts who specialize only in offshore drilling companies and nothing else. No offense to them—I'm sure they know a ton about offshore drilling—but I wouldn't trust them to make broader investing decisions. How could they if all they do is focus on one narrow topic?

Having an extremely focused knowledge set and being a student of capital markets and the economy is an irreconcilable paradox. I simply don't see how anyone could hope to understand markets and economies as a hedgehog.

I'm happy to admit most any insight I've ever had about my job as an analyst came when I wasn't thinking about my job. I make it a point to spend a lot of time studying things that aren't market related whatsoever. In doing so, I learn a lot about markets. I notice most great thinkers (investors included) have the habit of associating knowledge in unique ways. Some folks believe there is no such thing as a new idea, only new ways of saying the same things over and again. You know The Beatles line, "There's nothing you can know that isn't known"? Well, I'm not willing to go that far—seems to me new insights are made on occasion. (Maybe not in the territory of human wisdom, but at least in the scientific realm.)

In any case, often ideas and insights come from somewhere outside the field being studied, or a recombination of old ideas can make something new. I think it mostly has to do with context and perspective. Analyzing a problem from a new set of lenses offers greater insight and deeper understanding.

Don't get me wrong, great investors are quite focused on their jobs. But, almost inevitably, they have a broad perspective on the world in addition to a deep one. They are students of many things and many ways of viewing the same things. In short, they're foxes—they spend time ambling around the great expanse of human knowledge, seeing what they can find and generating perspective by association.

A few years ago, I was sitting behind a cameraman, watching my boss Ken Fisher being interviewed about how markets move. He said (paraphrasing), "You can think about stock market movements as something like a vector in physics—it tends to move in one general direction until some opposing force strong enough impacts and diverts it elsewhere."

It's such a simple and elegant idea to equate the movement of a market to physical laws. It tells you two things: Market trends tend to continue until something impedes them, and that something has to be strong enough to actually move the market's direction (not a trivial event). Of course, it's an imperfect comparison (all metaphors are), but it is also tremendously powerful. It's an insight one simply cannot have without a broad knowledge of many other fields.

The interview was taking place in Ken's library—a large room filled with thousands of books, few of which had anything to do with economics or markets. Books on science, religion, history (a lot of history books!), psychology, and many others. The stuff of foxes.

Current findings in neuroscience corroborate much of this idea. Memory and reason are increasingly being understood by the way the brain makes associations, not by the way brains "pull up" information as if from a databank.

We live in a world of progressively more hedgehogs. We're trending toward specialization. That makes foxes all the more valuable simply by virtue of their rarity. I think foxes are the ones who make the best investors in the long run. Myopia is one of the largest enemies in investing—explicitly the Achilles heel of hedgehogs. Get your head out of the dirt and look up to see the broad world around you.

Source: Kandel, 155.

BRAINS ON THE MARKET

Ok, we've covered some brain basics. Now let's examine how those neural functions can affect our investments.

WIRED FOR THE SHORT TERM

Folks sometimes forget the brain is just one part of the overall nervous system that reaches its tentacles into every part of the body. Bodily reactions are nervous system reactions. One of the most potent reactions is the way our bodies prepare for threats. Reaction to stress—or any perception of danger—is lightning-quick in the body. Notice its "perception" of danger. Our bodies produce a similar kind of reaction whether you're about to do public speaking or get in a fight—your nervous system doesn't know the difference. All sorts of hormones get pumped into the bloodstream, and you're breathing heavy, your eyes dilate, your palms get sweaty. Adrenaline! Ready for fight or flight!

Two important things are happening: First, the reaction to stress is a short-term solution—adrenaline rushes don't last forever. Second, the body has geared itself up to do something . . . now! *The reaction to stress is to take action here and now.* Now put that together with the notion we react with a similar hormonal response for any *perception* of danger. We perceive danger all the time when stock markets fall or are highly volatile. Stress comes from fear and the feeling of a loss of control—or heightened uncertainty.

The reaction? Take action! This is what I call the "do something" mentality. When we perceive danger in the markets we feel an involuntary need to make a move—relieve short-term discomfort. Countless studies have shown what a bad idea that is for investors.[3] Yet most just can't help themselves.

 When we perceive danger in the markets we feel an involuntary need to make a move—relieve short-term discomfort. Countless studies have shown what a bad idea that is for investors. Yet most just can't help themselves.

I was astounded by the number of otherwise rational people who, in the financial crisis of October 2008, did serious harm to their investment futures because they sold their stocks in panic near the bottom. It's one of the saddest things I've seen in my profession—watching people lock in losses on assets that took them their whole lives to save, all to alleviate stress in the short term. I'm not saying this is an easy one to conquer—it's not. Surmounting eons of evolution is a big obstacle. But few lessons are more important—when in doubt, do nothing. Take no action. Allowing time for that short-term "do something" rush to pass gives you a much better chance of making better decisions.

You've Never Been a Villain, Have You?

I love studying stories from all times and places. Specifically, I love myths of the world. One universal feature about stories is the villain never believes he's a villain. Even Lucifer thinks he's justified! We always find a way to believe we're in the right—that somehow it wasn't our fault.

Why is that important? Because rationalizing the world to fit our worldview is something we do naturally, but it can get us into big investing peril. The academy's term for this is "regret shunning." Often "pride" is worked into the equation as well. I see this frequently in my field. When someone gets a stock forecast right they're quick to tell us about it: "See! I told you so!" But then the next time, when they get it totally wrong, it's usually "Oh, I would have been right if it wasn't for . . . ." This is shunning regret—failing to see the world for how it really is and instead finding a way to rationalize it to our personal worldview. It's a fancy way of saying we always find a way to believe we're heroes—villains are other people, but not us. A wonderful psychological study of the nature of villainy is Philip Zimbardo's *The Lucifer Effect*, which examines how good people find ways to justify horrid behavior in certain environments and situations like war and prisons. Granted, shunning regret on a stock loss is undoubtedly different than the often heinous nature of war, but the psychological principles are similar.

This is another tough one to combat because a lot of successful investing has to do with acting against the crowd and taking a stand

My advice: Seek the opinions and counsel of folks who readily admit when they got something wrong, acknowledge it, and proceed to tell you what they learned from it. Those are great people to get advice from.

for what you believe to be true. That usually means adhering to an unpopular opinion for longer than you'd like while many will be telling you you're wrong. My advice: Seek the opinions and counsel of folks who readily admit when they got something wrong, acknowledge it, and proceed to tell you what they learned from it. Those are great people to get advice from. That's especially true because even great portfolio managers know they will be wrong only a little less often than they are right—so there will be plenty of opportunities to shun regret. See who irrationally holds on to their pride and who lets it go in search of the right answers.

Also, never mistake what's really a bad investment decision for bad luck. In the long run, there is no such thing as bad luck in stock markets—you either get it right or you don't. Don't be a villain—admit when you've screwed up.

Which brings me to my next point.

READ THE GENIUSES

A great way to become a great investing thinker and see how minds work generally is by reading the work of geniuses.

I noticed something about the greatest achievers in many fields: *All were independent thinkers*. Given the problems of innate behavior, simply being independent is a feat in itself and worthy of study. There are, of course, scores of investing books out there purporting to study the master investors. But in my view, most are quite useless because they mistake methodology for the process of thought that underlies it.

Still, I recommend reading and learning all you can about investing masters of the past. Knowing the territory that's already been tread is important so you don't have to do it all over again yourself and also know what has worked and what hasn't.

More broadly, we can benefit greatly from seeing how great minds work. Most theories will one day become outdated or somehow be proven false. All of them! That's true for anything in life—not just investing theories. Even most scientific "facts" are at some point proven wrong or amended. That's great because for geniuses long passed, we can study purely the quality of their thought—see how they reasoned, see their biases, see how culture influenced them, and view how they surmounted or succumbed to the natural biases outlined in this chapter.

Brains form "neural networks" very early in life. A neural network is, essentially, your brain solidifying a certain kind of thought pattern so it doesn't have to re-learn things. That's why you never really forget how to ride a bicycle—your brain makes a network for bicycle riding that it never fully forgets (even if you might be a little rusty after many years). Same for other skills like reading, driving, and so on. A problem with neural networks is they tend to solidify over time—we get stuck in our ways.

A philosopher like Descartes, a physicist like Richard Feynman, an artist like Picasso, an architect like Gaudi, a maverick like Socrates—they all saw the world differently than the rest. They challenged their own ingrained neural networking and the conventional wisdom of their times with new perspectives. Whether they were right or wrong, they forced us to consider an entirely alternate and wider view. As investors, that's a process we constantly need to be in touch with, particularly if we'd like to overcome the innate tendencies that often get us into trouble.

Investors are confronted daily by scores of investing theories and explanations on how the economy functions and the consequences. Most theories will be wrong and lead you astray. Ultimately, the only antidote is to learn to think through them for yourself. Study the greatest thinkers in human history to do it.

(See the Selected Bibliography and Further Reading section at the end of the book for suggestions on the geniuses to read.)

Lemmings, Herds, and Humans—Oh, But I Repeat Myself

One thing I really hate is people who always say they're doing great even when they're not. You know what I mean? You ask someone how they're doing, and no matter what's going on—could be Monday morning at 7AM, could be heading into the dentist's office for some molar drilling—they always say they're "Spectacular! Doing great!" Really bugs me. If you're not feeling that well today, just say so. Only genuinely crazy people *always* feel good. I'd rather know how you're really doing—that's why I asked.

But we say things we don't really mean all the time, don't we? We engage in and adhere to countless social mores—asking each other how we are and answering, "Great!" and a million other tiny obligatory behaviors because that's part of what it means to be in a society. We do those things because those are the norms.

Our brains are wired for norms—humans are social, communal animals. We're wired to want to have people like us, agree with us, and to feel like we fit in. That's fine and good insofar as it goes—we couldn't really have a civilization if no one were willing to participate in generally regular social behavior. But it can also lead to big investing mistakes.

I'm talking specifically about the *herd mentality*. We're capable of influencing each other heavily (that's the premise marketing's built upon!). We crave approval and to fit in—we generally feel awkward and upset when we're alone or the group disagrees. Social validation is a big deal. But the natural proclivity to fit in counters your best interests in investing—you must feel comfortable alone, or you're cooked from the start.

Herding and mimicry is more instinctual than we realize. Our brains are chock full of "mirror neurons"—a kind of brain cell specifically designed to observe behavior and mimic it. Consistently in MRI scan experiments subjects who observe a behavior in someone else actually mimic the observed action in their brains, even if they don't carry out the actual movement.[4] Scientists have pinned the causes of a huge range of behaviors on mirror neurons. Many believe it's a fundamental way we learn. Watch babies who are about a year old and you'll see they pick up a great deal—and quickly—from the interaction with their parents. Everything from how to clap, to, eventually, how to walk and talk. Particularly when very young, we learn from our parents by

We crave approval and to fit in—we generally feel awkward and upset when we're alone or the group disagrees. Social validation is a big deal. The natural proclivity to fit in counters your best interests in investing—you must feel comfortable alone, or you're cooked from the start.

mimicking their speech and movements. This is great for life generally, but what a dastardly thing for investors!

Chapter 5 will teach us markets work best with heterogeneity—diversity of opinion. Markets function poorly when homogeneity reigns—that's when extremes happen. Diversity is a vital component of a collective system's ability to solve problems. But we will also learn in Chapter 5 that all widely understood and discussed information is already reflected in stock prices. So going with the consensus makes no investing sense. Therefore, fight that herding mechanism in you. Mirroring the herd mostly makes for horrible investments.

Learning not to allow what others think to influence your choices is hard to do. The first time you go against the crowd, it's a strangely liberating and exhilarating feeling—like skinny dipping. It takes a lot of time to get used to and be comfortable in that territory—some folks never do. Then again, a few exceptional folks seem to innately feel good working against the crowd. Good for them, but the vast majority isn't so lucky.

A good way to see how this neural feature works is to study the greatest thinkers in world history—by definition, geniuses need to be somewhat maverick-like in their work because to change the world you have to be different. You'll see they don't do it just to be different—they're holding on to a worldview they believe to be right because they have good reason.

TIME TICKS BY SO SLOWLY . . .

Philip Zimbardo and John Boyd's 2008 book, *The Time Paradox: The New Psychology of Time That Will Change Your Life*, is an excellent study of how time is felt and understood psychologically. Time misperceptions lead investors astray, particularly in bear markets. *In times of stress our perception of time is materially altered.* It's easy to see in extreme cases. For instance, during the stock market panic of 2008, I noticed many folks developed a completely out-of-whack sense of how much time had passed relative to market events as they happened. In retrospect, the Fannie/Freddie nationalization, Bank of America purchase of Merrill Lynch, government bailout of AIG, and congressional passage of the $700 billion rescue package all happened in a mere 12 weeks or less! Extreme short term.

Yet, at the time, it felt like ages passed. Time felt like it slowed down. This is bound to have a material impact on perception of risk. My hypothesis is this happens because financial news is usually peripheral to daily life (particularly to non-professional investors), but during panics, events are hyper-analyzed and brought to the forefront of the collective consciousness—and for much longer durations. This excess time spent in our thoughts makes things seem to move much slower than they actually do.

This is bad because the "I can't take it anymore!" factor tied to stress is exacerbated in moments when time seems to have slowed—folks feel as if they've been hanging on for a very long time and enough is enough. They have to sell. My guess is exactly the opposite is true in a mania—time would seem to speed up and investors believe stocks haven't been up for very long and have further to run.

A time perception bias is an easy one to fathom, but few behavioral economists have noted it. The perception of time is an easy thing to distort in our minds, and time horizons for investors are a dicey and misunderstood subject to begin with. There are a lot of myths about the brain's internal "clock." There is no such thing. We can often become habituated or condition ourselves for certain expectations, but there is no mechanism in our heads to measure time.

Awareness of time slips from us very easily if things like clocks and sunlight are taken away—the stuff that constantly orients us. Investors would do well to remind themselves of their time horizon, in which case most market "crises" appear to be what they really are—fleeting events.

These are just a few examples of investing biases and problems our brains cause. At the end of this chapter, there's a list of even more. Using what we've learned about how brains work so far, you can come up with your own simply by observing the investing habits, thought processes, and reactions of yourself and those around you.

MY, WHAT A TERRIBLE MEMORY YOU HAVE!

Memory is the touchstone of intelligent life. If we can't remember, we're merely organisms capable of reacting to stimulus and little more. There are two kinds of memory: short term and long term. Short-term memory is much different physiologically than long-term memory. In the short term, we can usually remember a handful of things and keep them in our heads for a few seconds (like a seven-digit phone number, for instance). Not much happens in the brain with short-term memory, and before too long, the knowledge falls right out of our heads forever. That's a really good thing! You wouldn't want to remember every single trivial thing you ever encountered—it would be more than your poor psyche could handle—you'd be overwhelmed. It's an evolutionary feature that we retain some information and discard other information.

PROTEINS AND NETWORKS

Long-term memory has a specific biological signature and scientists are learning more about its intricacies seemingly by the day. Our brains start in infancy as a mass of neurons with relatively few synapse connections. As we gain experiences and learn, we actually *lose* neurons—pruning away those superfluous cells and strengthening those connections that have created the strongest networks. Brains are continually forming themselves all the way up until about 30 years of age, at which point, formation of new neural networks becomes more difficult, and we tend to get set in our ways. (But recent studies indicate brain changes can still happen throughout life, just not as easily.)

Once a neural network is formed and repeatedly reinforced, it becomes extremely difficult to break—these habits, feelings, sensations, and emotions are a vital part of memory formation. Hormonal reactions and other bodily reflexes reinforce neural networks and create proteins that further solidify those networks.

This is why, for instance, an emotion like love can literally be an addiction. If you are with someone for a number of years, your brain will form acute networks in response to the loved one—everything from voice to touch to scent. If you truly love that person, with each stimulus you're likely to get a reaction of "good feeling" hormones. Should that person go away, your body will experience withdrawals, anticipating that stimulus and hormonal fix, just like a drug addiction. This experience is catalyzed by way of memory.

Memory's solidification in the brain is done through the creation of proteins. Short-term memory, for instance, features a small biological reaction but doesn't create the proteins necessary to be stored for the longer haul. Thus, a long-term memory is made when the idea is reinforced or important enough for the brain to create the proteins necessary to bind neural networks together for long-term recall.[5] Intuitively, strong memories tend to be associated with strong emotions. Memory is often not what we decide it to be.

But how do we recall anything? What triggers a memory? Why can't we easily remember more than seven digits at a time or what we had for lunch a week ago, yet we can immediately recall our second-grade teacher scolding us for losing our homework? (That just pops right back into our minds like it was yesterday!) How does the scent of lemonade trigger images of lazy summer afternoons at your grandmother's pool when you were eight?

One of the greatest meditations on memory is wholly unscientific—French author Marcel Proust's masterwork, *Remembrance of Things Past*. There, we can see the strange workings of neural networks and memory:

> But it is sometimes just at the moment when we think that everything is lost that the intimation arrives which may save us; one has knocked at all the doors which lead nowhere, and then one stumbles without knowing it on the only door through which one can enter—which one might have sought in vain for a hundred years—and it opens of its own accord.[6]

It all has to do with association and emotion. Recall that general knowledge is wired in the brain by association via networks. Many things are interconnected in your head somehow. Neural networks, as they are recalled, can give rise to a number of memories and strange associations in the brain.

Remember from Chapter 1, we humans tend to think in categories and prototypes. A category like "women," for instance, conjures memories that can go off on a number of paths—your mother, girlfriends, wives, daughters, siblings, and so on. The thinking of the category alone triggers a number of networks and gives us access to all sorts of associations and thus memories. And while every experience leaves a trace in the brain, repetition and familiarity solidify it.

Another way the brain recalls information is by "chunking." It groups data together so we can remember many things at once, like seven digits in a phone number or 26 letters in the alphabet. We rarely recall facts in isolation.

FALSE MEMORIES

Most people never stop to think how faulty their memories really are. We don't remember anything exactly. False memories are not just common, they're ubiquitous. The brain isn't made for perfect recall. Scientists have even found that déjà vu is just an error commonly occurring in the hippocampus—a misfiring of neurons, mistaking something as familiar when it really isn't.[7]

Remember there is no such thing as reason without emotion—all thoughts are colored by emotion, and therefore so are memories. Emotions are a key player in our personal and communal histories because they influence how we remember, literally changing our perception of reality. Both at the moment of the event and years after, your mood will alter your memory.

Have you ever noticed how many biographies we have of famous people or how many disparate ways events like the Civil War have been retold? Why is there no definitive text to tell us the "truth" of what happened? The same is true for financial events. For instance, history commonly holds that scores of ruined stock brokers threw themselves out of windows during the 1929 stock crash. Not true! If you go back and check the headlines, suicide rates weren't much different before or after that period. Why such a macabre collective memory then? Well, there are many reasons history is more like fiction than truth, but one salient reason is because that particular memory about the financial crash is colored by emotions of death and ruin. Our brains shape experiences to fit emotions, not to preserve facts. Sometimes memories of an event are far stronger than reality because we imbue them with greater emotion and imagination, whereas in the real moment we may not recognize the significance right away.

As we will see in Chapter 7, history is by definition a *reimagining* of events and can only be told through humans—that is, colored with emotion and subjectivity. History is just as much fiction as fact because we must re-imagine events each time they are told.

Another reason memory is fallible is we do not remember in complete events—most memories return to us in fragments, little shards of something fuller. When we fill in those gaps of memory to complete the story, we often mistake imagination for a true event. Ease of recall is a huge bias in how we perceive the world. We can only remember what we already know, which by definition is a slanted, incomplete view of the world. Yet folks not only rely on memory, but use it as a kind of knowledge. Uncertainty makes us uneasy. It's tension. We hate it. We want certainty and will make stuff up (especially where there are memory gaps) just to ease it. This makes memory a kind of belief, for we know what and how we recall is truly a function of what is important to us, what we believe in, and what has significantly affected us. This is one reason our fictions can feel as real or more real than reality, and also a reason we are capable of easily deceiving ourselves with false memories.

 History is by definition a *reimagining* of events and can only be told through humans—that is, colored with emotion and subjectivity. History is just as much fiction as fact because we must re-imagine events each time they are told.

There are numerous lessons here for investors. An obvious one: Don't trust your memory—go back and see if the facts corroborate what you remember. Second, because memory is so colored by emotion, people often under- and overstate the future and extrapolate the recent past onto the present. The power to contemplate the future is a great ability of man's, but often abused. Sometimes, memory lapses can lead us to place a greater emphasis on information that is available to us than on information that is relevant but not known. That is, we place greater emphasis on what we remember rather than what might actually be most important. Market analysts do this often—falsely believing the information available, or the information they know about, is the most relevant. Often it is not.

Ultimately, you're doing yourself a great service if you can realize your memory wasn't meant for the kind of precision we think it's capable of—especially when dealing with markets.

YOU GOTTA BELIEVE

I'll make you a bet. I'll wager the vast majority of your decisions are made on beliefs and not facts. I'll go a step further—I'll wager every decision you've ever made is based on a belief. What, don't believe me? Convinced you're a perfectly rational human of the modern scientific world who decides on facts alone? You'd be wrong.

Any scientist worth his salt will tell you we don't know much of anything for sure. That's because in order to know something in the scientific sense, you have to scrutinize it from every angle and test it over and over again until it can't effectively be proven false. Even then, after scores (if not hundreds or thousands) of experiments, we still don't "know" if anything's true. (Remember the problems of induction from Chapter 1.) All we know in the technical sense is what we think to be true because we can't disprove it. That's how science is done.

This means acquiring real information is extremely expensive, and a scientific fact requires a herculean effort of testing and retesting. Truth is so mentally expensive, it's impossible to conduct our lives based on things we know to be scientifically factual. We don't have time to wait around for science to prove everything. We've got to live our lives! (If you dumped your girlfriend or boyfriend today, would that be the right choice or the worst mistake of your life? It's impossible to know and pretty darn tough to scientifically test. You're just gonna have to go with your gut.)

That's what life is mostly about: reliance on beliefs and assumptions to make decisions. Life evolved that way. Back in the Stone Age, we didn't really know if that mountain lion stalking us from across the field meant to kill us, but it was pretty safe to assume he did. So we ran like heck!

Brains are belief machines, and for the most part, we get along pretty well with this model. We're more comfortable acting on intuition and feeling than taking the time

(Continued)

(Continued)

to find proven truths. We even tend to ignore data that go against our personal experiences and beliefs. That can be bad because our beliefs often are false or skewed. According to neuroscientist Andrew Newberg in his book, *Why We Believe What We Believe*, humans are prone to false memories and beliefs because "beliefs appear to be based primarily on the emotional impact of specific experiences."

So while beliefs and assumptions might be how we conduct our lives, it's a perilous thing for investors. Sound investing is often opposed to a belief system. It's imperative to act on facts and against intuition. Yet investors' heads are chock full of false beliefs and theories, and too many folks act on assumptions and emotions—the culprits behind losing them a lot of money.

Like any scientific endeavor, there's been little actually proven when it comes to stock investing. Most economic and market theories are based on incomplete information or assumptions that haven't been rigorously tested enough to know if they're true.

P/E ratios are a classic example. Forever, folks have thought P/Es tell you something about how stocks perform. Yet it's been proven time and again P/Es have no predictive power for stock prices. Even with that knowledge, belief still tends to trump fact and folks scrutinize P/Es all the time in search of the next great stock.[8]

Capital markets are still in their infancy and continue to develop at record speed. It's vastly difficult to predict or understand how they function today, let alone what they'll develop into 10 years from now. But nobody would invest at all unless they thought over time it would lead to positive returns. But how do we know?

Well, you gotta believe.

BAD BEHAVIORAL FINANCE

A cautionary note: Focusing on all this brain science can get you into trouble as often as it helps you. Increasingly, folks are reliant on behavioral finance as a panacea of investing knowledge. It isn't. Like all fields, the behavioral sciences help us get perspective on investing, but they have their shortcomings. So before moving on, I'd like to illustrate the perils of behaviorism with a personal example.

About a year ago, I sat in on a behavioral finance conference, and I must admit to dozing once or twice. It happened somewhere between the crash course in *hedonomics,* the study of happiness and economics (happiness at a finance seminar . . . the very idea!), and a 40-minute presentation on the history of annuities.

In a moment of greater lucidity, I witnessed an inexplicable, if not truly bizarre, presentation. It had a two-pronged approach: First, to prove the US housing market was in a downturn (this was early 2008, mind you). Simple enough, and true. Second, to assert that—based on behavioral research—policy makers ought to force owners to hedge the value of their homes.

What!?

Never mind that housing prices have been rather docile over the long term and hardly justify the capital necessary to hedge. Never mind that nothing ever really stopped investors from hedging the value of their homes in the first place. None of that seemed to matter. Because the housing market was in a downturn and some were overextended and even faced foreclosure, the situation was "undeniable" behavioral evidence we need to mandate an insurance system to make sure no one ever loses money on their home again.

This presenter was not alone. I slowly realized most presenters (all brethren of the temple of behavioral finance) had a similar message: *We need to tell people what to do because they aren't clever enough to choose optimally for themselves.*

What's going on here?

Behavioral finance used to be a beautiful thing. A few decades ago it was a burgeoning field of study, linking observations on human behavior to how markets and economies function—even if some conclusions were a tad obvious. (Did we really need a team of PhDs to tell us our memories are sometimes faulty?) Behavioral finance's major contribution was to revise economic theory to account for human bias and irrationality based on innate neural wiring. This replaced the traditional model of rational man (AKA, "Homo Economicus"). Such findings are nothing to scoff at and today still have powerful implications.

But that golden era of discovery might be over. New insights in the field have given way to proposals to engineer public policy or "nudge" (to use their term) the populace into certain behaviors. That's a shame. To pervert the objective study of human behavior into justification for ideologically driven regulation is abhorrently contradictory to what real behaviorism ought to teach us.

> To pervert the objective study of human behavior into justification for ideologically driven regulation is abhorrently contradictory to what real behaviorism ought to teach us.

A popular ethos today is to believe rational individuals must be the basis for a rational market; therefore, if we know people aren't rational then markets can't be either. In fact, just the opposite is true: It's the sum total of all irrational individuals that create a wiser market (we'll cover this topic in detail in Chapter 5).

That we are imperfect is evidence that we should shun an elite central decision maker whenever possible. It's because investors are not always rational that free markets are a better way. Knowing we're all myopic and have a highly limited view of the world, any empowered elite group would surely and ultimately lead to inefficiency, if not ruin. And through history, it has.

Many of today's behavioral finance experts casually eschew free-market capitalism's demonstrated power to allocate capital where needed and create vast, interconnected wealth across populations. How many times must we bear witness to the constricting and suffocating grasp of socialism before we realize attempting to control people "for their own good" is not only a fool's errand, but immensely dangerous?

Though imperfect—and often brutal—truly free markets are a tumult of relentless competition. In markets, all viewpoints are given voice—many possible permutations and innovations are tried until optimal solutions are brought to market (and duly rewarded). No one group, even one with the power of behavioral science on its side, could possibly ascend to such a feat.

In looking back on the presentations of that day, I sensed a strong (dare I say, innate) propensity for humans to tell other humans what to do. I'd humbly suggest the behavioral finance experts endeavor to investigate that urge and start with themselves as the test subjects.

But either way, it's important to remember a field like behavioral economics is no panacea—it is *one* valid way to see investing behavior and should always be considered with many other factors.

BEHAVIORAL MISCELLANY

This chapter provided a mere taste of behavioral quirks and how they affect investments. Behavioral finance is a burgeoning field, along with much of the cognitive sciences. Throughout this book there are many additional examples. Below are a few more, in rapid fire.

- **Prospect Theory.** This is the idea folks hate losses 2.5× more than they enjoy gains. This theory is the foundation for much of behavioral finance and was pioneered by Daniel Kahneman and Amos Tversky—who won the Nobel Prize for this discovery in 2002. Prospect theory explains much about why bear markets affect folks as adversely as they do, often causing irrational decisions. It's often associated with *myopic loss aversion,* where investors avoid losses in the future and become overly conservative after an event like a bear market. A layperson's way to say this would be "gun-shy."
- **Overconfidence.** Investors are commonly overconfident in their abilities to judge a situation. Overconfidence was a great evolutionary development—hunters needed a good dose of confidence to go out on the hunt for food amid the dangers lurking in the wild every day. This translates today into us making decisions believing we have a better grasp of the situation than we really do.
- **Confirmation Bias.** We tend to confirm what we already thought or believed and shun evidence to the contrary. Investors who are diehard bulls, for example, will find a reason to be bullish in any situation, regardless of reality, and vice versa with bears.
- **Anchoring.** Investors tend to "anchor," or overly rely, on specific information. We tend to use the first thing we are presented

as a baseline, or context, for whatever comes next. Generally, once the anchor is set, there is a bias toward that value relative to any other information presented.

- **Scaling**. Brains weren't designed to think in millions or billions or trillions. Heck, we can barely think in hundreds and dozens. Often, we skew the reality of a situation by not scaling, or understanding proportion, properly.

- **Pattern Recognition and Repetition**. Brains see in patterns. Pattern recognition is important, but often we see patterns where there are none, leading to investor errors. (Chapter 7 will explore this idea further as it pertains to market forecasting.)

- **Hindsight Bias**. We tend to think of the past as "obvious." That the answers were clear when, in fact, things at the time were just as uncertain as they are today. This is close to the old maxim "hindsight is 20/20."

- **Operant Conditioning**. Behavior can be shaped by consequences. For instance, if a child gets an "A" on his/her homework and gets a reward of ice cream in return, the child is being conditioned to do his/her homework well. Sometimes though, behavior isn't rewarded consistently. Randomly occurring rewards can often force us to search more for positive feedback. This can be dangerous in investing because we may repeat or seek to repeat behavior that won't necessarily have a positive outcome each time. (And, if nothing else, telling someone they suffer from "operant conditioning" will make you sound really smart.)

- **Order Preference**. Brains often ascribe an importance to the order of things where there is none or misperceive precedence for function in an ordered list. For instance, we tend to categorize things in alphabetical order because we can remember and find filed items easier that way. But there is nothing about the order of the alphabet that is inherently significant; it's just a random order of symbols we've decided to adhere to for convenience.

CHAPTER INSIGHTS

Understanding universal features about brains can tell us a lot about how markets act and save us from common investing mistakes.

- Brains were made for survival in the wild, not in markets. Markets evolve much more quickly than brains can. Therefore, we need strategies to cope with our limited brains amid burgeoning markets and economies.

- Brains are:
  - Largely composed of leftover parts from previous species.
  - Hierarchical—most decisions our brains make never make it to our awareness.
  - Influenced heavily by instincts, sometimes called "modules."
  - Able to learn and remember via neural networks—evidence our brains can change and are influenced by culture and not only instinctual.

- Brain functions make for sometimes odd market behavior:
  - We are wired for the short term and tend to make short-term focused decisions. But most of the time, good investing keeps the long term in mind.
  - Brains are made to mimic and follow the herd. But we know information gets priced in; therefore, acting with the herd can often be a bad thing for investors, who often must go against the herd.
  - Our memories are heavily reliant on emotion and association, not facts. Often much of what we think we remember is wrong or colored by subjective feelings.
  - Brains often perceive time in warped ways, throwing off perception of reality and leading to bad investments.
  - Mental life is mostly belief-based, not fact-based. We often mistake beliefs for facts. When making investment choices, ask if the information is well proven and vetted, of if it's simply taken as "true" based on belief.

- Studying the behavioral sciences is no panacea—the field has its own biases and shouldn't be the only thing influencing investing decisions.

4

SENTIMENT AND THE MEDIA

The man who reads nothing at all is better educated than the man who reads nothing but newspapers.

—Thomas Jefferson

We can't quite decide if the world is growing worse, or if the reporters are just working harder.

—*The Houghton Line,* November 1965

Some believe the media controls sentiment. Others believe sentiment controls what the media prints. It's probably a little of both, and maybe neither.

What's most fascinating about the media and sentiment over time is its amazing consistency. For as long as news has existed, folks have had the same complaints about it and suffered from the same biases in consuming it—no matter the type of media (newspapers, TV, Internet). And for as long as there have been markets, there have been manias and panics. That speaks to something about us as humans generally, not just the mechanisms of the media.

Either way, the media has always played a large role in sentiment and investing. It cannot be ignored if you aim to understand how markets work. This chapter will delve into a few intricacies of the media and perhaps provide some insights you haven't before considered.

For years now I've been Managing Editor of Fisher Investments' financial news and commentary website, MarketMinder.com. At MarketMinder, we do two things. First, we have a group of analysts who sift through over 100 of the top print and online publications published throughout the world each day to find the most relevant stories and perspectives. Similarly, we take note of the stories we believe are the most egregiously wrong each day. We post both—good and bad—to the site. Second, we have an editorial commentary analyzing the day's market action. (Beyond that, the site has a number of little bells and whistles, including a cadre of regular columnists and more.)

It's been a fascinating and enlightening ride. MarketMinder represents part of the new "supra" structure to the financial press—we aren't just commenting and observing news and then reporting it; we're also observing and reporting on the media itself! This represents a vastly different endeavor than simply looking for good and bad stories or searching for relevant and esoteric pieces of news. It's about viewing the media as an entity in itself—studying its tendencies, biases, and other basic characteristics in addition to what it reports. Understanding the media as a whole can be—more than any single piece of news—far more enlightening than any hard-hitting exposé or breaking headline.

Most will agree investor sentiment can move markets—particularly in the short term. But after that things get jumbled quickly and we agree seldom on how to best gauge sentiment. This chapter is designed to help you think about sentiment and the media in a way that can help you make better investments. We won't recount how the media is structured in full, but we will conduct a cursory examination of how it's put together—thereby revealing some reasons the media behaves as it does.

This won't be a treatise on media-bashing. There's enough of that already. As we saw in Chapter 1, skepticism is good but cynicism is bad. Same for the media. This might be hard to believe, but *the media can be your friend in your mission to be a better investor.* The attitude "I know there's a lot of spin out there, so I'm just going to ignore the media altogether so I don't become biased or influenced myself" isn't going to work. You need to know what the world is thinking and why.

But the "how" to engage the media is the trick. We must observe not just the news, but what people think about the news.

SENTIMENT BASICS

Before we talk about the media though, let's first tackle the idea of sentiment. For this section, let's call sentiment by its other name: *Demand.* Those terms aren't perfectly interchangeable—but they're darn near close when it comes to investing, and it's useful to think of them as similar.

Let's be clear: Sentiment is not some magical, ethereal thing that holds the key to stock market outcomes. Sentiment is merely a concept—one that's useful in helping to think through how investors might behave. There is nothing magical about sentiment and it is no silver bullet. There is no need—and it can even be damaging—to think in terms like "stocks always go up when sentiment is optimistic," or vice versa. Like any good investing tool, sentiment can point to probable outcomes but is never foolproof.

> Let's be clear: Sentiment is not some magical, ethereal thing that holds the key to stock market outcomes. Sentiment is merely a concept—one that's useful in helping to think through how investors might behave.

Being too vague and abstract is one of the most common errors investors make in trying to gauge sentiment. As investors with practical goals like making profits, we want to discover ways to think that make the job easier and clearer. Sentiment is an abstract concept—so we want to ground it with something like real-world demand. As we saw in previous chapters, abstract thinking has its virtues for helping us understand concepts. But when thinking about sentiment, we want to ask questions that can be answered reliably and have applicable answers. For instance, asking "Will this story about recession on the front page of the *New York Times* change how people feel about the economy?" isn't a good question. It's too vague, and even if you could answer it correctly, the conclusion isn't worth much in terms of practical action. Instead, ask questions like, "How does this story affect the way people buy and sell stocks?" The answer to that question is much more focused and gets to the core of the issue. This might seem like semantics, but it's an important psychological move out of the vague and into a direction that helps investors judge sentiment.

Next chapter, we'll look closely at the reasons supply and demand are the most basic, and still among the best, ways of understanding how anything gets a price. Supply is relatively easy to measure (just take a count of what's available for sale), but demand is much more difficult. Actually, that's false. Folks just believe it's more difficult. Demand is just more abstract and qualitative than supply, not more difficult to know. This goes back to getting ourselves off the addictive tendency of desiring to quantify everything. Attempts to quantify demand have always been dubious. Maybe one day we'll get it right, but I doubt it. I'd argue most so-called sentiment indexes are more harmful than helpful. Why? Because, as with so many economic indicators, the only way to ascribe an accurate number to something is with existing data. That means, by definition, any sentiment indicator you can find is a statement about the past, which is of little use to investors who seek to forecast the future. At best, these indicators relay sentiment coincident to the market reaction. Extrapolating the recent past into the future is fraught with peril.

My advice is to get rid of all that quantitative thinking and simplify. Instead, imagine sentiment in terms of extremes. Most of the time, sentiment is fairly heterogeneous—you can find plenty of bulls and bears. That's normal and doesn't need to be monitored particularly closely. Since brains are wired to be alert and worry about danger (a neural survival tactic), it's common for sentiment to be skewed to the pessimistic. Sentiment becomes a real factor when it becomes near homogeneous—clustering at one far end of the spectrum or another. When the vast majority of investors are bullish, take note; same if most are pessimistic. That's usually when a sea change in stocks is nigh or already occurring.

Many investors think polarized sentiment is literally 100 percent. That's never how it is. There are always folks on both sides. Even in the Great Depression, the tech bubble of the late 1990s, and the panic of 2008, more than a handful of well-respected investors remained bullish. There are too many smart people out there not to have at least a few on the other side. So if you're waiting for 100 percent capitulation before you make an investing move, you'll be waiting forever. Instead, look for where the vast majority sit and observe when many are capitulating one way or another.

Sentiment becomes a real factor when it becomes near homogeneous—clustering at one far end of the spectrum or another. When the vast majority of investors are bullish, take note; same if most are pessimistic. That is usually when a sea change in stocks is nigh or already occurring.

SENTIMENT MEANS SHORT TERM

The "softer" theory of market efficiency (detailed in Chapter 5) says that widely known information is priced in to stocks, but not necessarily instantaneously and perfectly efficiently. Particularly in the short term, markets can over- and undershoot the fundamentals. This allows for sentiment to cause shifts in prices in the short and medium term, but over the long run, fundamentals are ultimately reflected in stock prices—so thinking about sentiment is always a short-term issue. This makes intuitive sense because sentiment can shift wildly in a short time anyway, and it is impossible to forecast over long periods because our moods are simply too fickle. Never make a long-term forecast based on today's mood—it will shift, even if it feels impossible today.

TRACKING THE CONSENSUS

Understanding consensus expectations for political and economic outcomes is important to making successful market forecasts. Markets don't move on absolutes—they move on the differences between what was expected (or priced in) and what really happens or will happen. This is called monitoring *relative expectations* and will be discussed more in Chapter 7.

Understanding where fundamental analysis and sentiment cross will feel counter-intuitive for many. We need to not only understand the data, but also what investors consider is most bullish or bearish looking forward and why. What countries or sectors are widely discussed in the media? What market segments have been bid up recently based on something other than fundamentals?

If the market's perception is different than fundamentals in the short term, stocks will eventually correct themselves to reflect reality in the long term. Your analysis of fundamental "drivers"—that is, your assessment of how the economy or specific company is really performing—is meant to identify market opportunities where sentiment is different than reality.

Let's say you observe the consensus expects a US recession in the next year. But you disagree and believe GDP growth will be stronger. This speaks volumes to future market prospects because the negative outcome is being reflected in prices. You can load up on stocks that will benefit from an economic boom few others foresee and watch the prices rise as the rest of the market realizes it much later and demands more stocks at that time. In short, a key to achieving profits above and beyond the market is by noticing a short-term disconnect between sentiment of the consensus and reality and taking advantage of it in your portfolio.

THE SHORT AND LONG OF IT

A natural question arising from the idea of relative expectations and sentiment is: *What exactly is short and long term?* After all, to say that sometimes short-term sentiment is dislocated with reality means we'd have to know how long the short term is and when the short term becomes the long term.

This is a surprisingly difficult question to answer. In order to say how long any period should be, we'd need a starting point. That's a dicey proposition in stock investing because markets are continuous—there is no start or end date for them. They go on and on. So picking a date for anything to "start" is arbitrary and will heavily bias results. Folks like to use the calendar year or the beginnings and endings of quarters as starting points, but those are arbitrary too—and have little to do with most fundamentals.

Here's a brain teaser to highlight the difficulty with this: When exactly does the short term become the long term? The answer is never! It is always the short term. The long term is a clustering of short terms. We are never "in" the long term, yet somehow it still happens!

Seems like an irreconcilable paradox. What to do? Get abstract again. A useful rule of thumb is the short term is anything less than a year, or maybe 18 months. Longer than that is the long term. I'm not willing to get any more specific than that and neither should you. Be very flexible with time periods—sometimes investing results may take much longer to develop, sometimes much less. If you hold a stock that you believe to be undervalued, but for, say, 18 months it still hasn't moved much, there is nothing magical about 18 months that says you should necessarily sell it. Maybe it will take 20 months . . . maybe three years! So long as you believe there is more value than currently priced in a stock, and so long as you don't believe there are better alternatives in the meantime, you should probably keep the stock.

Short and long term are merely useful abstract concepts for us to comprehend time periods and how sentiment moves markets, little more. If you try to pin them down too rigidly with specific dates, you'll make huge investing mistakes because you'll be basing decisions on arbitrary epochs.

Short and long term are merely useful abstract concepts for us to comprehend time periods and how sentiment moves markets, little more. If you try to pin them down too rigidly with specific dates you'll make huge investing mistakes because you'll be basing decisions on arbitrary epochs.

A NOTE ON BEING CONTRARY

Contrarianism is an age-old concept meaning to go against the crowd—if folks are bullish, a classic contrarian becomes bearish and vice versa. Seems intuitive, but it's wrong. Why? The market is a pretty efficient discounter of all known information, so if people agree on future market pricing, it by definition can't happen because it's already reflected in prices—something else must happen instead.

Only the truly unexpected can change demand and move markets. How the market moves need not be the exact reverse of what folks expect. Suppose most agree the market will rise. That doesn't automatically mean it will fall. Maybe it will, but it could also simply do nothing or rise much more than anyone expects—both of which would make everyone wrong.

Sometimes contrarianism is popular, and then it mostly doesn't work—because contrarians become the crowd itself. When, in history, contrarianism is very unpopular, it worked pretty well before long.

My advice is to avoid working yourself into a contrary frame of mind. Instead of thinking exactly against the grain per se, set your mind on determining what the consensus believes, and acting accordingly to take advantage. The right answer isn't necessarily the opposite, it's just most often different than what the consensus believes.

NEWS AND THE MEDIA

Now that we have a handle on the basics of sentiment, let's apply it to where it is observable: the media.

 I like the media—I think the more you come to understand it, the more you will like it, too. It's almost limitlessly useful. We can read the news to see what others are thinking so we don't have to think those things. Why? Because well-known information gets reflected in stock prices. That's a really wonderful function the media provides us.

It's time to start thinking about the media as our friends. If you're looking for a media-bashing bonanza, you've come to the wrong place. I like the media— I think the more you come to understand it, the more you will like it, too. It's almost limitlessly useful. We can read the news to see what others are thinking so we don't have to think those things. Why? Because well-known information gets reflected in stock prices. That's a really wonderful function the media provides us. Even better: Nothing challenges our views and keeps us sharp more than reading opinions from a multiplicity of sources . . . especially ones you disagree with.

But before we can make the media our friend, there are a few ground rules:

- **The Golden Rule**. The stock market reflects all widely known and discussed information. If it's widely discussed, it's priced in. Obviously, the media is the conduit through which you can judge this. But flip the issue around for a moment and look at it differently: Priced-in information can act as a media *filter* for you in deciding what is relevant and what is not. If we know what is already discussed is priced in, then we can ignore any redundancies in the media. Any new piece of information had potency *once*—after that it's old hat. The same stories will be regurgitated over and again, but you can ignore them because they're already reflected in stock prices. Believe it or not, in my experience, that simple heuristic cuts out well over three-quarters of what's reported. Life just got that much easier!
- **It's a game of relative expectations**. When it comes to forecasting stocks in the short term, reality can matter much less than what is expected to happen.
- **Don't be a contrarian**. Contrarians are investors who simply do the opposite of what most believe will happen. Studying the media for investment opportunity finds places where sentiment (people's beliefs) doesn't match reality. It may be simply a matter of different magnitude. Maybe folks are bullish but not bullish enough; maybe they're bearish but not bearish enough. And so on. Don't just do the opposite by rote.
- **Be politically agnostic**. It's downright terrifying how politics and ideology have crept their way into even the seemingly most benign reportage. Always put ideological biases at the front of your mind so you won't be blindsided by them. You may be a staunch elephant or maybe a lifetime donkey or maybe a free-wheeling independent, but the fact is your views will do nothing

but bias you and possibly blind you to things. I call this the "team bias." People tend to regularly root for their team and then hate their rivals simply because they're a rival (it's tough to find a Yankees fan who likes the Red Sox, and vice versa). Not everyone succumbs to this, but many do. For instance, I love the Lakers and generally despise the Celtics. Why? I really have nothing against the Celtics, but it's part of my job as a Lakers fan to not like them. The team bias can be easily seen in politics, nationalism, and so on.

WE HAVE NARRATIVE MINDS

Stories are universal, and all humans live by them. Narrative is the way we understand our lives—it's part of what gives us a sense of coherency. No matter the place or time, we interact with, gain meaning from, and understand the world as the story and ourselves as the characters. The media understands this and positions most news items, however random, in the context of a "story."

Often, the very framework of a story can mislead an investor into false conclusions. Really, life is much more random and chaotic than we imagine. We think about how things will "play out," as if all events from before will follow through in linear fashion, like a story. We link and assign meaning to our lives in a linear way—with causes and effects we believe we understand. We do not look at life as a series of random, unlinked events. Brains crave coherence and patterns, which leads to story making. But there is huge randomness in the world—much more than we usually recognize—especially tied to market outcomes. So we must be very alert to our story making.

Stories existed long before civilization. The first known human art was created at least fifteen thousand years ago at the Lascaux caves in France where over fifteen hundred paintings of animals called the "Great Hall of the Bulls" reside. (And there is strong evidence such art existed prior in other regions of the world as well.) The paintings are in fact a sprawling, though very basic, narrative. So stories aren't merely artifacts of civilizations (though of course civilization does have a large impact upon stories). *Stories existed long before civilized culture and are a naturally occurring phenomenon in humans, very likely part of the brain's wiring.* Mark Turner, in his book *The Literary Mind: The Origins of Thought and Language,* says:

> Narrative imagining, often thought of as literary and optional, appears
> instead to be inseparable from our evolutionary past and our necessary

personal experience. It also appears to be a fundamental target value for the developing human mind.

Stories probably emerged from our minds to help solve various problems of evolution. We imagine stories and construct meanings to help achieve the goals of our evolved selves. Stories are used for teaching and learning and memory. We remember facts more accurately if we experience them through a story rather than a list. Understanding a story, while natural to the brain, is a very complex task that requires all sorts of cognitive functions to interact with memory, language and image comprehension, emotion, and reason, to name a few. Story making and telling is a wonderful cognitive workout of sorts.

Aristotle, perhaps the oldest of the narrative theorists, believed *mimesis* is the principle behind our need for stories. Mimesis is mimicry, the ability to reenact what we observe. He believed humans have an instinct to imitate others and that we have a deep need for learning and mimicking what we have learned. He was more right than he knew. (Recall last chapter we noted the so-called "mirror neurons" as a principal way brains learn.)

Stories must be *interpreted* by the audience. That is, stories pass along knowledge or lessons obliquely and not directly. One cannot simply state the meaning of life or tritely pass wisdom on directly. These must be *experienced*. Stories are closer to real-life experiences than bullet-pointed facts.

The media will report on a "developing" story or cluster a group of related events together to make things seem coherent. Often they are, but many times they are not. This innate desire to take observations and make them fit a narrative can be damaging for investors—often incorrect correlations are made between stocks and budget deficits, trade, currency movements, energy prices, and so on.

It's just as important to critique the story structure as it is the facts within it. The study of drama—the common patterns of good stories—is an excellent place to see the implicit drama in the media. (A few worthwhile books are noted in the Selected Bibliography and Further Reading section at the end of this book.)

THE MEDIA IS A COMMAND SYSTEM . . . FOR NOW

How is the media put together? Maybe a better question is: Why should an investor care how the media is constructed?

Part of your job as an investor is to get the news, but also to view the media as an entity and observe its behavior. Understanding the media's disposition and motives is every bit as important as simply finding a good news source. You're looking to add a *reflexive* layer to the analysis, where you judge the folks who are doing the judging—a vital part of gauging sentiment.

This is not a comprehensive overview of the media, but a broad perspective to help you understand its motives and navigate it in the future.

Old-World Command Systems. The media, for as long as it's existed, has been a command system, where a few elites control most of what's ultimately reported. Media mogul Rupert Murdoch said in a 2008 speech:

> It used to be that a handful of editors could decide what was news—and what was not. They acted as sort of demigods. If they ran a story, it became news. If they ignored an event, it never happened. Today editors are losing this power. The Internet, for example, provides access to thousands of new sources that cover things an editor might ignore. And if you aren't satisfied with that, you can start up your own blog and cover and comment on the news yourself. Journalists like to think of themselves as watchdogs, but they haven't always responded well when the public calls them to account.

For many decades, local news sources in the form of newspapers, radio, and TV would produce some original content tied to local news, but the rest would be taken from the higher ups—the national news outlets from the major networks, the Associated Press, and so on. It's always been true that news trickles down from the big moguls to affiliates. When it comes to big, national stories, for many years, there was only a handful of outlets to cover it. There isn't anything necessarily sinister about this; that's just the way it was, given the technology and information-sharing capabilities of the times.

But things change. Where in the nineteenth century there may—literally—be just one local newspaper covering a story, today we have more, larger, and independent news organizations due to the proliferation of cable news, international newspapers, online reporting, and so on. Information today travels faster, cheaper, and in many more ways than it once did.

But mostly, major news is still controlled by just a few huge entities. NBC, and all its incarnations, is ultimately owned by GE. CBS is part of a much wider media umbrella and associated with Viacom. ABC is owned by Disney, which also owns ESPN and myriad other media outlets. CNN is just a fraction of the Turner system, which also owns Headline News, TNT, TBS, and others. And Fox News is a mere piece of Rupert Murdoch's media empire, which owns dozens of newspapers, satellite TV providers, and television stations across the globe . . . including the entire family of Dow Jones publications and the *Wall Street Journal!* Even the New York Times Corporation operates in many venues across the world under different names like the *International Herald Tribune.* Then, of course, there are public bureaus, like the BBC (one of the world's largest media outlets), that are expressly controlled by the government—it doesn't get any more centrally commanded than that.

Again, this isn't to say any of them are evil. It's simply to point out almost all our news comes from a handful of large entities, and most are for-profit organizations. Each of these larger entities is generally heralded by a central command structure. That very specific and narrow landscape dictates a lot of what gets reported and how.

In other words, the media is less dynamic and slower than a free-market economy or the stock market. Systems like stock markets are adaptive and complex—they are decentralized and share information widely via mechanisms like prices. They are therefore very agile. By that definition, today's media is the opposite of a complex system like the economy—today's media is a command system with limited information sharing and poor adaptability.

That makes the media somewhat predictable in a general, linear way—patterns are often detectable in their general behavior. More importantly, the best the media can ever be (under the command structure) is a coincident indicator for news, whereas markets are pricing in the future. The media is an indication about the present or past and never the future like markets are. *Media can only reflect what's already priced in.*

More importantly, the best the media can ever be (under the command structure) is a coincident indicator for news, whereas markets are pricing in the future. The media is an indication about the present or past and never the future like markets are. *Media can only reflect what's already priced in.*

To see just how homogenous the mass media really is, test it yourself. Take any of the major media outlets and see how comparable the lead stories are over some stretch of time. You'll find similar news is reported in similar ways. Such homogeneity is in itself a statement about the media's lack of dynamism. Moreover, it's an incestuous bunch. It's a community. Reporters on the same beat and rival editors all know each other, and many probably worked together at some point. They mostly have the same methods and were taught to be journalists in similar ways. Thus, their philosophies and worldviews will tend in similar patterns, too.

A truly diverse system should theoretically run myriad top headlines and have large divergences in what makes it to print. Fortunately, technology might be putting the traditional media to the test.

Information Age Revolution? In the last decade or so, something has changed in traditional media. It's possible the media is on the way to shifting into a more complex, decentralized structure like a stock market, but it's not quite there yet—in fact it may never fully get there. Old-world command systems tend to die hard, but they do evolve.

A truly dynamic complex system needs *a critical mass of free-flowing information among individuals* in order for that larger structure to "emerge." That means it's built from the bottom up—individuals need the ability to provide and consume information and to give feedback. Where once it was only a few elites at the top of the superstructure who controlled media information and dissemination, new technology is allowing individuals to have a voice. Today, via methods like laptops, blogs, Digg, wireless devices, and the Internet generally, folks are *pushing up* news from the bottom that the elites at the top cannot ignore. This phenomenon is evolving at an accelerating pace. Glenn Reynolds' book, *An Army of Davids: How Markets and Technology*

Empower Ordinary People to Beat Big Media, Big Government, and Other Goliaths, is an insightful glimpse inside these methods.

Any popular blog is an example. So is YouTube. Heck, the very existence of Google is something of a threat to the command system. New technology is creating immediate feedback from readers, influencing much of today's content. User ratings for online stories are common—much of CNN.com's content is influenced by feedback, not editorial decisions. The important feature is that technology allows feedback to be near real time. At the very least, there's now interplay between reader and editor.

Thus, editors—outside of opinion pages—have become something different than they ever have been: responders to feedback. Where once their job was expressly to decide what news to report (command-system elitism), editors today are reacting to and filtering reader feedback. For the first time ever, the command system is crumbling. It reacts to data and user numbers as often as selecting news based on limited information and bias.

This represents an important change—the media could in fact be presenting information that is relevant and correct in the same timely way markets price in information since they both are locally *pushing up* a systemic result not decided upon by elites—a dynamic, emergent system of news.

Irrefutably, we have more access and are exposed to more media today than decades ago. It makes a difference—the question is what kind of difference. Think of how revolutionary it is that, via audio and video and in near real time, we are able to experience things outside our personal lives all over the world. It's hard to underplay the importance of this. Just a half-century ago, most people still only had newspapers and radio. Technology alters culture and how we feel and even how our brains wire themselves. The notion of "continuous partial attention" (AKA multitasking) has been floated by many psychologists as a profound change in the way our minds work from just a few decades ago.

But for all that, complex systems like the stock market also require timely feedback mechanisms to evolve, adapt, and maintain efficiency.

Stock markets have that feature via highly liquid pricing mechanisms. The media is showing signs of versatile feedback via ratings systems and the ability to track usage with advertising tools, but this is a far cry from the efficiency of stock markets. Media systems with built-in feedback could theoretically be as efficient in delivering relevant information as markets.

This is hugely important for investors. If the media were to become closer to a complex system, it could reflect known information in the same way a stock market does. That change could mean one day we won't think about sentiment like we used to.

Clearly, this change hasn't been total. In my view, it probably never will be. Media elites still control most of the game—their control just isn't as stifling or dominant as it used to be.

Thus, I do not think the age-old lessons of sentiment and media have changed for all time, nor do I believe the consensus will have everything right going forward—no more than they ever did. Today, the mainline media very obviously continues to preserve inane worries and fear-mongering tactics as much as it ever did. But what's clearly happening is the old-world media is being forced to deliver news readers and viewers find most relevant, and that is profound for gauging prevailing sentiment. More than ever, it's vital to understand the reality of the situation relative to how it's being perceived.

WHAT'S THEIR MOTIVE?

Read these four headlines:

1. *Stocks Tumble as Worries Persist*
   —CNNMoney, September 29, 2008
2. *US Stocks Plunge as Global Credit Crisis Spreads*
   —MarketWatch, September 29, 2008
3. *Grip of Paralysis Adds to Threat of Recession*
   —*Financial Times*, September 28, 2008
4. *A Nightmare on Wall Street*
   —*The Economist*, August 28, 2008

These are real headlines from major media sources, all published within weeks of each other. What do they have in common?

Emotion!

Let's be clear: These headlines aren't pulled from the editorial or opinion pages. These are supposed to be news—as in, level-headed, unbiased reportage. Yet it doesn't take a genius to see these headlines are nothing of the sort.

The media's stated goal is to inform, not tell you what is relevant. Yet, by definition, we know that has to be false—the simple act of editing is about deciding what to print and what not to print. That means editors are deciding relevance.

The media's stated goal is to inform, not tell you what is relevant. Yet by definition we know that has to be false—the simple act of editing is about deciding what to print and what not to print. That means editors are deciding relevance.

The media knows its readers will react to things that arouse emotion. It's the oldest trick in their book. Today's media is jammed to the gills with adjectives to produce an immediate reaction from you, and thus keep you reading.

Why? The landscape is more competitive than ever. Editors can't afford to do it by the book and present an unbiased story. In the last years, many new media outlets have emerged. Newspapers and the evening news compete with the Internet, mobile devices, and cable TV, to name a few. Once upon a time, media was extremely elite because it had huge *barriers to entry*—only a few very rich and resourceful entities had the wherewithal and access to broadcast nationally or conduct mass printing and mailing. Basic economics says that once barriers to entry fall, competitors come rushing in. Today, technology allows many competitors to rush in to the media game.

Remember, we noted earlier most media is *for profit.* So editors have to think about their jobs and their businesses—they have to keep readers and viewers! How? Use emotion. Pull at the heartstrings. Finding emotion in headlines is virtually inescapable today. But instead of attempting to avoid it, you're best served being cognizant of it so as not to let it sway you. Always keep these two motives in mind:

1. **The Profit Motive**. Most media outlets of the world are for profit. That's great! But it also has consequences. By definition, their motive is to make money, not preserve fidelity of the news. They may say differently, but the bottom line is the bottom line, always.

2. **The Fear Motive**. The media knows it will get more viewership/readership when it has something scary to report. To see this even more clearly, flip the issue around: Would you buy a newspaper that consistently ran with headlines saying, "All Clear! The World Is Great!"? Of course not. Happy news isn't news that sells for very long. Need proof? Some of the best ratings in the history of the financial media came during the panic of 2008.

TIPS AND TRICKS TO NAVIGATE THE MEDIA

By now, we've come to at least a tacit understanding about investor sentiment and the media. But how to apply that knowledge? How does an investor go about monitoring the media? There is so much information out there that just the thought of keeping up with everything can feel tremendously daunting. From my years of sifting daily through the world's media, I've come up with a few tricks to help you gain the most relevant data and interpret it correctly in the least amount of time.

WHO ARE YOU GETTING NEWS FROM?

Not all stories are created equal. Through what delivery systems and outlets do you get your information? How diverse is it? Who's writing it? Is it a cub financial reporter from the *Fresno Bee* or an editorial in the *New York Times* from Warren Buffett? Authorship makes a big difference.

Read What's Popular, and Also What's Fringe

Remember, the media becomes your friend when you read what everyone else is reading because that's the news getting priced in fullest. If you're looking to understand sentiment and communal thought, get intimate with the world's biggest, broadest publications. The *Wall Street Journal* and *New York Times* are a good start. But even these are somewhat limited because they are so US-focused. Once you know what the biggest outlets are saying, then you can dig deeper and search for news and trusted sources that are off the beaten path for new ideas.

Read the Headline and First Two Paragraphs, Then Go

I read a lot of books. I mean a lot. Like several hundred a year. (I fully expect to be semi-blind from eye strain by 50.) But I don't finish every single book I read, and the same is true for articles and essays. There's a really weird bias people have about "finishing what they started" when it comes to reading. I hear it all the time: "I started this book, so I'm going to finish it." It's totally irrational. A high-quality paperback costs about $15 these days. Let's say it takes you five hours to finish. That's a measly $3 an hour! Which means the book is not very expensive (per unit of time spent on it) if you decide to ditch it. By contrast, a two hour movie at 10 bucks a pop is $5 an hour—67 percent more expensive per unit of time! Of course, since you pay the money upfront for both, it's a sunk cost (meaning, you're out the money) either way. But the point here is relative costs.

Anyway, forget about the cash, *time* is by far the most important of all assets. Ditch the bad books and articles and move on. Spend your time on the best ones. Most non-fiction books have their pertinent information upfront and spend the remaining pages detailing or bolstering their argument. That's fine if you're a hedgehog-like expert in a narrow field, but investors are foxes seeking general information.

It's especially true that journalists and financial writers in particular put the majority of pertinent information in the first couple paragraphs. Feel free to read them and then bolt. In many cases, financial articles turn anecdotal in the second half, with "expert" interviews and comments from the "man on the street." If anything, anecdotes can bias you and not help you. Ignore them. Only carefully peruse those articles most pertinent and enlightening to you. This will seem difficult at first, but with enough experience you'll spot them easily.

> It's especially true that journalists and financial writers in particular put the majority of pertinent information in the first couple paragraphs. Feel free to read them and then bolt.

LEARN TO SKIM AND LOOK FOR KEY WORDS

Some folks think speed reading is a panacea (those weird infomercials where the guy reads 10 pages of *War and Peace* in five seconds), and some think it's totally bogus. Both views are right. Sort of. Speed reading is one of the greatest skills an investor who tracks the media can have—when used wisely. Just as risk and return are connected, there is always and everywhere a trade-off between speed and comprehension.

The nice feature is most news stories only make a single point or two—that means you can skim. I'm not going to give you a course in speed reading, but I will say this: Speed reading is really a misnomer for skimming. Skimming is a greatly useful skill for folks who need to read in large volumes. Learn to pick up on keywords in the text—those will clue you in to important passages. Also, think about the structure of the article before diving in. Most journalists are trained to put the "thesis" statement of their paragraph at the beginning—just like your third-grade grammar teacher taught you. Theoretically, a soundly written piece of journalism can be understood just by reading the first sentence of every paragraph.

BE CONSCIOUS OF ADJECTIVES VERSUS FACTS

This is a biggie. There is so much sensational and unnecessary verbiage in today's press. Train yourself to recognize and ignore it.

Always make a distinction about whether something is interesting or informing. It's possible to be both, but in the case of columnists and editorials, most authors are aiming for entertaining. After all, that's what ultimately sells advertising. Many mistake something that is "fascinating" for something that is true or factual—a common behavioral bias. There are infinite theories, many tremendously titillating. But that doesn't make them worth your time. We tend to spend more time on what is interesting to us and less on what bores us. Maybe that seems obvious, but think of the biases that can create. Good columnists are paid for being controversial and, above all, entertaining—those are what drive readership. Be aware if you're spending an unnecessary amount of time on something you like but isn't necessarily relevant.

What's the Point of View?

Journalists are taught to "connect" with their readers via some standard conceits. One of them is to give the perspective of the "common man." They are writing in a way they believe an Average Joe would understand. Again, nothing wrong with that—but remember framing and context are among the most important cognitive factors in understanding an issue.

Being aware of the frame journalists use helps you think through what they're saying. Data get distorted when they get reported. "Strength and weakness" are vague, almost useless descriptors and can lead to wrong inferences. For instance, when you read "GDP was stronger than forecast in the third quarter," dig deeper and find out what really happened. This isn't necessarily a statement of growth. Maybe GDP was negative, but just not as negative as many thought. Another great example is how often I see headlines about some economic indicator or another "falling" when really it's just the rate of growth that slowed. Big difference.

Instead of taking their word for it, look at the data and see if something is really as they say it is. Get your own context.

Anecdote Is No Antidote

News is story; news is narrative. Facts are not interesting; data dumps are bores. What's riveting—what really gets the juices flowing and sells papers—is narrative. Journalists' jobs are to tell stories—that's the business they're in. They actually prefer anecdotal evidence over abstract figures because those feel more "human." But an investor should never make a judgment based on anecdote.

Notice two things about our language: One, reporting is literally "story"—that is, information with a plot. Never mind that most stories don't have so neat and tidy a structure as we'd like—journalists will find a way to frame it as such. This leads to empathy. Empathy is another characteristic of a good story—journalists have to make the thing hit home, people must be able to relate to what's going on, otherwise it falls flat. Next, news is literally, well, "news." It's designed to be new. Every day, there's "new" news to fill that *new*paper, whether relevant information has come to light or not. Whether today is a slow news day or not, the media will do its best to convince you there is something that's a "must read." In truth, there simply isn't much of interest that happens on most days.

Seek Diversity and Multiplicity

In the end, the best thing to do is seek news from many places and switch sources regularly. I think you should always read the biggest of the big, like the *Wall Street Journal* and *New York Times*, but outside of that, get many points of view from many places. Ultimately, this is the best way to keep from becoming too biased or blinded by a single news source and will go a long way in revealing the natural slant of any single publication.

Ignore the "Could" Headlines

Most days there isn't much news. Seriously! We are needy for news—and the media will create news every day, even if there isn't much to report (are front page exposés about Paris Hilton not sufficient evidence?).

When it comes to the right investing advice, it's about discipline—which means executing the same strategies day in and out. It can seem monotonous. Fact is, people do tire of hearing things over and over again—that's why the media has a habit of re-reporting old news with new language whether there is something relevant to report or not. For instance, in 2007, there were countless headlines—daily—about defaults in sub-prime mortgages. Yet information about those is released no more than once a month. That the media reported daily on sub-prime is more of a statement regarding folks' moods and what they're worried about than it is about sub-prime per se.

Most inane news takes the form of what I call the "could" headlines. You've seen these—news about something that might happen masquerading as a legitimate story. Anytime you see a "could" headline, you're best off ignoring it because not only is it speculation, but it's also direct evidence the market is already cognizant of it and therefore already pricing it in.

When it comes to the right investing advice, it's about discipline—which means executing the same strategies day in and out. It can seem monotonous. Fact is, people do tire of hearing things over and over again—that's why the media has a habit of re-reporting old news with new language whether there is something relevant to report or not.

DON'T FALL PREY TO "THE MYTH OF ONE"

Maybe the strangest of all media behavior is the media's fetish-like need to cite a "reason" the market moved each day. Just think about how dumb that is—there are literally millions of things acting on the markets daily. To believe we can single out one event every single day that moved the markets is absurd.

True, there are sometimes identifiable events large enough to move markets—but they're rare. Things like giant investment bank bailouts or major terrorist attacks don't happen often. Most days, nothing truly important happens, but the media will say something like "stocks down as oil climbs" on a day oil rose half a percent and stocks fell half a percent. What hogwash! Never forget markets are full of noise, or *stochasticity*. Most daily market moves aren't attributable to anything identifiable. Good investors don't manage their portfolios day-to-day anyway, so it's not worth your time thinking about it to begin with.

METAXIC BALANCE

There are infinite ways to interpret the world. The Greek philosophers had lots of strange ideas about thinking we still use today. One particularly interesting idea is *metaxis*, where two or more distinct realities in paradox with each other vie for attention. Metaxic balance means living with conflicting points of view in a way that's helpful and constructive to understanding and learning. Ambivalence is the opposite of metaxic balance, where two points of view pull at us and we cannot reconcile them. Maybe we could call this the quintessential "Hamlet" point of view.

Far out philosophy? Hardly. We're faced with paradoxical views of the world every single day in the media. Everyone has their way of seeing things. In my days as an analyst, I've been through some pretty heated debates about how the world works. Debates between analysts can be intense, which is a good thing—I respect someone who challenges what the group thinks. The only way to strengthen an investing idea (or any idea, really) is to put it to the test—temper it by fire, see if the minds of those you trust can punch holes in it. Then see if the world corroborates it.

It's fascinating to me how sure we are the world works one way, but then if we're presented with a compelling case, we can switch and see things completely differently. Our brains have the ability to see things from many different points of view, which is quite problematic for an investor looking for the "right" way to get rich.

My advice? Don't search for certainty. Remind yourself any theory is a way of seeing things, not "the" way to see things. Over time, you'll find the ideas that work best and discard the ones that don't. Seek metaxic balance in investing by reading many different publications and opinions, and always find and consider the counterpoint.

METAPHORS WE INVEST BY

Does this sentence strike you as odd?

The markets are up today!

Probably not. It's a very ordinary way to speak. But if you really think about it, this sentence is a truly weird thing. Consider: By making reference to the position of a physical object in space, I've expressed an outcome (and my feelings toward it) about an object that doesn't tangibly exist.

Saying the market is "up" is a metaphor. Nothing is physically moving upward. It's just an expression to say the value of the market is larger than it was.

Maybe all that strikes you as mundane, but simple sentences like that one can tell us a lot. In fact, an understanding of linguistic basics can help you be a better investor. The media in particular traps us with various metaphors, and those metaphors govern how we think about things. Politicians do this all the time by creating euphemisms for things they don't really want to say. For instance, is it "spreading around the wealth" or a "tax hike"? Depends who you ask!

Language is an evolutionary adaptation—a means for us to communicate. Think of what a tremendous advantage it was tens of thousands of years ago for humans in the wild who could transfer ideas, thoughts, and commands into another person's head by simply making sounds! Those poor wildebeasts didn't stand a chance in the long run.

Metaphor is most often understood as an indirect comparison between two or more seemingly unrelated subjects to create a new meaning. This is true enough, but many think of metaphor as merely a tool of poetry. This is wrong. Nearly the entirety of human thought is metaphor. It is a mistake to believe we understand the world "as it is." *We understand everything as it is to us.* Metaphor is pervasive in everyday life and central to the way the mind works. Our natural methods of thinking and comprehending are metaphorical. Metaphor is not reserved for the poetic moments of life; it is for all moments of life from the most rational and calculated to our most spiritual. Heck, we couldn't understand capitalism without it—Adam Smith's "invisible hand" is just a metaphor to describe capitalism in a way we can better comprehend.

Whether with literature, everyday conversation, a technical scientific analysis, or a simple description of our surroundings, we liken subjective experiences to things outside ourselves in order to attain meaning and understanding relative to our environment.

These comparisons aren't accidental gleanings from the brain's inner workings. Metaphor is a natural function of mental activity and seems to be as universal and innate as language itself. Metaphor even bears a biological signature: Certain types of metaphorical thinking can be detected in the brain during functional magnetic resolution imaging (fMRI) scans.[1]

Because metaphors create relationships in terms of things we understand (and from a very specific human perspective), they're most often grounded on the basis of our own motivations, goals, actions, and characteristics.[2] The mind wants to reduce things to categories to easily determine and compute information.

Let's take the concept of economic recession as an example. When we say we're "in a recession," we're not truly "inside" anything—it's merely a way for the brain to describe the abstract state of the economy in a physical context. This is a very strange thing to say, yet everyone understands it. Cognitive scientist George Lakoff says, "Inevitably, many primary metaphors are universal because everybody has basically the same kinds of bodies and brains and lives in basically the same kinds of environments, so far as the features relevant to metaphor are concerned."[3]

The basic domains of experience are our bodies and our physical interactions with the environment. We most easily understand metaphors in relation to nature because that's where most instincts were developed through evolution—our brains were made to understand the world in terms of our position in it. So metaphors are based mostly upon things we naturally understand. To take an abstract concept, whether it be recession or an emotion like fear, and liken it to something we all implicitly understand is a basic strategy of human thought.

We must take caution: Life and stock markets are full of bad metaphors. Remember, our minds can deceive us—we often see what we want to and not reality as such (recall Chapter 2)—and bad metaphorical thinking can be the culprit. The way we frame our metaphors is very important to how we think and how we view the world.

Studying market metaphors can tell you a great deal about investor sentiment because they reveal how people understand (or misunderstand) more complex topics.

As an example, let's look at inflation and how people tend to describe it metaphorically. (These are a smattering of real quotes I've gathered over the years from the media.)

- Inflation has *attacked* the *foundation* of our economy.
- The Fed's biggest *enemy* is inflation.
- Inflation is *robbing* me of my savings.
- Inflation is *lowering* our standard of living.
- We need to *combat* inflation.
- Inflation is *taking its toll* at the checkout counter and the gas pump.
- Buying gold is the best way of *dealing* with inflation.

The words betray our attitudes and fears toward inflation—we think of inflation as something that can attack us, hurt us, rob us. We often try to describe something conceptual, like inflation, as literally human in order to understand it. This is called *personification*. Sometimes, inflation isn't just personified as human—it's an adversary, a sworn enemy, something to "combat" or "deal" with. And this is a common way of depicting inflation in the media. Why? Because inflation by itself is highly abstract and not intuitive. Therefore, our brains want to search for ways to understand it in terms that are natural to how we think. When we are experiencing the effects of something due to complex economic or political factors that few truly understand, the "inflation is an adversary" metaphor allows the mind to believe it's receiving a coherent account of what is happening.

But a good economist knows inflation isn't necessarily an adversary at all. In fact, a low, but positive, level of inflation is widely considered to be a necessary part of a healthy, growing economy. It's only high inflation that harms economies. And what if inflation were to go negative (deflation)? Actually, that's where it can really get bad! Yet, because the system of metaphors we use refers to inflation as an "adversary," it's hard for most people to see that. In this way, metaphors can both reveal and influence people's beliefs. A savvy investor can recognize how bad metaphors influence widely held, incorrect attitudes about the markets and use those insights to invest better.

 A savvy investor can recognize how bad metaphors influence widely held, incorrect attitudes about the markets and use those insights to invest better.

Language is an incredible technology for humans, but in truth it's still very crude. For hours, I've sat at my desk, lamenting the difficulty in trying to share an experience or insight about investing via words. Some experiential knowledge is simply ineffable—beyond language.

CHAPTER INSIGHTS

Gauging sentiment is mostly done through monitoring the media, and cannot be ignored by investors.

- Sentiment can also be thought of as "demand." Judging how investors are feeling is a different way of judging the perceived demand for stocks.
- Sentiment can swing rapidly and is thus always to be judged in the short term.
- Part of tracking sentiment is tracking consensus expectations.
  - Much of stock market forecasting is about understanding reality relative to the consensus, so knowing what most people believe is imperative to forecast correctly.
- The media is a command system traditionally controlled by a few elite companies.
  - Some forms of technology are empowering better real-time information, feedback, and reportage from non-media civilians.
  - It is important to study the media itself and not just the news being reported.
- Behavioral quirks affect how the media reports and how we perceive it:
  - Brains are trained to understand the world in a coherent way via story.
  - Most news is designed to achieve an emotional response from readers/viewers.
- Some tips to navigate the media:
  - Ask where and who you get your news from.
  - Read what is popular, but also read what's fringe.

- Make a habit of only reading the first few paragraphs of a story.
- Learn to skim.
- Be conscious of adjectives versus facts.
- Ask yourself what point of view the story propagates.
- Learn to ignore anecdotal reporting and use aggregated data more readily.
- Seek diversity in where you get your news.
- Ignore stories that report things that "could" happen.
- Don't fall prey to "the myth of one"—stories that try to explain market action based on a single event.

- Humans understand ideas, and especially abstractions, via metaphors.

  - Most metaphors are imperfect and can be misleading.
  - There is no getting around metaphor, but it is good to be cognizant of prevalent metaphors in the financial press.

5

HOW STOCK MARKETS
REALLY WORK

*Prices are important not because money is considered
paramount but because prices are a fast and effective conveyor
of information through a vast society in which fragmented
knowledge must be coordinated.*

—Thomas Sowell

*It is the fundamental wisdom of the capitalist system
that it functions irrespective of the wisdom or the stupidity
of the capitalists.*

—Gustav Stolper

This chapter won't give a usual view of how stock markets work. We're not going to cover the basics of trade, or how the Federal Reserve works, or financial statements, or any of that. Those are fine and great things, but they're not what this book is about.

This chapter provides a way to understand how markets work for investors. Too many folks believe that if you can understand how the economy functions, perfect vision of markets will naturally follow.

Nope! Markets and economies are mechanically different beasts, requiring completely different approaches to understand.

This book is about how to think about markets and understand them better, but it isn't to say you can just disregard economic things. It's important for investors to know how the economy works because otherwise one cannot critique or corroborate other assessments or determine what is relevant and irrelevant for stocks. For guides on how to analyze and understand how sectors of the economy work, I recommend the *Fisher Investments On* series. Each volume covers a specific sector of the global economy and strategies for stock investing in that sector.

We won't do that here. Instead, we're looking for a point of view—a new way to think—about how markets function to make us more successful investors. The first thing to do toward that goal is correctly understand how free markets work.

CAPITALISM BY ANY OTHER NAME

It's fascinating how humans pass on knowledge and experience by continually reinventing—we often say the same things over and again but in a slightly new way. It's typical in academia, but just as prevalent with society generally. Over and over again, variations on the same themes are repackaged to audiences in film, books, and other forms of mass media. (Long before Obi-Wan Kenobi taught Luke Skywalker wisdom about the cosmos, Merlin did it for King Arthur. And Superman couldn't exist without scads of messianic figures like Jesus and the Buddha to arrive before him.)

Re-messaging widely held wisdom updates the lesson for a new generation or culture, but also forces us to revisit and rethink an idea. I believe deeply in seeing issues from as many sides and perspectives as possible to tease out unseen contradictions or problems, or simply to strengthen what we already knew.

A philosophical debate for the ages is whether there is any such thing as an "original" thought. Whether you think so or not, one of the best ways to make any non-original idea your own is by interpreting it uniquely. When you get your own set of metaphors about a concept, you truly make it your own. Of course, and importantly, the metaphors we use matter greatly, and the wrong ones can get us into deep trouble (as we saw in Chapter 4).

So to understand how an economy or free market works, the best place to start is to see how some of the best economic thinkers of the past described capitalism's mechanisms in their own words.

ADAM SMITH

Adam Smith, often thought of as the original theorist of capitalism, emphasized the role of autonomy in capitalism—that individuals, pursuing their own self-interests, ultimately make a larger, efficient system. Yet the individuals do not play an active role in defining the larger system of capitalism, nor do they ever really think about capitalism—they just think about their own needs and transactions. Instead, capitalism is guided by the "invisible hand":

> As every individual, therefore, endeavors as much he can both to employ his capital in the support of domestic industry, and so to direct that industry that its produce may be of the greatest value; every individual necessarily labors to render the annual revenue of the society as great as he can. He generally, indeed, neither intends to promote the public interest, nor knows how much he is promoting it. By preferring the support of domestic to that of foreign industry, he intends only his own security; and by directing that industry in such a manner as its produce may be of the greatest value, he intends only his own gain, and he is in this, as in many other cases, led by an invisible hand to promote an end which was no part of his intention. Nor is it always the worse for the society that it was no part of it. By pursuing his own interest he frequently promotes that of the society more effectually than when he really intends to promote it. I have never known much good done by those who affected to trade for the public good. It is an affectation, indeed, not very common among merchants, and very few words need be employed in dissuading them from it.[1]

JOSEPH SCHUMPETER

A famous economist in the twentieth century, Joseph Schumpeter emphasized capitalism's ability to work in cycles. Capitalism weeds out inefficiency, innovates new solutions, integrates and distributes those solutions to the wider populace, and thus rebuilds the system stronger and bigger than before. He called this archetypal cycle "creative destruction":

> The opening up of new markets, foreign or domestic, and the organizational development from the craft shop and factory to such concerns as US Steel illustrate the same process of industrial mutation—if I may use that biological term—that incessantly revolutionizes the economic structure from within, incessantly destroying the old one, incessantly creating a new one. This process of Creative Destruction is the essential fact about capitalism. It is what capitalism consists in and what every capitalist concern has got to live in.[2]

FRIEDRICH HAYEK

In his time, Friedrich Hayek was highly controversial. Throughout the twentieth century, he insisted capitalism (much like Adam Smith) was a system that operated outside any single individual or government's ability to understand or direct.

> It may indeed prove to be far the most difficult and not the least important task for human reason rationally to comprehend its own limitations. It is essential for the growth of reason that as individuals we should bow to forces and obey principles which we cannot hope fully to understand, yet on which the advance and even the preservation of civilization depend. Historically this has been achieved by the influence of the various religious creeds and by traditions and superstitions which made men submit to those forces by an appeal to his emotions rather than to his reason. The most dangerous stage in the growth of civilization may well be that in which man has come to regard all these beliefs as superstitions and refuses to accept or to submit to anything which he does not rationally understand. The rationalist whose

reason is not sufficient to teach him those limitations of the powers of conscious reason, and who despises all the institutions and
customs which have not been consciously designed, would thus
become the destroyer of the civilization built upon them. This
may well prove a hurdle which man will repeatedly reach, only
to be thrown back into barbarism. . . . Common acceptance of
formal rules is indeed the only alternative to direction by a single
will man has yet discovered.[3]

MILTON FRIEDMAN

Libertarian-leaning and monetarist-championing Milton Friedman
made his mark in the twentieth century. Friedman's influence was
wide as an economist, but his voice carried even further via best-
selling writings about the relationship between capitalism and freedom. Hence, his seminal works, as expressed in *Free to Choose* and
Freedom and Capitalism:

> A major source of objection to a free economy is precisely that
> it . . . gives people what they want instead of what a particular
> group thinks they ought to want. Underlying most arguments
> against the free market is a lack of belief in freedom itself.[4]

In some form or another, each of these titans of economic thought
describes capitalism's ability to provide goods and services to individuals in the most efficient manner possible. They continuously note
there is no central command to govern capitalism—it's simply a system that emerges as a result of the aggregated activity of many individuals. Capitalism seems to be something greater than its individual
parts—a supra-system that's stronger and more versatile than any elite
decision-making body could be. Even in times where capitalism fal-
ters with excess or mistakes, it ultimately (though often harshly) holds
the power to correct itself and move forward.

Now, under no circumstances will I count myself among these
titans, but I do have my own way of thinking about capitalism
that reflects all of these ideas, just described with a new set of
metaphors.

Whatever your way of viewing capitalism, studying these concepts can provide context and lead to greater understanding and adept investing decisions.

IT'S COMPLICATED . . . A CRASH COURSE IN CEAS

In my opinion, what links all these views about capitalism, and the reason markets and economies are vastly more efficient than any government, individual, or central command system of any kind, is that they are **Complex, Emergent, Adaptive Systems.** We'll call them **CEASs** for short.

Theories of complexity and emergence are relatively new and find their origins in social science and physics. They are only just now being thought of for systems like economies and markets. Some of the leading studies in this subject are being conducted at the Santa Fe Institute, and I highly recommend Michael J. Mauboussin's book, *More Than You Know: Finding Financial Wisdom in Unconventional Places*, or Eric Beinhocker's, *Origin of Wealth: Evolution, Complexity, and the Radical Remaking of Economics*, if you wish to delve further into these subjects. Today, CEASs are being used to understand everything from how a simple DNA strand can create a vastly more complex human organism to how the weather works, how cities develop, how the universe and its matter behave, how ant farms work, how the ecosystem and natural selection work, and yes, even how stock markets work.[5]

For whatever reason, folks have always regarded markets and economics as if they're some special thing exclusive from the rest of the natural world. I think this is a poor way to study economics because it disallows us from using vast amounts of human knowledge gleaned from other areas. True, economies and markets are unique in the sense there isn't anything exactly like them in nature, but a wider understanding of natural systems goes a long way toward understanding markets and economics better. It is an error to think markets are unique to all of life, but pitfalls also lie in making too many comparisons to outside systems. We must tread cautiously.

So let's be clear about something upfront: CEAS is a way of describing markets, not some discovery of a "law" about how they function. It is a new and updated way of understanding capitalism with much the same foundation as the masters of old.

Ants Get Us Started

At first, CEASs can seem a bit abstract. What exactly are they? They're organizations in which high-level patterns arise from local behavior and create a system that is autonomous from the individuals that are a part of it. *That means collective behavior and individual behavior are different things and need to be analyzed separately.* In other words, individuals who act autonomously and in their own interests in a market environment will eventually begin to produce a larger, more complex system. That's just another way of saying Adam Smith's "invisible hand." Let's define each piece:

- **Complexity**: The study of how relationships between parts give rise to the collective behaviors of a system and how the system interacts and forms relationships with its environment.
- **Emergence**: The movement from low-level rules and interactions to a higher-level system of macro-behavior. A system where agents, acting locally, start producing discernible macro-behavior not controlled or planned by a central authority.
- **Adaptive**: The change in living organisms or systems allowing them to survive in a dynamic (or changing) environment. Adaptations cope with environmental stresses, changes, and threats.
- **System**: We're talking about macro-behavior—looking at group behavior and not individuals.

Maybe that seems a bit convoluted. Think about an ant farm. Ant farms are great examples of a CEAS. Individually, ants don't have any idea about what's going on with the farm they're a part of. They have no nervous system or detectable awareness other than their ability to leave and follow hormones. If you observe an ant farm for a while, you'll see an individual ant only knows how to follow a couple simple rules tied to leaving a strong hormone signal or following one. When ants go out searching for food, they follow all sorts of random, non-linear paths. As they do, they leave hormones based on whether that path was successful in leading to food or not. As more successes happen, more hormones get left behind, and eventually, from just a few rules, huge networks of communication, hierarchy, and food transport are created—a complete, emergent, and complex system based on local interactions between ants.

Not a single ant—including the queen herself—knows anything about this vast, dynamic system that's been created. They only know their few hormone-based rules. The complex system operates on a level above and outside the constituent ants.

Even better? Ant farms are adaptive. When ants encounter obstacles or disruptions, the simple rules they follow locally can often help them cope with a changing environment. This is evident simply by noting ant farms can exist in many locales, not just one specific environment.

So, ant farms are CEASs in a nutshell. Sound strange? Not at all! It happens frequently in the world. Just think about evolution. That is explicitly the process of going from low complexity to higher complexity without any individual animal/species doing it deliberately or centrally planning it. Primordial soup created single-celled organisms, which gave rise to multi-cellular organisms, which generated amphibians with nervous and circulatory systems and that could walk on land, and so on, until eventually you get people. The ecosystem itself is perhaps the highest and most grand of all CEASs—not a single individual or group oversaw the process—its patterns and structure simply emerged over time via adaptation.

Evolution reveals something key to CEASs—it's not a neat and tidy process. There's an incredible amount of "creative destruction," as Schumpeter might say. In evolution, there are mutations, inefficiencies, and zig-zagging paths full of randomness to get to a "higher" species. It's important to understand that creating a "higher" species is about a better way to cope with the environment than it is a progression. Nature doesn't know what improvement is—it just knows survival.

We're Not Ants! But We Are a Community

Maybe by now you're saying, "But humans aren't ants! We're thinking and self-aware beings!" And you'd be right! But self-awareness only adds profoundly by many magnitudes to the complexity and adaptability of the economy and markets. The fact remains an economy and stock market are examples of CEASs—where individual humans create a dynamic system vastly more complex, diverse, and smarter than any individual is actually aware of or could be.

Friedrich Hayek was a pioneer in this field, arguing strongly humans are not equipped to understand the systems they create. He was more right than he knew, and his argument is consistent with our earlier observations on the limitations of human awareness in Chapter 2. Any cursory examination of the stock market reveals there was never any real central command that "planned" how Wall Street would develop over time—it simply "emerged" as individuals built it step by step, not with some grand schema in mind, but in pursuing their own interests.

When it comes to investing in stock markets we have to think *communally*. And no, I don't mean we all become communists. I mean that we must take note of the fact that *individual behavior gives rise to a more complex system with its own characteristics and patterns.* So an attempt to understand markets by individual or localized behavior is an error. Yet think of how often we do this—we commonly mistake our own experiences or local interactions as proxies for what must be happening everywhere else.

This fact is also generally startling and abhorrent to most traditional scientific thought. Traditional thinking says

When it comes to investing in stock markets we have to think *communally*. And no, I don't mean we all become communists. I mean that we must take note of the fact that *individual behavior gives rise to a more complex system with its own characteristics and patterns.*

that if you can understand how individuals act, then all you have to do is aggregate that individual behavior and, thus, understand how the bigger system works—the amalgam of micro makes the macro. But CEAS says otherwise—it says the system might act much differently and in unforeseeable ways than individuals do.

Another conventional mode of scientific thought is, if we are given a set of initial conditions and a set of proven overarching principles or rules, we can predict how the system will behave through time. These are examples of *linear, reductive* thinking—hallmarks of mathematics and the scientific method (which we studied in Chapter 1). Our brains are designed to desperately want cause-and-effect logic, but the basics of CEAS show us that cannot be true because the overall system is different than the individuals it's made of. Ants and their farm; people and their economy. Just as there is no way to know exactly how an ant farm will develop based on observing one ant (even when we know the hormone-based rules it will act upon), there is also no way to know how an economy will develop by simply understanding the initial conditions.

Carl Jung, one of the forerunners of psychological thought in the early twentieth century, was to my mind among the first to envision something like this when he described the *Collective Unconscious*. Of course, most of Jung's theories today are defunct, but the idea that we should think about the community and its patterns as separate from the individual continues to hold merit.

This is fantastic news for investors! It means we don't need to be burdened with understanding how every individual acts (something that varies and is often predicated on individual situation and intention), but we can instead focus on the big system—the market itself. Understanding stock markets and economies as CEASs allows us to sharpen our investing focus.

IRRATIONAL AND EFFICIENT IS EASY . . . IF WE SHARE INFORMATION

Often people say, "It's easy for ants because they just follow rules. Humans don't—they can often be irrational and don't necessarily follow any discernable pattern like ants do via simple hormones." This is certainly true. What's more, the behavioral sciences have shown individuals are often irrational and erratic (at least, by the standards of classical economics). Thus, the system humans are a part of by definition can't be rational or efficient simply because its constituents aren't rational. It follows too that, if investors are often irrational, then stock markets must often be irrational as well.

While that seems logical, it simply can't be true. CEASs don't work like that. Highly efficient and complex systems can emerge from simpler (and even irrational) people who are a part of it.

To see this, let's think about the notion of "rationality" for a moment. It assumes only one right answer, which means there should be unity, or *homogeneity*, of opinion between "rational" people. But we know that very smart people often disagree. We also know that seemingly smart, or rational, people can often be flat wrong. That's ok; in fact, it's great because markets take all the opinions—smart and dumb and everything in between—and digest them to reflect all the known information and opinion via *the mechanism of pricing*. A better way to think about markets is they provide the *best* answer in an uncertain world based on known information, which is not necessarily the *right* answer, but a better answer than any individual could come up with.

As long as any CEAS has *high information sharing* with lots of *heterogeneous, independent* agents acting within it, high efficiency can happen. That's the crux of stock market efficiency. Let's throw out this notion about markets either being "rational" or "irrational." It's that kind of yes/no thinking that gets folks desperately in trouble. Humans are neither rational nor irrational—they can be both. Market pricing is not about omniscience—too many critics want to saddle it with that too-heavy burden. Prices move around to reflect how the consensus is feeling about it at that moment, based on known information. That's not omniscience; it's just a mechanism that's vastly more intelligent and efficient—most of the time—than any individual can be.

James Surowiecki described in his book, *The Wisdom of Crowds*, how groups of decision makers are often much better than individuals.

But how? Let's think through the components. Stock markets by defini-tion aggregate local information into a central place (prices). There are millions, if not billions, of investors taking one side of a stock position or another at any given moment via trading. Those bets are representative of what people believe about the stock they're buying or selling. That means, through the mechanism of a stock price, all the known informa-tion about the stock is being shared. But also see that each trade is an *independent, discrete* event. No one knows for sure the motives of the counterparties. There is a wide dispersion of knowledge and opinion and analysis coming from all directions—no unity whatsoever.

That's why markets are far more efficient than individuals—information sharing and diverse opinion based on all available knowledge is getting digested in the system at lightning speed. Information is being shared via prices. That so much knowledge can be represented in a single data point—the stock price—is to my mind one of the great innova-tions of human achievement. Even if some, or many, of those trades are "irrational," the sum total of all trading activity balances out if the sys-tem is big and deep enough (stock markets definitely are). Thus, mar-kets can still be efficient even in the presence of individual irrationality.

Incidentally, many believe rising stock markets are the "natural order" of things. Untrue. Profits aren't a foregone conclusion, neither are stock price rises. Stocks can't go up unless there's someone willing to pay more than the last person did. Meanwhile, a seller believes the cash he's getting for the sale is worth more than the share he's selling it for. That dance between buyers and sellers is where the information is shared and reflected in prices.

Let's go back to our ant farm example for a moment. At first, scout ants form extremely crooked patterns toward food. There is a huge amount of randomness and misinformation as ants try all kinds of fruitless directions to reach food. Eventually, however, with enough instances—that is, enough ants going through the trail to the food—the path begins to smooth, and the direction to the food becomes straighter and more efficient. The same is true for stock markets—the more trades that are done (AKA volume or liquidity), the more infor-mation is digested. In the short term, stock charting patterns are jag-ged, haywire things with countless indiscernible bumps and bobs. But over the long term, the chart is smoother, reflecting after much time and trading what the market believes to be the correct price in a more discernible, straighter pattern.

The important thing to see about all this is that the system itself—via pricing in the case of stocks (or hormones and food trails in the case of ants)—creates a more efficient system than any one individual can. That's why it's really, really hard to beat the market—it's essentially you versus the aggregated opinion of the world.

All that diverse information is called *heterogeneity* (the presence of many different items or opinions, often not easily sorted or separated, though clearly distinct). This is an absolute must for CEAS to work properly. Manias and panics happen when heterogeneity diminishes and investors start to think alike—the system becomes truly irrational because there isn't enough diversity of opinion to ballast the other side. This is the difference between negative and positive *feedback loops* in CEAS, which we'll discuss momentarily.

CHANGES . . . TURN AND FACE THE STRANGE

Another important feature of CEAS—and thus markets—is they adapt and change independently of the individuals comprising them. That is, markets take on a life of their own, turning and growing and shifting in ways few can foresee. How?

We've discussed evolutionary theory a few times already, and nowhere is it more important than here. It happens via the principle of *feedback loops*. There are two kinds:

- **Negative Feedback**. This is what evolutionary scientists would think of as natural selection. Businesspeople think of it simply as competition. A trader would call it arbitrage. A negative feedback loop sounds bad but is a great thing. It regulates the system. For instance, why don't rabbits rule the world? Because foxes hunt them and eat them and keep their population lower—negative feedback. But then why don't foxes rule the world? Because mountain lions eat them. And so on. Nature is the greatest of all negative feedback mechanisms—constantly regulating the system. So too with markets and economics.

The reason Dell can't rule the computing world fully is because companies like Apple are hot on their heels. The reason a stock trades at the levels it does is because there are plenty of bets on both sides—buying and selling. These factors push and pull against each other constantly, causing adaptation and change that no single individual can see clearly. Actions trigger reactions and on from there. The more complex and deep the system, the greater the adaptation, or negative feedback. It builds on itself. It may even diminish *stochasticity*, or the noise and randomness of local interactions (more on this next chapter).

- **Positive Feedback**. Or the opposite of negative feedback, where instead of regulating the system, feedback builds on itself. This is what happens in market panics and manias, for example. When the vast majority of investors all become bearish—or want to sell—prices plunge, and the selling perpetuates the drops with few or no buyers there to stem the losses. With such deep losses and pervasive fear, maybe mutual fund managers get many calls for redemptions and thus have to keep selling. And so on. The same can happen in euphoric times, when folks become so bullish, stock prices can soar to irrational levels simply because there aren't enough sellers there to stem the tide.

NOT DRUNK, JUST BUZZED

Particularly in the short term, markets tend to stagger up and down charts like a guy staggering home after a few too many—zig-zagging along without any real direction. That is, there is the appearance of randomness. Maybe, but more than likely the market is doing something you cannot see or currently fathom.

A common investor mistake about markets is the belief in *linearity*. Most of the time, CEAS cannot be understood via linear logic. Many believe in their gut there has to be a discernible cause and effect for everything—a precedent action to every observed reaction. It's Newton's third law for goodness sake! This is taken as such dogma, most forget to ever question the premise or what it really applies to.

We've visited the problems of math and reductionist thinking many times already in this book. The belief in action/reaction and cause/effect comes from an erroneous belief that CEAS should work in the same ways basic physical science works. For whatever reason, over the years, investors and economists think we ought to be able to deduce market movements the same way we calculate stuff like gravity, velocity, and acceleration. That's probably because we want to believe mathematics somehow contains concrete and precise answers for everything. It seems intuitive—like we're making it all "scientific"—but if you understand how CEAS works, it simply cannot be. Linear reasoning and mathematics will often fail.

With CEAS (stock markets and economies) there is no requirement of linear cause and effect. Seems like blasphemy! But it's true. Daily journalists and pundits try to explain "why" stocks did what they did. If you watch those explanations for just a few days you'll see how contradictory they are. One day stocks are up because oil is lower, which is supposedly good for consumers. Then the next day, stocks are up because oil is higher, indicating high demand for energy, which points to a more robust economy. Hogwash, all of it! *It's trying to assign causality where causality isn't discernible or even necessarily possible.*

If you think about it, a well-functioning CEAS should rarely produce an easily predictable result. Things are dynamic and evolve

STOCKS AND ECONOMIES ARE DIFFERENT

Remember, the stock market and the economy are different things. Some of the best professional investors I know believe to this day the economy and the market are different ways of saying the same thing—that stocks are a direct reflection of the economy. They are not. Stock markets are the sum of what investors believe shares are worth, traded on the public market. An economy is the sum product of all output of a country or society. The vast majority of "economic" activity is private and has little to do with stocks, and a big chunk usually comes purely from the government. Anyway, most companies do not sell stock to public markets. This alone points out a big potential difference between stocks and the economy. There are many others. For instance, it's entirely possible to have earnings sink but the economy grow, or vice versa.

because of competition and the struggle for survival (again, something nature and free market capitalism have in common). Thus, one could argue evolving systems must be inherently unpredictable because if they *were* predictable, they'd be gamed very quickly and everyone would get rich. Just so, organisms that are easily understood are easily hunted and become extinct very quickly.

Like a biological organism, economies evolve in such a way that their predictability often disappears. Things literally get "priced in" and thus don't have the power to affect markets in the way most investors believe they can. There are always more parameters and possibilities in a stock market and economy than can be measured. When viewed as an interconnected system, the probabilities of possible outcomes in an economy explode. Today's world is so vastly connected, market adaptation and flow of information happen faster than ever. That means markets are more nimble than ever at digesting widely known information.

 Like a biological organism, economies evolve in such a way that their predictability often disappears. Things literally get "priced in" and thus don't have the power to affect markets in the way most investors believe they can.

The economic modeling experts come up with to explain the economy or any other complex system is usually flawed. Such models often rest upon a number of assumptions and are far too simple to account for the greater complexity of the economy. Usually, how you fiddle with the assumptions in such a model is how you get the model to work—which is dubious because the whole point of the model is to help explain something when, in fact, all that's been done is push the uncertainty into the variables. With a CEAS, the slightest error in any variable throws the whole thing way off. As we've seen many times already, there are too many variables in an economy or market—and all acting upon and influencing each other simultaneously—to have any economic model function the way we know math today.

We simply do not have the equations—possibly, we don't even have the brainpower—to predict where CEAS will be or what will happen with exactitude or very far into the future. The only way to come close is via probability (much more on this next chapter). Thus, simplistic valuation assumptions invite a lot of danger, and cause-and-effect thinking can be anathema to you in market forecasting.

The Power of Observation

Probably the best amalgam of investing advice I've ever seen is from the Sherlock Holmes stories. I'd wager Sir Arthur Conan Doyle would have been one heck of a portfolio manager.

My favorite part? Everyone thought Holmes was a genius, but all he really ever did was notice things others didn't and interpret those things in a slightly different way than the rest. Seldom if ever did Holmes have any extra information—he was usually privy to the same data as his faithful Watson. So how did Sherlock glean the answers when everyone else failed? Elementary! Holmes didn't know more, he *observed* more than others and used logic to make deductions, allowing him to see things in plain sight no one else could.

So much of investing is this way. Too many believe it's some special secret or data set or software program "only the pros" have that creates outsized stock returns. No way. Most investing insight comes from widely public and available information. It's about careful observation and seeing what the crowd misses.

Folks tend to focus on one thing and block out the rest. Behavioral scientists sometimes call this *anchoring* or *framing*, but it's a concept old as time. Knowing people will focus on something that draws the most attention and ignore the rest is the principle most illusionists (or magicians) make their living on. The solution is simple: Be aware. When a big market-moving story emerges, ask yourself what the market is focusing on and see if there are details or other factors being ignored. You can never stop yourself from having biases, but if you're aware of them, you have a fighting chance of surmounting them. Deliberate observation is a great tactic toward that goal.

Here are a few of my favorite Holmes quips—all tremendous investing advice.

"On the contrary, Watson, you can see everything. You fail, however, to reason from what you see." —From *The Adventure of the Blue Carbuncle*

"We balance probabilities and choose the most likely. It is the scientific use of the imagination."—From *The Hound of the Baskervilles*

"It is an old maxim of mine that when you have excluded the impossible, whatever remains, however improbable, must be the truth."—From *The Adventure of the Beryl Coronet*

"It is a capital mistake to theorize before you have all the evidence. It biases the judgment."—From *A Study in Scarlet*

"Everything in this world is relative, my dear Watson."—From *The Dying Detective*

THE NEW GOLDEN RULE

When viewing markets and economies as CEASs, one thing becomes very clear: *You can't know everything—and don't need to!*

No one understands everything about how the economy or the stock market works. Not a single person—ever! Why? Markets and economies are both far too large and deep for any individual to fully comprehend and have been so since people were trading cattle in exchange for jars of wine in Ur millennia ago.

There's so much confusion on this issue. Most economic and market theories are tough just to conceptualize in your head, let alone compute and execute. The fact is you need hardly any of it. Many see this fact as limiting, but I find it truly liberating.

Perhaps you don't believe me—you were trained to carefully analyze everything before doing anything. Try this on for size: Today's global economy comprises some 6.7 billion people, each going about their business every day in billions of unique ways. The sum total is the global economy. So to understand it all in some fashion, you'd have to have some conception of how those billions of folks did things every single day.

Then, realize an economy is an *interconnected web of activity*, which means you'd not only have to understand all those people individually, you'd have to understand the different ways they interact, too. Any good statistician knows that with just three possibilities, or options, the number of potential combinations begins to expand very quickly. Adding a new variable to just about any model tends to make things almost infinitely more complex. The economy has billions of people with many available options each day—making the potential interconnections and outcomes incomputable. The same logic applies for stock markets, where trillions of dollars worth of stock trades are transacted daily—each with a different motive and point of view. Heck, science hasn't yet really figured out how a single brain works, develops, or comes to structure itself to attain consciousness, let alone billions of brains working together in an infinitely interconnected global economy.

Another way to think of it is like a chess game—a board with finite squares and pieces and rules for moves. Even in such a contained area, within a few moves, the potential numbers and combinations of moves become almost infinite—and the possibilities shift because they are dependent on how the pieces on the board shift. It's impossible to fathom or come up with a system to exactly forecast the next move, even within such a small, enclosed system as a chess board!

Now consider this: Human brains were designed to conceptualize up to maybe 10 to a few dozen of anything. Try to actually visualize a million of anything. You can't! In your head, it becomes an abstraction almost instantly. Fact is, the gray tissue in your melon isn't made to understand markets fully. Even our slickest, fastest computers aren't powerful enough to approach comprehending the whole system yet. Maybe one day, but we're still nowhere close. And it's not just a matter of computing power—we don't have the math for it either.

It takes some courage and gumption to accept that we can't know everything. It seems impossible that humans could beget systems like markets and economies and not be able to understand them fully. Most investors I observe fail because they're overconfident and think they can understand it all and thus end up understanding very little. They fall in love with their explanations, their views of the world—which by definition have to be limited and myopic at best, or more often downright wrong. For my part, I've been as guilty of this as anyone (we all are), but at least I know it.

> It takes some courage and gumption to accept that we can't know everything. It seems impossible that humans could beget systems like markets and economies and not be able to understand them fully. Most investors I observe fail because they're overconfident and think they can understand it all and thus end up understanding very little.

This all must sound pretty limiting and sad. How can you possibly invest successfully with obstacles like these!? Actually, if you learn to roll with it, <u>understanding our ignorance</u> can become our greatest investing ally. <u>Understanding markets</u> and economies as CEASs helps you cut through the clutter and see investing more clearly with one important rule—saving time, hassle, and worry.

As demonstrated in our review of CEAS, *stock markets are discounters of widely known and discussed information.* If you can learn and believe markets digest information better than any individual— really sear that into your soul—the rest becomes much easier.

BY MANY NAMES, STILL THE GOLDEN RULE

The Golden Rule has been around for a long time—*Do unto others as you'd have them do unto you.* Most of us probably learned that in kindergarten or on *Sesame Street.* It's so basic and obvious, we forget or eschew it often. Some folks think the Golden Rule originated from the Bible—it didn't. The Golden Rule is way older and more universal than that. As religious studies scholar Karen Armstrong demonstrates in her book, *The Great Transformation,* the Golden Rule is basically universal among world religions and was likely independently conceived as civilization developed well before the Common Era. Here are a few:

- **Buddhism**: "Hurt not others with that which pains yourself."—From *Udana-Varga*
- **Confucius**: "Tzu-Kung asked, 'Is there a single word which can be a guide to conduct throughout one's life?' The master said, 'It is perhaps the word *shu.* Do not impose on others what you yourself do not desire.'"—From *The Analects*
- **Hinduism**: "This is the sum of duty: do naught to others which if done to thee would cause thee pain."—From *The Mahabharata*
- **Islam**: "No one of you is a believer until he desires for his brother that which he desires for himself."—From *Hadith*

The Golden Rule seems to be universal wisdom about human life, transcending place and time. There have been countless approaches explaining it—commentaries, fairy tales, philosophies, and so on. But in the end, it's all the same basic message: *Do unto others as you'd have them do unto you.*

Well, I'm not going to go against millennia worth of human wisdom. But I have an investing Golden Rule for you: *Markets are discounters of widely known information.* <u>What is known is already</u> <u>reflected in stock prices and therefore doesn't have power to signifi-</u> cantly move markets looking ahead.

I realize this isn't too provocative—market efficiency theory has been around a good long time. In fact, it's really had some staying power as theories go (most theories about markets come and go without much fanfare or potency because they work "in theory," only to be proven useless in the real world). Market effi-

Well, I'm not going to go against millennia worth of human wisdom. But I have an investing Golden Rule for you: *Markets are discounters of widely known information.* What is known is already reflected in stock prices and therefore doesn't have power to significantly move markets looking ahead.

ciency is universal wisdom for investors that everyone has heard but most (sadly) ignore.

A SOFTER, GENTLER KIND OF GOLDEN RULE

A point of clarification: Our golden rule of market efficiency is the "soft" kind. It's important to understand markets are not omniscient, nor are they always right. A current market price is a representation of what the market believes about a company via all well-known and discussed information, not what is necessarily actually right. It's just prone to be more right than any individual because it has the advantage of pricing in the totality of what the whole market believes.

Some people believe in the "hard" version of market efficiency, which means markets are so good at discounting information that it's utterly and unequivocally impossible to beat them. That's also known as the "random walk" version—where you'd be better served throwing darts at a newspaper page of stock quotes to make your portfolio than employing any strategy.

That simply cannot be true. Markets are discounters of all known information, but not everything is known nor is it necessarily understood correctly. Often what is priced into the market is the aggregate belief about an outcome. Those can sometimes go haywire (often do, actually). That's where opportunity lies.

We'll get much further into the guts of why later on, but for now realize markets are only capable of reflecting widely discussed and disseminated information. That's nothing to scoff at—it's remarkably powerful. Markets are incredible information aggregators. Think about how important that is to us individuals—just a few pages ago we observed how myopic and limited a single brain is. But markets are able—better than any individual—to aggregate and communicate all that information we can't hold in our brains in a succinct, simple way via prices. Classic CEAS stuff.

THE LONG AND SHORT (TERM) OF THE GOLDEN RULE

Particularly in the short term, it's reasonable to say markets undershoot and overshoot reality pretty often. Think of it this way: On a really good day, where world markets move, say, 2 percent up, ask yourself: Did something fundamentally change in the world on this exact day that makes the world's stocks fully 2 percent more valuable than they were yesterday? Unlikely.

In the short term, there are shocks, manias, panics, fads, and randomness. In the short term, capitalism can seem vastly destructive or abnormally rewarding. Money, capital, and assets of all kinds can get realigned and dislocated.

But in the medium to long term, it's uncanny how markets ultimately reflect the wider reality and discount it far in advance of most anyone's ability to see it. Figure 5.1 shows this relationship—where stock prices over- and undershoot in the short term, but reflect the value created by companies via earnings in the long term.

THE GOLDEN RULE'S BIG BENEFIT

Knowing markets reflect widely known information makes it pointless to worry about what others worry about. Basing judgments on common worries will make you wrong far more often than right. Put another way: If others worry about something, it becomes priced into

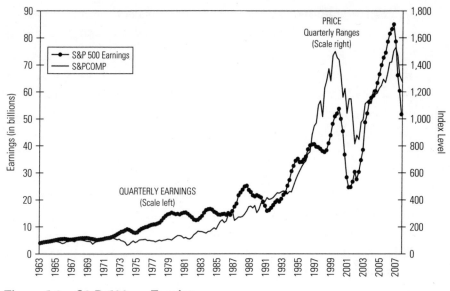

Figure 5.1 S&P 500 vs. Earnings

markets, and you're relieved of that duty. You don't have to do any of the worrying yourself because the crowd is doing it for you.

Instead, you should worry about something else—namely, whatever the crowd isn't fretting. This will often feel counterintuitive and somewhat painful in practice. That's a main reason invest-

> Basing judgments on common worries will make you wrong far more often than right. Put another way: If others worry about something, it becomes priced into markets, and you're relieved of that duty.

ing is so darned difficult—people don't like pain and uncertainty and most of the time feel more comfortable with the support of the consensus rather than being on their own.

Even most long-time professionals fail to beat the market year after year, including those with access to incredible databases of information. Why? Many view investing as a craft. They think, "If I learn the craft of investing and all its rules in and out, then I can be a successful investor using the method of my choice." But that can't work because by definition all the conventional ways of thinking about, say, value versus growth investing will already be widely known and thus priced in.

In fact, most investment strategies are very well known and are already widely practiced. Never forget there are literally millions of investors out there much like you, looking at the same metrics and information you are—even reading this book. Unless you know something they don't, you're out of luck.

There are ways to figure out stuff no one else recognizes and profit from it. Luckily for you, my boss already wrote it. If you want to know the methods to consistently beat the stock market over time based on the notion of market efficiency, read Ken Fisher's *New York Times* bestseller, *The Only Three Questions That Count.*

You might think, based on CEAS, we don't need to pay attention to the news or even bother to understand how companies operate or what's going on in the world. Wrong! The Golden Rule isn't a license not to read the news or study earnings reports. After all, how can you know what's priced in if you're not paying attention to what's going on in the markets and economy?

In my view, CEAS is the most potent way to understand how markets and economies work from an investor's perspective. But a point of view is all it is. It is just a theory—a way to help us comprehend how capitalism works. Just because capitalism fits into the definition of CEAS doesn't mean it has to follow all its rules. Remember, at the beginning of this chapter, I said seeking tried and true perspectives is key—often seeing contrasts is just as important as similarities. One day, undoubtedly, there will be a new and even better way to think about how markets work.

A FEW TIPS FOR USING THE GOLDEN RULE

As we've seen, under the Golden Rule of market efficiency, we don't have to worry about what everyone else is worrying about. This begins to solve the problem of trying to navigate and understand an entire economic landscape—we can let the broader market do that for us.

Instead, you're free to focus on deciding what's important and analyzing that fully. In a world where information is so abundant we nearly choke on it, the right strategy is to seek the best, highest quality, and most pertinent information. It's been proven time and again more information isn't better—in fact, it tends to cause worse decisions over time![6] Don't seek more for its own sake—seek *better* information. Here are a few rules of thumb that result from Golden Rule thinking:

- **Ignore lagging indicators**. An easy one. This heuristic knocks out at least 95 percent of the data out there. Ignore any report that gives you backward-looking information. If we know markets are pricing in all well-known information and doing it swifter and better than most any individual, then past economic data are of very little use, if any. This is doubly true because we know stocks are always pricing in the *future*. Markets always and everywhere look forward. Yet, just about all economic "indicators" describe the past! They don't actually "indicate" anything in terms of market forecasting! As an investor you have very little use for the past. The future is what matters to you. (Although, history sometimes can actually be a great tool for forecasting, as we'll see in Chapter 7.)
- **Pay little or no attention to daily/weekly/monthly reports**. Too many data points only cause huge confusion. Most indicators flop around quite a bit and give a lot of false positives about direction. Again, the more temporal the data point, the more stochasticity, or random noise, you will observe that will only confuse you. Instead, look at the longer, smoother trends and don't let the short-term stuff trip you up. Market pricing can be erratic in the short term as the consensus digests information.

Against the Guilds

Most folks (educated ones, mind you) are never taught how to think. Isn't that strange? Only a few very narrow disciplines ever teach an actual method of thinking. It's one of the great tragedies of education, and it trickles into investing. Most investors are so intent on getting their hands on some handy heuristics (or rules of thumb) that seldom if ever do they take the time to focus on the thought behind them. That is, if the method makes sense.

When I started as an analyst, I noticed most of my peers set themselves to learning all the technical skills of the craft—things like how to create complex spreadsheets, modeling financial statements, and so on. I thought, how could I possibly be any better at investing than these guys by learning exactly the same things they did and in the same way? Seemed absurd! So I took a different route—I decided to focus my effort on learning not just the "hows," but also the "whys" behind what's going on.

A different way to say that is, I chose to focus on thinking. Many experts call *critical thinking* a type of thought. I regard critical thinking not as a type of thought, but rather a skill set for thinking. Critical thinking isn't just for investors—it's a skill for life. It is a process, not a rule of thumb to follow. It's about learning to discern and evaluate, sort of an attempt to pair science and logic with reality. A good critical thinker uses findings from as many perspectives as possible. Some attributes are:

- Clarity
- Rigor
- Credibility
- Accuracy/Precision
- Relevance/Significance
- Breadth and Depth
- Logic

Those are good generic categories. Critical thinking for investing will require approaching a problem from economic, market, historical, statistical, qualitative, theoretical points of view—or some other method entirely. All are valid in some measure—they're ways to help you understand an issue.

Craftsmanship is a tradition that goes back to the Renaissance—when guilds trained artists of all kinds in a certain method so apprentices could learn from a master and maybe one day become masters themselves. Same for martial arts, architecture, the sciences, and many other vocations. It's perhaps the oldest and most tried method of human learning—except it doesn't work for investing. I learned from Ken Fisher that investing can't be learned as a craft. Simple logic defies it! Any widely practiced method can't work for long because the more the number of people who know it, the quicker it becomes priced in to the market. And therefore the method loses its potency. A simple derivative of the Golden Rule.

Nevertheless, "schools" of investing like "value" investors or believers in the "random walk" theory continue to exist and probably always will. A common investor pitfall is mixing and matching heuristics from different schools—taking one set of thoughts from the "monetarist" camp, another from the "Keynesian" camp, and maybe another from the "supply side" camp, creating a hodgepodge of theories loosely held together without understanding how or why. The only way that can work is via critical thinking—that is, understanding when a heuristic is appropriate and in what context. Otherwise, mixing theories becomes vastly dangerous because most theories don't jibe with each other—each has its own way of viewing the world and undetected contradictions ensue.

Just don't yoke yourself to a single guild, make sure you know which territory you're in, and use critical thinking to help you.

OLDEST AND STILL THE BEST: SUPPLY AND DEMAND

This brings us to good old supply and demand. You never really hear much about supply and demand anymore. I scour the financial press every market day and, in a year, maybe find one or two analyses explaining market moves in terms of supply and demand.

Yet the price of any good or service can be traced back to this rock-solid principle. Supply and demand is particularly potent for analyzing stocks, yet most never think to use it. That makes it even more powerful if you do your analysis right because that viewpoint may not be priced in fully.

Supply and demand is particularly potent for analyzing stocks, yet most never think to use it. That makes it even more powerful if you do your analysis right because that viewpoint may not be priced in fully.

I've always believed there is a "genius mentality" on Wall Street. Most analysts want to sound super smart on TV or in the paper, so instead of retreading old and basic economic theories like supply and demand, they spout all sorts of sophisticated and sexy new theories on how stocks are priced. After all, who wants to hear about boring old supply and demand? Everyone knows that! You can't look like a genius if you talk about something everyone knows!

But supply and demand remains perhaps the most potent way to view the macro workings of any market. Now, I realize supply and demand is old hat for experts in the finance biz, but it's well worth the refresher.

BALANCING ACT

Studying supply and demand is about understanding the relationship between them (AKA *equilibrium*). Let's separate those three concepts and consider them individually:

Demand: Represents how much of a good buyers are willing to purchase at various prices. The demand curve, shown in Figure 5.2, is almost always represented as downward sloping—that is, as price decreases consumers will buy more of the good.

Supply: Represents how much of a good suppliers are willing to sell based on the price and amount of goods produced. As Figure 5.3 shows, the supply curve is typically upward sloping—as the price increases, sellers will supply more.

Equilibrium: Equilibrium is where the supply and demand curves meet: the quantity and price where suppliers and demanders agree

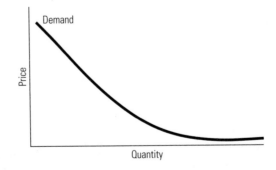

Figure 5.2   Standard Demand Curve

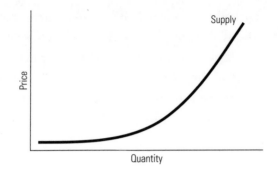

Figure 5.3 Standard Supply Curve

in a competitive environment—the market price. Equilibrium is simply a different, though simplistic, set of metaphors for understanding how information gets priced in. Figure 5.4 shows a basic equilibrium between supply and demand.

Remember, we said free flow of aggregated information is a key component for a CEAS. In a market environment, prices are the conduit for all that information. The equilibrium point resulting from supply and demand is one way of viewing how market prices are established.

It's worth noting the relationship between supply and demand works best in highly liquid markets like stock markets. Things become distorted when there is little liquidity, which can cause problems in understanding what the true price of something is. This can be easily seen in the sparse trading of collateralized debt obligations (CDOs)

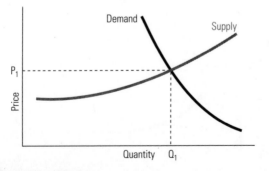

Figure 5.4 Basic Equilibrium

and mortgage-backed securities (MBSs). Sometimes thought of as the culprits behind the financial crisis of 2008, CDOs and MBSs had problems largely because no one knew what they were worth. Why didn't we know what they were really worth? Because they traded seldomly—a different way of saying there wasn't much known and priced-in information about them.

A Different Kind of Equilibrium

We just saw the basic, traditional kind of supply and demand equilibrium. For stocks, however, it looks a bit different.

The demand curve for stocks is a backward-bending hyperbole. At one extreme, when the price of securities is low enough, demand becomes infinite for securities. At the other extreme is the backward-bending part of the curve, representing irrational demand. Leading up to the backward bend is the part of the demand curve most would consider rational: As prices increase, demand falls. However, for "glamour" stocks (where there is a "mania" or homogeneity of opinion about a stock or stocks), as prices rise, demand also rises.

For example, prior to the Tech bubble of the late 1990s, most investors believed Tech stocks were stocks they *had* to own—regardless of the price paid for them. It's within this realm the market becomes "irrational" as higher prices actually lead to higher quantity demanded (where a negative feedback loop switches to a positive feedback loop). This is an interesting behavioral quirk that marks the end of many bull markets, as shown in Figure 5.5.

Figure 5.5 Hyperbolic Demand Curve

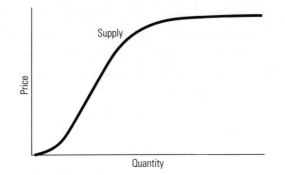

Figure 5.6 S-Shaped Supply Curve

The supply curve for stocks is an S-shaped curve representing an increase in aggregate supply as prices increase. At a certain price level, supply becomes virtually infinite, as investment bankers have every incentive to create as much new supply of securities as possible (again, a switch from negative feedback to positive feedback). This is represented by a flattening of the supply curve, running out to infinity in Figure 5.6.

These can represent supply and demand for a stock, a sector, or the market as a whole. In the short term, demand (sometimes thought of as a proxy for sentiment) has the most influence on pricing, while over the longer term, pricing is almost completely a function of supply.

DEMAND IS ONLY A TWO-WAY STREET

As we saw last chapter, measuring demand is tricky business because it's highly, if not totally in some cases, qualitative. Time after time, attempts have been made to gauge investor sentiment and tie it back to stock market movements. These have always proved coincident at best and never predictive.[7]

I think the problem lies in the desire for precision—folks want a numerical and precise number for demand, but I think it's unnecessary. Demand is basically a qualitative thing, so let it be. Instead, make things easy on yourself and create a binary decision set—a yes/no proposition. Think of it like a spectrum: At one pole you have complete pessimism (lack of demand for stocks). At the other is complete optimism (ubiquitous demand for stocks). All you need to know is whether sentiment has swung to one pole or another—homogeneously (or, near completely) optimistic or pessimistic.

Everything else in between is normal and offers little information for you as an investor. Why? Because the "in between" is the territory of *heterogeneity*—which is where markets are versatile, adaptive, and largely able to discount well-known information.

If the market is homogeneously optimistic—like in 1999 with tech stocks—you know sentiment (demand) is out of whack. Conversely, in times of homogeneous pessimism—when investors are declaring the "death of equities" like in early 2003—you know sentiment is way out of whack on that pole as well.

Don't Ignore Supply

The demand side usually gets a lot of attention when it comes to stocks. People use all kinds of sentiment indicators, market breadth indicators, and countless others to try and gauge demand. Less thought of is supply—yet it's just as vital. The supply of stock on the market matters very much for long-term market outcomes.

In the short term (less than a year), demand tends to rule. Why? Investor demand can fluctuate quickly and wildly in the short term. Supply of stocks is not so nimble; it remains relatively fixed in the short term. It takes time to offer new shares to the public—due diligence and regulatory approval processes that require months and years, not days. But over the longer term (where supply is free to expand or contract infinitely), supply is the dominant factor in setting stock prices.

When you have more of something (higher supply), prices go down (holding demand constant). So if there's a lot of new stock supply coming online, that's a major red flag that prices are likely to suffer in the period ahead. Stock supply can grow in various ways, including:

- IPOs
- Stock-based mergers
- New share offerings
- A corporation granting employee options or warrants

The best and most recent example is the now-infamous tech craze of the late 1990s. There were IPOs aplenty, gigantic stock-based mergers (e.g., AOL/Time Warner), and option grants were the new form of compensation for tech employees. That kind of rapid expansion of stock supply swamped demand and ultimately contributed to the bear market of 2001–2002.

Supply and demand are a great way to understand the interplay between buyers and sellers at the aggregate level and how prices and quantity can play a role. If you can gauge these two factors—supply and demand—accurately, you've got an excellent shot at investing success in the longer term.

A Bit of Criticism . . . Just like CEASs, supply and demand is no panacea for stock predicting. It's just another way of understanding how prices are set in a CEAS market environment. It's largely abstract and theoretical. Look through any economics textbook and you'll see how convoluted and warped supply and demand analyses can become in trying to account for all situations—a classic case of trying to make reality fit the model and not the other way around. When your models begin doing that, it's time to throw them out.

CHAPTER INSIGHTS

Now we've got a great system for understanding how markets and economies work—updated, but still reflective of the classical views on the "invisible hand" theory developed in the eighteenth century by Adam Smith. In the next three chapters, we'll apply these principles to forecasting market activity and some rules of thumb for managing a portfolio of stocks.

- Capitalistic, free-market economies form complex, emergent, adaptive systems (CEASs for short).

- CEASs:
    - Emerge from the sum of individual behavior, but form a system *distinct* from the individuals who act within it.
    - Are not controlled by a central command structure.
    - Can be efficient even though their participants might not be.
    - Adapt on their own via negative and positive feedback loops.
    - Are non-linear and not necessarily predictable based on logical cause and effect.
    - May display some consistent patterns over time.

- CEAS-based markets reflect all well-known and discussed information via pricing mechanisms. This is the new "Golden Rule" for investing.
    - Market efficiency means an effective, but imperfect, aggregation of well-known information, not an omniscient system.
    - The substantial benefit of market efficiency is that most worries and big issues are already priced in to the marketplace, so investors don't need to spend a great deal of time on those issues.

- Supply and demand is another tried and true way to understand how markets price information.
    - In the short term, demand rules, but in the longer term, supply dictates prices.

- Neither CEAS nor supply and demand is perfect, but they're metaphors for describing how the stock market works.

6

FORECASTING, PART 1—THE PRINCIPLE OF PROBABILITY

Prediction is very difficult, especially if it's about the future.
—Niels Bohr

Weather forecast for tonight: Dark.
—George Carlin

Stock market forecasting is a difficult subject. To understand how it works we're going to have to dig into some esoteric ideas and sometimes vexing logic.

Forecasting is not a footnote to market analysis—forecasting is a kind of analysis that has its own set of methods independent of economics and markets. So the first thing we must do is explore ideas about how forecasting works generally before considering stock market forecasting specifically.

This is the first of two chapters about forecasting. This one is about probability; the other is about pattern recognition. Both are

147

discussed in context of CEAS—Chapter 5's topic. These two ideas—probability and patterns—can sometimes contradict one another, and there are many experts who sit squarely in one camp and disparage the other. Ultimately though, pattern recognition and probabilistic thinking can be used together to help us forecast stock market outcomes. Understanding them both, then putting them together, is the project of these next two chapters.

FORECASTING IS STRANGE ALCHEMY

In the dark ages, alchemists had formulas and strict rules for making potions and alloys. Proportions and measurements were quite precise. But at the same time, alchemic rituals were also about the unquantifiable, the spiritual—it was about getting an alchemist's mind in a certain place to make the alchemical processes work. Their minds had to be right for the method to be potent.

Alchemy holds a strange but important place in pre-Enlightenment history because it's quasi-science, quasi-spiritualism. Market forecasting is similar strange alchemy. You have to get your mind right and see things the right way before you can apply any formula or method. Most of this book so far has been about getting started toward that end—understanding the limitations of our methods, the limitations of our minds, and viewing markets and economies as complex, emergent, and adaptive systems (CEAS) that can function independently and beyond our reckoning. Unfortunately, forecasting CEAS isn't like eighth-grade chemistry, where just following the textbook rules ensures the right chemical reaction. There won't be any analysis in this book about using valuations to determine when stocks are cheap. Why? Well, mostly because they simply don't work.

Forecasting stock markets is like alchemy because there's no definitive formula and never will be. That freaks out most folks pretty good because we

Forecasting stock markets is like alchemy because there's no definitive formula and never will be. That freaks out most folks pretty good because we tend to crave certainty—we want a rule book with instructions leading directly to a known outcome. Markets won't let you have it that way.

tend to crave certainty—we want a rule book with instructions leading directly to a known outcome. Markets won't let you have it that way. There are, however, detectable patterns that tend to recur in the system, and studying those can help us forecast.

Any book about investing correctly is ultimately a book about forecasting. It's a dicey subject because so few have ever done it consistently well in market history, and no one has ever always been right.

Particularly in times of high market volatility, I inevitably read headlines proclaiming "forecasting has never been more important than today," or that "it's never been more difficult to forecast market moves than now." Well, I'm here to tell you forecasting is always important and always really difficult. Uncertainty about the future is for all time. You cannot find an era when we ever had certainty about what's to come. If there was, we'd all be trillionaires, we'd never get caught in the rain, and divorce wouldn't exist.

We seem to have a tough time accepting this. Humans are constantly looking for certainty. Right forecasting techniques are methods for dealing with the unknown, not methods of making the unknown known—there's a big difference. There's so much hubris and overconfidence in forecasting. Folks can scarcely say where their lives will be in a few years, let alone where the world will be in a few years. The first (and maybe most important) lesson about market forecasting is: *It's not about knowing where the world will go, it's about going along for the ride in the right way.*

In Chapter 5, we discussed the oddity of thinking stock markets and economies are discrete from the rest of life's systems. Forecasting is the same way. Stock market prediction shouldn't be so different from forecasting in any CEAS. That is, forecasting is a genre of study in itself. Be it weather, genetics, economics, markets—whatever— there are tactics to forecasting that are similar across almost anything being forecasted. So instead of thinking "What are the correct methods for stock market forecasting?" think "What are the methods of forecasting that are best applied to stock markets?"

Through most of history, forecasting has been known as "prophecy"— oracles, astrology, palm reading, tea leaves, crystal balls, tarot cards, and crazy (sometimes blind) men ranting on a corner in the town square. If they were good, we called them prophets. If they were bad, society found them a nice padded cell or worse.

Admiral Robert FitzRoy is usually credited with coining the term "forecast." He didn't much like the idea of "prophecy" because it sounded to him too much like a sorcerer's spell or oracle's decree. He wanted a word exuding the lofty exactitude of science and math! So, in 1863, he published a book about weather prediction and called his subject a "forecast." From then on, the weather was "forecasted" and not predicted. Forecasting had become a science.

I've studied just about every predictive model and theory I could get my hands on—from how weather is predicted, to genetic outcomes, to economics, to how stock markets move, to how the universe was formed (prediction of the past!).

The crux of forecasting in a CEAS is the same whether you're looking at the weather or stock markets: It's establishing a degree of belief about the future and knowing you will be wrong some substantial portion of the time. That is, it's about pattern recognition and probability. The game is simply to be right more often than wrong and build in features so that when you're wrong, you're wrong in the right ways.

TYPES OF PREDICTIONS

But before we can talk about stock market forecasting, we need a primer in forecasting basics. Too seldom do we stop to analyze the basics—we take a simple thing like a "prediction" for granted. We just think of a prediction as some kind of statement of belief about an unknown outcome. But if we take a closer look, it becomes apparent that just the type of prediction we choose to make will have a big effect on what our prediction will be.

There are types of predictions, and the appropriate kind depends on what's being predicted. Let's go through a few of them—not just to see which apply to the stock market, but also so we can become cognizant of their benefits and limitations.

Independence: Many outcomes are *independent* of the predictions made. This would be like betting at the roulette table in Vegas. No matter what number or color you bet on, it (theoretically) shouldn't affect the result. A prediction on something with an independent outcome will not affect the situation.

Dependence: This is the opposite of independence: Predictions have an effect on the outcome. Outcome-dependent predictions are much closer to how stock markets work. What people think about what will happen is ultimately what makes the stock market move—investors bet on where they think the market will go. So the results of the predictions are based upon how people bet on them.

Event Order: Sometimes the order of events matters to the outcome. This is called *path dependence*. For instance, it matters little if a baseball team scores all their runs in the first inning, ninth inning, or across many innings. The sum total is all that matters. But in many cases in life, that's not true. For instance, the rule-of-thumb definition of a recession is two consecutive quarters of negative economic growth. So if in one year, the first and fourth quarters see negative growth, but not the second and third in between, then we didn't technically have a recession even though there were two quarters of negative growth. This is precisely what happened in 2001, though most still call it a recession anyway. Strange but true! So to predict a recession, at least in the traditional sense, one would need to be able to predict the order of the events, not just whether they will happen.

Initial versus Changing Conditions: Will changing conditions make a difference in the final outcome? For most mechanical systems governed by the laws of physics (like throwing a ball), knowing the initial conditions is sufficient to predict the final outcome. But conditions change quickly in CEAS—factors interact with each other and their environment. In a complex system the initial conditions quickly become irrelevant to the outcome. For instance, one reason it's so difficult to predict genetic traits is because we need to know much more than just a person's DNA. Scientists are coming to realize DNA's interaction with the environment is what determines the "phenotype" or genetic outcome. The initial conditions (DNA) probably can't itself lead us to the final traits that manifest. Same with markets. Every company interacts with its environment, and that influences its behavior and alters the outcome continuously.

Holistic: Can the situation be taken apart and viewed in pieces? Or will all the factors involved play a role? With a car motor, we can take it apart and deal with each piece discretely—not worrying about the other parts, knowing they will fit back together as expected later on. But in an economy, most often all the factors involved will affect each other—they can't be easily separated. So market and economic prediction is a holistic business—the different parts influence each other and aren't discrete.

This is just a taste of prediction types. The point is to see that the type of prediction we make can influence what we believe will happen. And we haven't even looked at a single piece of economic data yet!

Pretty clearly though, stock markets require a holistic view of the world, with changing conditions, where the order of events matters, as does the fact that stock market outcomes are dependent on how we bet on them. These simple observations mean we cannot forecast stocks as the vast majority of folks try to—as independent, discrete events that ought to follow from principal causes. Stock markets do not work that way and never will. So any method of prediction that doesn't account for CEAS isn't a good type of prediction.

FUN WITH LOGIC

Logic got its formal start with the Greeks, and we've been using it ever since. But it tends to scare people today. It feels mechanical, inhuman, cold. Thus, sadly, it's rarely studied outside esoteric rhetoric courses and philosophical systems. Perversely, these days, folks seem to associate logic with flighty intellectualism—as if it were something for only the aristocratic academics to think of. That's a tragedy because logic is a skill set that can shield investors from the vast majority of investing myths. Investing is about practicality, and there are few things more pragmatic than logic because it helps delineate useful information, particularly when dealing with abstract concepts.

On the whole, logic can be very useful for investors, but like anything, there are pitfalls and limitations. The important thing is to be aware of what kind of logic you're using so that you're aware of the potential problems or whether your reasoning is appropriate for the situation.

Here are some basics:

Syllogism: Where the conclusion is inferred from two or more premises. For example:
Premise 1: All beers have alcohol in them.
Premise 2: Whiskey has alcohol.
Conclusion: Whiskey is a beer.

Wait, that can't be right! What's the problem? The categories. The premise "all beers have alcohol in them" is true, but not narrow enough to follow to the correct conclusion given the second premise. Without sound premises, the conclusion is always dubious no matter how sound your reasoning. This is a common mistake in investing, where we tend to assume premises like "a weak dollar is bad for US stocks" are true without knowing if they're really so. Syllogistic logic is an important foundation of human thought, but make sure your premises are rock solid, otherwise the logic isn't worth much.

Deduction: To conclude something by going from general premises to specific conclusions.

A deduction is a kind of syllogism where the premises are "principles," or understood to be immutable facts. This logic style is used often by market forecasters. Let's say we're in a bear market today and are trying to determine what stocks will do. You hear an analyst on TV say a bull market will come soon because bull markets follow bear markets. That's an example of deductive logic. It is taking a general principle (that all bears are followed by bulls) and applying it to today's specific circumstances. This is valid thinking insofar as it goes, but can lead to wrong

(Continued)

(Continued)

conclusions. Why? For one, remember not all market outcomes are linear. That is, there often isn't a perfect cause-and-effect relationship. Second, markets don't necessarily always adhere to generic principles—specifics matter and anomalies happen.

Usually, only the simplest problems can be solved via deduction. In problems involving many factors and dependent variables (like markets and economies), there is too much noise to arrive at specific conclusions—based on generic principles—with any great precision. But don't throw out deduction altogether! It can be useful in thinking through probable outcomes.

Induction: To gain a conclusion by going from specific facts to general principles.

Induction is something like the reverse of deduction: going from specific observations to generic principles. Let's go back to our previous example about bears and bulls. Instead of simply saying "bulls follow bears" is a principle, maybe we can go back in history and see if it's true. By looking at all the instances, we can induce an answer. And lo and behold—it is true, throughout history every bear is followed by a bull. The inductive method is essentially the scientific method—using observation to corroborate hypotheses and create principles.

Induction is mostly about spotting patterns in data. The most common pitfall with induction is humans see patterns everywhere—often where there are none at all. Using only inductive thinking can lead you astray because we sometimes talk ourselves into believing there is a pattern where really none existed.

(To learn more about logic, see the Selected Bibliography and Further Reading section at the end of this book.)

PROBABILITY THEORY, OR HOW MARKETS ARE NOTHING LIKE COIN TOSSES

In Chapter 5 we learned a CEAS is usually different from the people working within it—the sum of the parts doesn't make the whole. But that raises a big and interesting question: Are markets (that is, CEASs) random or do they exhibit regular patterns we can successfully predict? This may be the most difficult—and important—question in all stock market analysis. Much rests upon it, and it's hotly debated to this day.

If markets are totally random, then the best we can do is use probability theory to make tentative guesses about what may happen. But if they have detectable patterns, can we actually do something with them?

To solve this riddle, we must first investigate probability theory.

Probability is the mathematical way of coping with randomness. It's a functional way of measuring *stochasticity*, which is Greek for "noise." Probability theory plays a big role in helping understand systems where there are random variables and noisy data in non-deterministic (where the outcome isn't certain) environments. Probability can be used for situations involving large sets of data and for a mathematical description of complex systems when we have less than full knowledge of what's going on—which is always the case in stock markets.

That sounds an awful lot like our definition of a CEAS, doesn't it? We already know from Chapter 1 that linear mathematical functions often don't work in CEASs. Is this evidence of randomness in markets? Many think so. Believers in complete randomness are legion—they're called the "random walkers," made popular by Burton Malkiel's classic study, *A Random Walk Down Wall Street.*

But I don't think the debate ends here. We need to consider much more before jumping to conclusions. There are very good reasons to believe stock markets exhibit regular patterns and are not totally random, which we will cover in the next chapter.

THE SPECIFIC AND THE GENERAL

A good market theorist who uses probability should be more interested in "the history that never was" than the history that actually happened. Why? Most folks tend to think *deterministically*—that is, that things are preordained. We want to think the thing that happened is the thing that was "meant to be," that "had to happen."

Wrong. Instead, think of history as a spectrum of possibilities where one result happened and the others simply did not—they could have, just didn't. Thus, to think probabilistically, the first thing to do is know the possibilities—they are often just as important as what actually happened.

One of the most fascinating scientific problems of the modern era is the rift between quantum mechanics and Einstein's theory of relativity. Quantum mechanics insists we can only understand matter through probabilities. At the quantum level, there's no way to know what is happening or what is going to happen. We can only know where tiny particles "jump to" at any given moment based on probability. The more specific we try to get, the further away a concrete answer becomes. In quantum physics, this is known as the *Heisenberg uncertainty principle*, where certain pairs of values for an observed particle cannot be known precisely at the same time. For instance, the more exactly we know a particle's velocity, the more uncertain its position in space becomes, and vice versa.

That's a gross generalization, but it's the general idea. The really interesting part of it is that the two ways of seeing the world work on completely different levels—the traditional theory of relativity doesn't connect with quantum physics. Folks have tried for decades to make both systems work together, but so far they haven't. (Some believe Einstein's relativity has in fact been falsified, but the debate goes on.)

Yet both systems describe pretty well how the world works. Different, yet both right! That alone tells you something about the nature of theory—how it helps *describe* the world and isn't in itself the "law."

Part of what quantum mechanics does—and why it is so useful—is it makes room for anomalous or incalculable behavior without destroying the theory or the patterns of particle behavior. In other words, quantum mechanics is a CEAS that can generally predict how some particle *is likely* to move, but in some specific cases, it may not.

Probability theory has two important concepts:

- **The law of large numbers.** This says the long-term mean (or average) of a random variable should even out to an expected value. A different way to say this: The odds of an outcome in a coin flip are 50/50, but if you only flip the coin three times, it can only come out 2/3 at best (either heads or tails will end up with at least two results). So 50/50 is impossible. If we flip the coin many times (as in thousands), eventually the outcome will approach 50/50. The law of large numbers means the expected value will be achieved after many coin tosses, not a few.

- **Central limit**. Similar to the law of large numbers, a sufficient size data set will eventually distribute itself in a "normal" way. This is often referred to as the "bell curve." (More on this and its problems later.)

Don't worry about understanding either of those concepts exactly for now. The key takeaway is that in probability theory, we must have many observations—the only way to get to a statistically probable outcome is by compiling many results.

This has huge implications for forecasting because it says *there will always be a difference between the general and the specific.* As it pertains to real-life outcomes with markets, probabilistic theories can only describe general behavior rather than predict a specific outcome. That's a major shortcoming because we are always forecasting in a "specific" time! A classic example of this problem is the notion of "average" market behavior. On average, markets return something like 10 to 12 percent nominal annually. But you'd be foolish to actually predict 10 percent in any specific year. Most of the time returns are way off that—down big or up big. That is, the average doesn't describe specific instances but only results of the longer run.

Point predictions, or exact predictions in stock markets, are not possible in CEAS. There is too much noise and random outcome in the short term. Also, we know sometimes the least probable event does in fact happen. With probabilities, we can emphasize process over outcome because *good decisions can lead to bad outcomes, but with a consistent process that uses probability in its favor, the expected and desired results ensue over the long run.* Another way to say this: Good strategies are sometimes wrong and that's ok because, over the long term, the probabilities bear out.

By knowing the only absolute is that there is no absolute, we know decisions are a matter of assigning and weighing probabilities—especially since forecasting is always and everywhere made upon limited and incomplete information.

Always Test

Whenever thinking through a problem, I try to take my logic one step further by testing it. If your logic is sound and your thinking is right, your conclusions should hold up to this additional step—or as many steps as necessary.

Here's an example: Many believe trade deficits are bad for an economy and thus the stock market. Intuitively, it certainly seems frightful that a country (like the US) would consistently import more than it exports.

But take it one step further.

If trade deficits were really so bad, two things ought to happen: (a) the stock market of that country should suffer while deficits were high or going higher, and (b) so should its economy, right?

Now take it one step further and test it.

The US has run a trade deficit consistently for decades and has seen consistent stock market growth and economic growth. So the logic doesn't work.

You can validate or disprove all kinds of things with this simple little rule.

EXPECTED VALUE

Before we can get to the business of assigning probabilities, we first need to explore how probability works. *Expected value* is the mathematical idea underpinning just about everything in finance. Expected value is the average value some experiment will produce if it is repeated a large number of times.

To see it and understand it, let's flip some coins. I'm going to flip a coin, and if it comes up heads I'll give you $100. If it comes up tails, you get nothing. How much do you think the right to play this game is worth? Or, said another way, what is the *expected value* of a one-in-two chance of winning $100?

In *general,* the expected value of a coin flip ought to be the total values of all possible outcomes multiplied by their respective probabilities. So our coin flip game has an expected value of $50, which is the probability of success (50 percent) multiplied by the payout on a successful outcome ($100).

Easy valuation based on probability! But this calculation gives us a false sense of what the outcome really could be. Why? According to the law of large numbers, if the coin toss is repeated many times, eventually we will get to 50/50—the expected outcome of the coin toss. The only way to ensure that outcome is if we flipped the coin many, many times (remember the law of large numbers). Flipping just a few times, anything can happen—maybe there's a run of heads or tails and it doesn't come back to the average for another hundred flips, or maybe a thousand! Maybe by then, you've gone broke.

Also, each flip is *independent* from the one before. This is a classic misconception about probability: If heads comes up this time, many folks will believe the probability is actually higher that tails will come up the next time. It isn't. Folks do this with stocks all the time. They'll believe if stocks are down big now, then that only means they'll be up big soon! Maybe, but there's no "law" to corroborate such a notion. Such a thing can only be probable, not pre-determined.

Coin Flips or Sports Books? Pretty clearly, stock markets aren't like coin flips. Sports books are an imperfect but better metaphor. In a sports book, the "odds" are the market's way of establishing a probability about the outcome. It's a statement about expected value—the payout relative to the probability of the event happening. The price, however, is arrived at via the beliefs of the bettors, not through a probabilistic model like the Monte Carlo (more on that soon). The odds are determined by those betting on the outcome of the defined event, wrapped up into a single data point—not so different from the pricing mechanism for stocks. In a way, stocks are a kind of "odds" about what the market believes the company is worth in the future.

But the so-called odds can be wrong. That's because odds are based on highly limited information and expectation of performance. Odds give us a good idea about what will happen and usually end up pretty close. Most of the time, the favored team wins. But odds also make room for variability and failure. This is not all that far from how markets work. Expected value in a CEAS can't be exact because it's based on unknown, dependent variables—totally different than a coin flip. Odds are a closer kin.

With sports books, the betting itself affects the payout structure. This is also true for stock markets, where the equilibrium price for a stock is based on perception of the outcome and limited information. Sometimes it's right, sometimes it's wrong; sometimes prices overshoot, while others undershoot. However, sports betting always has an outcome—at some point we get to see if our bets were right or wrong. With stocks, alas, there is little such luxury. Over the long term, though (getting from the specific to the general), aggregate stock market returns end up being close to the underlying earnings growth they track. In a way, that's pretty close to an outcome.

Let's Go Gambling, Monte Carlo Style

One way to find patterns in random data is via a set of algorithms called the "Monte Carlo." The name alone says a great deal about the method—its hardcore adherents believe stock price movements are little more than random events.

Monte Carlo takes data and produces many outcomes, not just a few discrete possibilities. It is the ultimate of all "what if" scenario generators.

There are many kinds of Monte Carlo—experts tweak the mathematics to make the models do all sorts of things for different kinds of systems. Monte Carlo simulations work in quantum physics, studies on entropy, emergent systems, genetic development, evolution, and stock markets, to name a few. Financial planners will often employ Monte Carlo analyses to past market performance to generate probabilistic outcomes for investors over their time horizons. This helps create a framework for understanding what expected values might be, and therefore some context on how to plan retirement or how much a portfolio might grow over time.

Monte Carlo is the mathematical opposite of the traditional way to calculate future or present values. Here are the equations for future and present values, where PV equals present value, FV equals the future value, r equals the expected rate of return, and t is the time period (usually in years).

$$FV = PV(1 + r)^t$$
$$PV = FV/(1 + r)^t$$

Notice that future value equations—the foundation of the capital asset pricing model (CAPM), net present value calculations (NPV), and much of modern portfolio theory, generally—are linear, reductive, and based almost solely upon principle causes. Therefore, they are near worthless as predictive measures in a CEAS system like the stock market. We can't use them in a practical way to predict where stocks will go.

In some sense, Monte Carlo is the epitome of probability theory, whereas future value theory is the epitome of linear math. Let's see exactly how Monte Carlo is done to get an idea of just how different it is versus traditional linear thinking.

Calculating Monte Carlo. To do a Monte Carlo analysis, you need a few things:

- Define the parameters. (For instance, the stock market from 1926 to 2008.)
- Generate data randomly and use a "deterministic" calculation, usually a set of algorithms. (For instance, get monthly stock market returns in the defined period.)
- Aggregate the results of the individual calculations and see what you get. (For instance, see how often and in what cases stock market returns were "average" or above or below.)

Usually, a Monte Carlo requires thousands of calculations, so I wouldn't advise doing it by hand. There are plenty of places you can get a Monte Carlo model to use in an Excel spreadsheet, or you can simply run them on the web. Here are some good places to learn more:

- Basics for Monte Carlo simulation: www.chem.unl.edu/zeng/joy/mclab/mcintro.html
- How to set up a Monte Carlo analysis in Excel: www.vertex42.com/ExcelArticles/mc/

The main point, though, is that a Monte Carlo is a different (and some believe better) way to arrive at a conclusion about random data than linear, traditional math. As a quick example, let's say we wanted to find the value of π (3.14), which is the constant ratio of any circle's circumference to its diameter. Can random data really tell us how to find such a precise number? Let's see.

We could go through all the mathematical proofs (a process of deduction using principles) and get to π the standard way. But it's been done many times before by mathematicians and we won't do it here.

Or π can be found (or at least approximated) via the Monte Carlo method. Here's how: Draw a square of any size then draw a circle within it, with the edges touching the squares' four sides. Now, close your eyes and make a bunch of random dots in both the square and the circle. So long as you weren't biased in your dot-making (they are uniformly distributed), and also assuming you made enough dots, the proportion of dots within the circle versus dots in the square will be close to $\pi/4$, or the ratio of the circle's area to the square's area, which leads you directly to π. Magic? No! Just probability in action. All we did was define the area (circle in the square) and generate enough random data within those parameters to achieve the answer.

Of course, it gets vastly more complex in stock markets, which have many variables. But the same basic structure can apply in calculating probabilistic outcomes.

AGAINST THE STRAIGHT LINE

Our brains desperately want to see things in a line—cause and effect, point A to B. We were built that way—eons of evolution designed brains to solve simple problems as quickly as possible (generally to avoid being eaten by predators). Our brains were designed to think mostly in terms of binary, two-dimensional problems.

Linear thinking is great for stuff that involves steps. That's how humans build things. We give instructions: 1, 2, 3. Each step follows from the last one and builds upon itself. There is logic and order.

We'd like to apply that same kind of thinking to stock markets, but unfortunately they don't work that way. Stock markets are full of noise and non-linear results where causes and effects are sometimes fuzzy and inputs don't always return the expected result.

The way we choose to analyze stocks reveals a lot about how we think, not necessarily how things really are. For instance, our brains aren't good at handling more than two variables at a time in relationship to each other, so simple stock charts make sense to us—they're a two-dimensional way of seeing the world. Of course, a stock chart doesn't tell you very much—it says little about the many forces that could be affecting the stock price. Similarly, most financial valuation metrics ultimately make comparisons, or ratios, of two variables (think price-to-earnings or price-to-book ratios).

There are exceptions, of course, but the point is we don't naturally think in many dimensions or in ways that include many variables. That is, we don't naturally think in the way stock markets work. Understanding the inherent limitation of our minds (that we want to think linearly) will allow us to keep a healthy level of skepticism—and to question our usual ways of attacking problems.

THE BIGGEST PROBLEM OF THEM ALL

Having learned a bit about probability, it's pretty safe to say CEASs (that is, stock markets) exhibit some randomness—daily, monthly, quarterly, sometimes *annual* returns are full of noise and produce results well outside a reasonable expected value. But surely there are some patterns in the system! After all, stocks tend to go up over time! So which is it: random or patterned? And how can we know?

This brings us to the heart of the issue: *the problem of induction.* This is a philosophical debate that goes way back through time—all the way to the Greeks!—and still isn't settled and likely never will be. The question: *Is inductive reasoning valid?*

A few pages ago, we studied how theories are formed—via the logical formulas for *induction* or *deduction*. Creating a theory based on induction means coming to a conclusion based on a number of observations. That is, *it assumes all past observations will resemble the future.*

The classic example is the problem of the black swan. For decades, scientists observed only white swans in the wild. They saw many thousands of white swans and never a black one. All those observations led them to use inductive logic and declare, "We have seen only white swans; therefore, all swans are white." And for a long time, they seemed right. Except . . . eventually there was an expedition to Australia, and lo and behold—they saw some jet-black swans! Thus, their inductive reasoning was destroyed.

The black swan problem has come to be a euphemism for unpredictable market events. This idea is described by Nassim Nicholas Taleb in his book, *The Black Swan: The Impact of the Highly Improbable*. In it, Mr. Taleb details a number of times unprecedented things happened in markets and economies that inductive logic could not account for.

What does the black swan problem mean? That no logical inductions can ever really be proven. All we can do is corroborate an observation as many times as possible. There never will be true certainty because you never know if the black swan is lurking out there somewhere. We don't necessarily know all the possibilities just based on observations we've made. There may be many possibilities we simply haven't observed yet. That is precisely how the "unprecedented" happens (and happens relatively often in stock markets, I might add.)

 What does the black swan problem mean? That no logical inductions can ever really be proven. All we can do is corroborate an observation as many times as possible.

Why does any of this matter for stocks? Because induction might be the only way to detect patterns in stock markets. But seeing this very vexing problem with induction, we should really have our doubts!

INVESTING LESSONS FROM PROBABILITY

In Chapter 8, we'll discuss some specifics on how to use probability to forecast with a well-constructed portfolio of stocks. Here, however, we'll address a few salient lessons of probability for markets.

MAKE ROOM FOR ANOMALY

If we can learn anything from probability theory and CEAS, it's that the expected outcome isn't always the one we get. Therefore, any good investing strategy is built to be wrong with some frequency.

My boss Ken Fisher likes to call stock markets *The Great Humiliator*, or TGH for short. That's a fine name, but I see it slightly differently. I call markets *Tricksters*.

Most every mythology of the world has a trickster figure. Loki for the Norse, Hermes for the Greeks, Anansi the spider in Africa, and so on. Tricksters don't play by the rules. They're agents of chaos who continually show us the reliable and stable world we believe we live in is full of exceptions and anomalies. Tricksters are made to break rules. They do things outside the guidelines. They teach you lessons by tricking you.

CEASs, and stock markets in particular, are tricksters. Because they price in well-known information, they're constantly tricking the populace, going against the consensus, defying accepted reasoning, breaking the norms. Thus, the vast majority of folks can never really beat a trickster. Tricksters always get the better of you in the long run unless you're uncommonly and eternally vigilant and savvy. The best you can hope to do is win a few battles with the trickster and for the most part let him have his way. That's a potent metaphor for navigating stock markets. We know they will rise over time, but they'll do it chaotically and in ways we often can't predict.

Knowing that allows you to pick your battles with the trickster and never have the hubris of thinking you can dominate him fully. Always make room for anomaly no matter how ironclad you believe your forecast is. The best way to do it is to think about the future via probability.

No Science Is True: The Philosophy of Sir Karl Popper

Twentieth-century philosopher Sir Karl Popper argued a scientific idea can never be proven true, because no matter how many observations seem to agree with it, it could still be wrong. Yet a single contrary experiment can prove a theory forever false. This is the classic problem of induction.

Thus, he argued that science advances over the long run as tests are made and failures are accounted for—it's a process of getting to narrower and narrower possibilities by elimination via experimentation. He described science as "the art of systematic over-simplification" and concluded, "Our knowledge can only be finite, while our ignorance must necessarily be infinite."

Popper's philosophy is good reason to invest using probability instead of principles or rules. We can only know anything about markets via experimentation, which means we can't know anything for sure about the future but rather eliminate some possibilities and generate likelihoods.

For more on Popper, see the Selected Bibliography and Further Reading section at the back of this book.

Normality? No Such Thing

Another important lesson of probability theory is that there is no such thing as "normal" in stock markets. Particularly in the short term, anything can happen.

One of the biggest investing myths is the idea markets follow a "normal distribution." Sometimes called "bell curves," normal distribution is, essentially, the idea that over time and a large number of obser-

 One of the biggest investing myths is the idea markets follow a "normal distribution."

vations, results will fall into a bell-shaped pattern, as shown in Figure 6.1. Most of the time an "average" result happens (the middle of the bell curve), and rarely do events happen at the tails. In sum, it's a fancy way of graphically depicting average and unusual behavior for a system or group of data.

It's believed that most days, months, or years, the markets will return something in the big part of the bell—an average result—and events "at the tails" will be relatively few. A part of the bell curve theory includes the idea of *mean reversion*. That is, if/when an unusual event

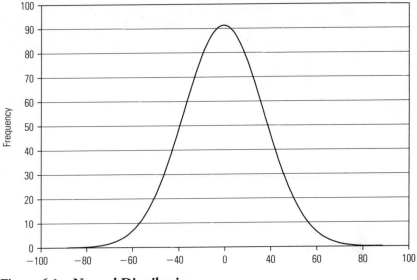

Figure 6.1 Normal Distribution

happens, market results eventually will regress back to the average. For example, if stock markets return 10 percent annually on average, but the last 10 years have only returned an average of 7 percent, those who believe in mean regression would say the period ahead is likely to feature higher than average returns to make up for the slower period and get back to the average. That is, to literally regress back to the mean.

Mean reversion and bell curve theories are important discoveries in statistical analysis and are excellent tools for many things like population analysis. But they are widely misattributed and misunderstood when thinking about stock returns.

Mean reversion essentially says there is something that is "normal" or baseline for stock returns. But insofar as I know, there is no such thing in stock markets. To say markets average a certain return over time is really just saying what they did—it is not necessarily a statement about what the expected return *ought* to be. There is nothing that says they have to keep doing what they have done in the past. There is no mathematical or financial "law" that says stocks must return 10 percent annually. So thinking of the average as the mid-point of a normal distribution that stocks must always revert back to is a false application of the principle.

Folks often get the idea of mean reversion mixed up with ideas like equilibrium in physics and homeostasis in biology. That is, that there is some balance point for stock returns and they should ultimately deliver over time. That *could* be true for markets, but it is impossible to say for sure whether there is a baseline for stock market returns. Ultimately, stock values are tied to growth in earnings and the expectations for growth looking ahead. But even if a reversion to that baseline exists, it doesn't tell you when or how it will happen. Very often a trend lasts a lot longer or shorter than anticipated.

The result of this erroneous mean-reversion thinking is that real short-term risks often go unappreciated. This is easy to see if we just observe what markets actually do—in the short term unprecedented and highly volatile activity rules.

The technical term is *kurtosis,* which means the tails on the bell curve are fatter than a regular "normal" distribution, as seen in Figure 6.2. Higher kurtosis means more variance is due to infrequent but extreme deviations. The fatter tails mean there are many unusual outcomes. For example, there are many businesses that operate under the "80–20" model, which means 80 percent of revenue comes from just 20 percent of customers. This is also true for taxes, where the vast majority of taxes are paid by a very small portion of the population. Both these examples are manifestations of a fat tail distribution underlying the data.

This is another way of saying volatility is typical in stock markets. Magnitude matters, not just the number of observations. Extreme

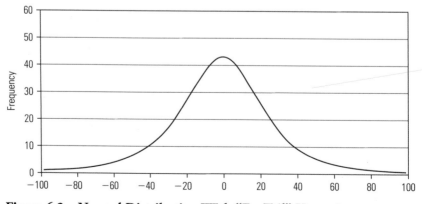

Figure 6.2   Normal Distribution With "Fat Tail" Kurtosis

single-day returns play a huge role in stock market outcomes. Table 6.1 shows that a big percentage of bull market returns happen in a short time and often in a matter of a few days. The same is true

Magnitude matters, not just the number of observations. Extreme single-day returns play a huge role in stock market outcomes.

for bear market losses—the biggest down days tend to be clustered and do the most damage.

Table 6.1   S&P 500 Daily Returns 01/01/82–12/31/07

What If You Missed the Best Days?	
If You Missed the Best:	Your Average Annualized Return Dropped to:
10 of the 6,771 trading days (.15%)	8.11%
20 of the 6,771 trading days (.30%)	6.40%
30 of the 6,771 trading days (.44%)	4.90%
40 of the 6,771 trading days (.60%)	3.53%
50 of the 6,771 trading days (.74%)	2.31%

Source: Thomson Datastream.

This represents a classic problem with using averages to make an analysis: They tell you nothing about a specific situation. All situations are in some form unique, and the "average" never actually happens—it's simply an amalgam of all that has happened.

SEARCH FOR ASYMMETRIC RISKS

Alice Schroeder, in her book *The Snowball: Warren Buffett and the Business of Life*, was once asked if she believed Mr. Buffett was a gambler. She said:

> No, he's a handicapper—big difference. A handicapper is somebody who understands odds-making. A gambler is somebody who bets but may not even understand the odds. Warren believes in a margin of safety, he doesn't bet unless the odds are overwhelmingly in his favor. When he goes to Vegas he does not gamble, he goes to see the shows.[1]

This is another way of saying Mr. Buffett seeks out what he believes are *asymmetric risks* (AS). This is one of the best ways to use probability as a point of view for forecasting. An AS is when the potential for one outcome is significantly different from another outcome. For example, the potential gains associated with purchasing a call option on a stock are significantly different than the potential losses. If you own a call option, if the underlying stock price goes down, the loss is limited to the cost of the option contract. But if the stock rises, your gains are potentially unlimited. That is, there's a floor on potential losses, but no ceiling on potential gains.

Try to find situations where the risks of a certain outcome are substantially less than the potential payoff.

In choosing stocks, such a situation will never be so tidy and clear. However, it is good to think in this way about risks relative to potential returns. Try to find situations where the risks of a certain outcome are substantially less than the potential payoff. If nothing else, this will help you create a more cogent analysis of the situation.

LOOKING AHEAD . . .

In the next chapter, which serves as Part 2 to this treatise on forecasting, we'll look at the flipside: *pattern recognition.* We'll explore the patterns of stock markets and see why it's possible (but still very difficult) to use both probability and pattern recognition to help predict stock market outcomes.

CHAPTER INSIGHTS

In this chapter, we learned that forecasting tactics and theory matter as much as prediction itself. As a CEAS (complex, emergent, adaptive system), prediction of stock markets can be compared to similar methods of prediction of complex systems—namely, probability.

- As a CEAS, stock market prediction requires a holistic view of the world, accounting for changing and dependent conditions, where the order of events matters. In such a system, there cannot be a simple, linear way to predict (like a mathematical equation) based on principal causes.
  - This has led many to believe in a "random walk"—that probability is the only way to predict in CEAS.
  - However, many CEASs do exhibit repeatable, predictable patterns.

- Probability theory is a common way to attempt to predict systems that feature some randomness, like stock markets. From probability theory we find:
  - There is a difference between the specific and the general. An average outcome based on many examples doesn't necessarily provide good information about a specific event.
  - Over many observations, an expected value—or average value—will tend to occur.
- All of this leads to the *problem of induction*.
  - Inductive theory, or pattern recognition, can never be proven, only bolstered by observation.
  - Yet induction may be the only good way to detect patterns in a CEAS.
- The next chapter will show some reliable patterns in stock markets do exist, but we'll also use the principles of probability to help us.

7

FORECASTING, PART 2—RECOGNIZING PATTERNS

The four most expensive words in the English language are, "This time it's different."

—Sir John Templeton

The fact that people will be full of greed, fear or folly is predictable. The sequence is not predictable.

—Warren Buffett

Last chapter, we looked at methods of market forecasting using probability. In this chapter, we're going to study the other side of forecasting—pattern recognition.

In Chapter 5 we observed CEASs sometimes show repeating and recognizable patterns. For instance, it may not be possible to know exactly which traits a strand of DNA will produce in a person, but we do know it's overwhelmingly likely to produce a human with two eyes, two ears, a nose, a mouth, and so on. We can even produce fairly reliable probabilities on eye, skin, and hair color, height, sex, and so on. Those are recognizable and probable patterns.

Or it might be impossible to predict the exact weather on a given day, but the earth's meteorological systems are consistent enough that we can know in a general sense what the weather will be like. Those are demonstrable patterns of the larger system and reasonably predictable. In both examples, there is a great deal of randomness, or noise, but in that noise there are patterns.

Many believe this is how stock markets work. For instance, over the long-term (where there is less noise in the data than daily or monthly observations), stock markets tend to go up over time, tied to the profitability of the underlying companies they track (like we saw in Chapter 5). That's been true for as long as markets have existed. This pattern appears to defy randomness. This chapter will outline some of the most prevalent patterns and drivers of stock prices.

But how can we prove these patterns are real and likely to repeat? We can't! Because of the problem of induction (discussed last chapter), we can never prove a pattern will repeat in the future; we can only say something *tends* to happen. And that is where the principle of probability comes in. Since there is in fact noise and randomness of outcomes in CEASs (particularly in the short-term), the only reasonable way to state a future expectation—even from a known pattern or driver—is via probability. Next chapter, we'll speak a bit about using both pattern recognition and probability to forecast and construct a portfolio.

 Ultimately, the question isn't whether stock markets are completely random or ordered. The real question is: How can we use probability to sort out the randomness from the real patterns and effectively use them to invest?

Ultimately, the question isn't whether stock markets are completely random or ordered. The real question is: How can we use probability to sort out the randomness from the real patterns and effectively use them to invest?

A PATTERN BY ANY OTHER NAME

Some call them economic drivers, others prototypes, archetypes, models, valuations, guides—there are a million names. But in the end it's all the same: patterns. Market forecasting using either the past or cause-and-effect relationships can always be reduced to a quest for patterns.

I've heard more than a few portfolio managers say, "I don't believe in managing money via historical patterns. I believe in understanding earnings and economic drivers. Those will eventually translate into share prices." Joke's on them! That's really just another way of saying, "I believe the pattern of earnings translating into share prices will hold." Pattern recognition has a pejorative connotation—it sounds trite and mundane. Portfolio managers would rather be super-smart economic analysts! But in the end, practically speaking, it's all patterns, in my view.

Using valuations to predict the market's future is another example of pattern recognition. So is using sentiment. Heck, if you think about it, the whole of economics is a quest to find patterns in an economy. In fact, most fields of study are quests to find patterns that are identifiable and repeatable (math, for instance).

Instead of calling ourselves economic forecasters, we're going to call ourselves pattern recognizers. Why? Because that makes our task easier to understand, more identifiable, and simpler to solve.

How do we identify patterns? Just like forecasting generally, proper pattern recognition isn't just for markets—it's done in many fields. This means much of our approach can mimic other widely held practices—principally, science. The scientific method is the best way to detect and corroborate patterns. If you think you've identified a pattern that could make for an effective market forecasting tool, the only way to know it works is via proper application of the scientific method. (For a refresher, see Chapter 1.)

STOCK MARKET PATTERNS

There are some specifics we need to keep in mind when it comes to pattern recognition and markets. Foremost: *The stock market itself is the ultimate leading economic indicator.* Not vice versa. A CEAS digests all widely known information before any one person (our Golden Rule from Chapter 5).

Stark evidence of this lies in the track record of most professional stock market forecasters. Their poor success rate points to the notion markets are generally efficient. If all well-known and widely discussed information is already reflected in stock prices, that means all commonly known and used patterns for forecasting are priced in, too. So theories about how PE ratios can predict future stock prices, or for knowing where we are in a Fed interest rate cycle, don't make a lick of difference. They're priced in! If you see a headline about a stock you follow, there's no use trying to trade on that information—it's already priced in. You missed the move.

 If all well-known and widely discussed information is already reflected in stock prices, that means all commonly known and used patterns for forecasting are priced in, too.

Some other pattern-seeking basics for stock markets:

Layering it on: Maybe the most important rule of thumb in detecting market patterns is to practice being "the layer on top of the layer." A good investor who understands the Golden Rule must do two things:
- Observe what is happening in the economy and markets and judge those factors.
- Observe and judge what investors *think* about what is going on in the economy and markets.

Those are two discrete types of patterns. Recall Chapter 2, where we learned about self-awareness. Investors need to be hyper-aware of what is happening in the world and what folks think about what is happening in the world. That is the only way to understand which patterns are being priced in and which are not.

Is it significant?: From the modern era (let's begin at 1926) to date, there really aren't that many market cycles. In most cases, there aren't nearly enough data to be "statistically significant." That is, there aren't enough data for us to really make a solid and reliable analysis about a pattern. What might seem like a pattern could just be happenstance and randomness. Don't make a judgment without enough data.

Market environments change: Markets are different today than they were a decade ago, let alone 80 years ago! That means they aren't necessarily comparable in every way. Back in the nineteenth century on into the early twentieth, railroad stocks dominated and car companies were like tiny technology stocks made for speculators. Since then, the global economy has undergone numerous changes—autos have come full circle from juggernauts back to small players again! So you must decide if periods from long ago are comparable enough to really say a pattern is valid.

As we discovered in Chapter 3, economies and markets evolve, but human behavior is a relative constant.

Remember your brain: Our brains are not wired for probability; they're wired for similarity. We see patterns in everything—real or imagined—which means we need to be doubly sure the patterns we identify are significant and use the scientific method whenever possible. *Don't ever use your eyes or intuition to corroborate a pattern—they can easily fool you.*

In Chapter 1, we discussed categorization as a method of reducing complexity so we can understand the world easier. Our brains are always trying to reduce a situation or stimulus to be as simple as possible. We don't say, "This is a mass of dead cellulose, cut in angular forms, stained, and nailed together." We say, "This is a chair."

One of the brain's favorite things to do is reduce a category to something *binary*: a yes/no decision. Our brains turn as much of the world into dual categories as possible and have to expend extra thought and energy to see the gray areas of life. Children, for instance, make distinctions between good and evil very quickly and intuitively. They do not think in gray areas (Superman is good, Lex Luthor is evil—pretty simple). When we're older, however, the lines between good and evil are clouded with gray areas and full of paradoxes. If our primal brains had their way, we'd make everything as stark as a yes/no decision.

Our brains also like repetition. In Chapter 3 we discussed how the brain creates and reinforces "networks" between neurons to enhance memory and learning. The more we do or think something, the more it becomes reality to us.

All these little quirks can influence the way we think we see patterns in the world. Don't trust them—seek corroboration in the scientific method before acting.

Correlation and causation: Never make an investment with a pattern you don't understand. Most patterns are "casual" correlations—happenstances. If you can't understand the causation behind the pattern, it could be a trap and lead you into a bad decision.

Is it big enough to move the market?: In your search for patterns to predict with, you generally want to find things that have an impact great enough to move the whole market or economy. Small patterns may be interesting, but if they're not big enough, they're not worth your while.

Know what the pattern points to: Make sure you don't mistake a pattern that works for a narrow portion of the economy for the whole thing. Perhaps a certain economic "driver" like strong economic growth will help energy stocks because folks will buy more gasoline. Great! Just don't make the mistake of thinking that driver will necessarily pertain to all sectors. Economic growth may not help, say, healthcare stocks, in the same way as it does energy stocks.

Never forget the Golden Rule: Part of finding the right patterns includes making sure they're not already reflected in stock prices. Well-known patterns are worthless because they're already priced in to the market—the epitome of the Golden Rule. Making good investing decisions is lonely. It takes guts. Finding a pattern that no one else recognizes or widely misunderstands—that is, being against the crowd—is tough work. It's difficult to understand how tough that is until you've been through it. Humans are communal, social animals. We are wired to want people to like us, to be comfortable fitting in. You have to fight that instinct with every ounce of you to be a successful investor. It's an extremely uncomfortable thing to do.

PATTERNS THROUGH THE NOISE

Let's investigate a few market factors big enough to create patterns with high probabilities of repeating. A couple of examples include:

- Bull markets follow every bear market.
- Regular booms and busts (bear markets happen about every four years).
- Small-cap stocks tend to outperform at the beginning of bull markets and big caps outperform near the end.
- Stock markets tend to perform better in the second two years of a US presidential term.

Some of these might seem easy and obvious. My advice is to keep it basic and obvious because the more granular you get, the more difficult things will become. Our brains love to see patterns where there are none, so it's vital to be very careful about the patterns we identify and use. The vast majority of patterns folks believe exist simply don't.

Economic and market cycles are among the most common patterns. Through every epoch in market history, booms have followed busts and back again. But I don't like the term "cycle." It's a misleading metaphor for understanding the economy. A circle starts you in one place and then you end up in the same place by the end. No real economies (well, maybe communist) work that way over time.

It's better to think of markets and economies in a *spiraling* pattern. There's a lot of trial and error and advances and

It's better to think of markets and economies in a *spiraling* pattern. There's a lot of trial and error and advances and pullbacks—a lot of going around and around (like a circle). But it's also moving *up*. A spiral captures the nature of real progress and market evolution. Progress is never a straight line down or a laser shot up. It's more like two steps forward, one back. Over and over again. Spiral-like. Economies grow; markets tend to move up over time.

pullbacks—a lot of going around and around (like a circle). But it's also moving *up*. A spiral captures the nature of real progress and market evolution. Progress is never a straight line down or a laser shot up. It's more like two steps forward, one back. Over and over again. Spiral-like. Economies grow; markets tend to move up over time.

Ditch the cycle of circle thinking. That metaphor only helps you remember there will always be pullbacks (bears). But a spiral also helps you recall every bear is followed by a bull, and most often, the bulls are much bigger. Economies and markets grow over time. Let's take an example.

What can you make of Tables 7.1 and 7.2? They show bear and bull markets in the S&P 500 since 1932.

Pretty clearly, through time, bulls follow bears and bulls are bigger and last longer. There are few exceptions, and they've proven true for nearly 80 years—through many changing economic environments. That makes the notion that bulls follow bears a pretty reliable stock

Table 7.1   Bear Markets in the S&P 500 Since 1932

Bear Market Bottom	Duration (Months)	S&P 500 12-Month Returns from Bottom
06/01/1932	33	120.9%
04/28/1942	62	53.7%
06/13/1949	36	42.0%
10/22/1957	15	31.0%
06/26/1962	6	32.7%
10/07/1966	8	33.2%
05/26/1970	18	43.7%
10/03/1974	21	38.0%
08/12/1982	20	58.3%
12/04/1987	3	22.8%
10/11/1990	3	29.1%
10/9/2002	30	33.7%
Average	**21**	**44.9%**

Source: Global Financial Data.

Table 7.2 Bull Markets in the S&P 500 Since 1932

Start	End	Months	S&P 500 Change
06/01/1932	03/06/1937	57	324%
04/28/1942	05/29/1946	49	158%
06/13/1949	08/02/1956	86	267%
10/22/1957	12/12/1961	50	86%
06/26/1962	02/09/1966	43	79%
10/07/1966	11/29/1968	26	48%
05/26/1970	01/11/1973	32	74%
10/03/1974	11/28/1980	74	126%
08/12/1982	08/25/1987	60	229%
12/04/1987	07/16/1990	31	65%
10/11/1990	03/24/2000	113	417%
10/09/2002	10/09/2007	60	102%
Average		**57**	**165%**

Source: Global Financial Data.

market pattern. Notice that this is a general observation and not a "point" prediction. Using the lessons from the last chapter, we know we can't make an exact forecast with any good reliability. There will always be noise and randomness in the data. But through that noise the trend is very clear.

IT'S A GAME OF RELATIVE EXPECTATIONS

Once we've identified a useful pattern we must then understand it in *context*. Facts without context are essentially meaningless. For example, what if I said to you, "six billion"? What information can you glean from that? What can you do with it? Not much of anything. Is six billion a lot? A little? What if next I said, "three trillion"? Now, does six billion still seem so big? No. We have a little context and we can say that six billion is not very big relative to three trillion. What if then I said "ten." Now we have even more context. We know that six billion is big, but ten is tiny, and three trillion is really huge. All just on context.

It's good to apply this sort of contextual thinking to pattern seeking. Is a $20 billion bank bailout by the Fed big? Seems huge, right? Really, it isn't. They do trillions in lending every year. $20 billion is a drop in the bucket.

Context is sometimes called *framing*, and is essential, because in a world that's constantly changing we can only understand things relative to other things. Market history provides a useful framework (or context) for better understanding future market direction.

Context is sometimes called *framing*, and is essential, because in a world that's constantly changing, we can only understand things relative to other things. Market history provides a useful framework (or context) for better understanding future market direction.

Perhaps we're worried about inflation today and want to see if there's an identifiable pattern between inflation and how markets work. If we go back in history and see inflation was much higher in the past and markets still muddled through, then we have some context letting us know it's relatively not as bad as currently believed.

Culture, society, capital markets, economies . . . they're always in flux. There are simply too many variables out there for a theory or model to hold for long. More importantly, markets and economies evolve and adapt rapidly. Evolving things

Culture, society, capital markets, economies . . . they're always in flux. There are simply too many variables out there for a theory or model to hold for long.

are always context dependent because the foundation from which we judge them changes, too.

Consider: If John is six months old, it isn't reasonable to assume he can swim. But as John grows and gets to 20 years old, it's much more plausible that he can. Over time, the situation changes again, and when John is 100, it's again unlikely he can swim. John's expected ability to swim is entirely context dependent on his age—which shifts over time.

Things that happen in CEASs, and economies specifically, have a *reflexive* quality. That is, they act and react upon each other in real time—which is a fancy way of saying everything is interconnected.

That interconnection is key because it means as something changes, it's probably having an effect on the rest of the world around it—in ways many can't fathom or detect because the world is so vastly interconnected.

The same logic must be applied to markets, or any CEAS. Most mathematical thought can only account for "first principles" and can't deal effectively with a changing environment. But economies and markets always have changing contexts—the principles that drove something before will change over time, so simple cause-and-effect logic often doesn't work.

> But economies and markets always have changing contexts—the principles that drove something before will change over time, so simple cause-and-effect logic often doesn't work.

Again, this is something many investors forget or ignore. Most economic models try to examine variable factors like interest rates or money supply in a vacuum. As in, "If you raise interest rates by X, then the money supply will fall by Y." That logic may serve as a valid way to help our brains conceptualize an idea about how interest rates and money supply interact in theory, but there's no way it could consistently work in practice because the interconnected circumstances of the economy at any given time would affect the outcome.

This is a fallacy of applying the rules of physical science to stock markets. First causes and linear cause/effect relationships can only work if the system is very simple. Markets and economies are not; they are complex—so searching for patterns in such a simplistic way can't generally work. In a complex system, nothing exists in a vacuum—most everything is somehow, some way dependent on everything else.

So all the analysis you do for investigating patterns must also account for *relative expectations*. Professor Jeremy Siegel, in his book Stocks for the Long Run, had it right when he said "markets respond to the difference in what the participants in financial markets expect to be announced and what is announced."

If we know the market reflects what is already expected, then it's the contradictory information that is of material value to investors. Think of the consensus as a baseline. For instance, economists might have a consensus view that next quarter's GDP growth will be 3.2 percent. Days and weeks before the official announcement, markets will reflect this view in stock prices. But on reporting day . . . GDP goes up only 2.9 percent! Yikes! In the short term, investors are likely to be disappointed by the news and adjust stock prices accordingly—even though 2.9 percent GDP growth is quite a respectable number. It's not the absolute that counts—it's the market's expectations relative to reality that makes the difference.

The same logic holds true for valuations. Numerous studies have shown absolute P/E ratios have no ability to predict stock price returns (and so too with many similar valuation metrics).[1] To see why that must be so, forget the absolute level and think relative. Let's say a certain kind of stock has a P/E ratio of 23. Is that high or low? Standing alone, the number is close to meaningless—it only becomes meaningful when compared to something else. That something else might be other stocks—particularly its peer group (or stocks that are of similar type in business and scope).

There is a more basic reason relative expectations are important: Humans get acclimated to new information very quickly. Think of oil prices from about 2003 to 2008. In 2003, the prospect of $50 oil/barrel was widely feared as a sure way to sink the economy. But through those years, oil ran up—higher and higher. By mid-2008, oil prices hit $150 a barrel! That had folks plenty worried. But then, by the end of the year, oil prices returned below $50 per barrel and people began fretting that such a huge depression in oil prices must translate into low demand—which means the economy is about to sink!

Now, put aside for a moment the irrational logic of somehow believing high and low oil prices are *both* symptoms of a sinking economy (perverse as it is). Just the fact that oil was suddenly viewed as "cheap" at $50 a barrel is fascinating in itself. This has everything to do with relative expectations.

Jarring effects on an economy—a sudden change in a significant factor—cause the most immediate dislocation and often result in the most severe market effects simply because the market has a lot to digest in very little time. With little understanding of the issue, homogeneity of sentiment among market participants often ensues, causing overshooting or undershooting in the short term.

An example is the 2008 financial panic. Wall Street investment banking was wiped out so quickly few had any idea what the longer term effects might be. Thus, for some weeks, markets entered a true panic (a very rare event)—deciding the end could be nigh and markets may be headed to zero. But in fact, it was an overshot of reality by quite a lot. The market eventually got it right—that things had worsened but it wasn't nearly Armageddon, as was widely feared. But it took some time to price all of it in. One day we woke up and Wall Street as we knew it went *poof!* Relatively speaking, everything had changed.

When it comes to economic and market data—or anything priced by a free market—always consider *relative expectations*.

ACCELERATING CHANGE IS THE GREATEST OF ALL PATTERNS OF DEVELOPMENT

What do these have in common?

- Evolution
- Technology
- Economies
- Capital Markets
- Human Knowledge
- Medicine
- Civilization

They all evolve under the principle of *accelerating change* (AC). This is a prevalent idea in futures studies and the history of technology. Accelerating change is defined as an increase in the rate of change through time.

The principle of AC was made popular in 1965 when Intel co-founder Gordon Moore described a long-term trend in the development of computing hardware. Moore noted that, since the invention of the integrated circuit in 1958, the number of transistors that can be placed on an integrated circuit has increased *exponentially*, doubling approximately every two years. That is, not only has change been constant, but the

(Continued)

(Continued)

rate of change is accelerating at a constant rate and in an exponential fashion. So far, "Moore's Law" has proven true and many expect it to continue for decades longer.

This pattern has been applied to many CEASs and proven potent across many fields. Amazingly, the rate of progress of economies and development of capital markets has followed a similar pattern of accelerating change over time.

The lesson? Change is one of the only patterns we can count on. Not just change, but increasing change—ultimately faster than anything our small minds can keep up with.

Ray Kurzweil, a leading inventor and author of the groundbreaking 2005 book, *The Singularity Is Near*, gives an exhaustive account of how the principle of AC works, and he even describes how it works for economics and stock markets. (Mr. Kurzweil is also the founder of the Singularity Institute, and much knowledge about AC can be gleaned from his website, www.kurzweilai.net.)

Consistently (and paradoxically), we tend to feel as if things are progressively getting worse, not better. Greg Easterbrook, in his book, *The Progress Paradox*, offers a detailed analysis of how things continue to get better even as we continue to feel worse. Here's a short list (which goes on and on in the book) of what's consistently trending better across the globe:

- Democracy
- Human freedom
- Per capita wealth
- Free trade
- Standards of living
- Life expectancy
- Poverty
- Economic growth
- Crime
- Environmental pollution
- Armed conflict
- Education

This provides an important lesson: Take a step back from daily media haranguing and see the bigger picture once in a while. There, it becomes abundantly clear those who truly believe things are getting worse are suffering from myopia.

But gloom has its uses. One of the great features of the American way is the *pursuit* of happiness. Notice it's never enough for us. We want more, we strive for more.

Sure, poverty might be near all-time lows, but we want it eradicated. Yes, crime might be anemic, but we prefer it didn't exist altogether. This house is okay, but we want one with a pool and a rec room, too. And the old TV was fine, but it would be great to have a 42" flat panel.

America's forefathers were more right than they knew in calling it the pursuit of happiness. *Pursuit* is precisely what it's all about. It remains a human universal that we are not ever satisfied. And contentment, happiness, whatever you want to call it, is a matter of relative standing. Behavioral studies have shown this time and again. There's an innate and irrepressible drive to continually get better from where we were yesterday and in comparison with our peers. If we get a 10 percent raise, but our peers all got 15 percent, we will actually probably feel *worse* than before. That truth helps explain why we continue to feel angst even as things continue to get better.

BACK TO THE FUTURE: USING HISTORY TO FIND PATTERNS

History is the "research lab" for detecting stock market patterns. History can be a great tool to help with forecasting, but can also be a great enemy if abused or misunderstood.

I think history is best used for context—it gives us a sense of what's happened and whether something today is truly unprecedented. History is no panacea and it isn't an exact science. Since markets evolve and the world changes, each new day is basically unprecedented in some way, and history never exactly repeats itself. Then again, very few things are truly unprecedented. Most market events are comparable to past situations in some way. Simply understanding what is different between then and now is helpful.

In my view, knowledge of history is one of the ultimate competitive advantages in investing. Why? Because few study it or take it seriously anymore. Today, history is something of a hobby or pastime—particularly for market analysts. Remember, anything not well known or understood in markets isn't fully priced in. In my experience, one of the easiest ways to perceive market overreaction is when folks believe something is truly unprecedented, yet isn't. There's no way to know unless you study history.

Here are a few pointers for using history in identifying market patterns:

Context and probability: History helps frame situations. For instance, if today there is a credit bust, you can study past credit busts and see what is similar and what is different. What was the market reaction? What were people saying back then? If you can see that, then you have a baseline for understanding how people might react today. You have context.

Human reaction is fungible: In my view, the most potent form of learning is experiential learning. Over the course of modern market history, human instinct won't have changed very much. As generations pass, similar events will occur, but new people will be there to experience them—people who will not have studied or digested events of the past. This is one reason why panics and euphoric manias happen about once a generation—in some sense, we all have to live through them in order to know them. It's amazing how closely history tends to repeat itself—not necessarily the events themselves, but the human reactions to similar events. That's one of the real values of history—seeing the repeatability of human behavior.

The accepted view isn't always the right one: We need to be careful about how we get our history and from whom. Most historians aren't economists—many historical accounts will fail to find the proper view simply because historians aren't equipped with the right skills. Interesting fact: Fed Chairman Ben Bernanke is regarded as one of the most learned students of Depression-era economic history. He's probably a pretty good candidate to be a Depression history buff because he's also a trained economist, and I'd be more apt to listen to him than a PhD history student writing his/her thesis on the subject.

History is a point of view: The idea that there is objectivity, or even "truth," in accounts of history is one of the longest-held myths about the field. Think of it this way: Why hasn't there ever been a "definitive" account of anything? Because the only thing a historical account can ultimately do is give a perspective. History is not an objective science—it is an interpretive one. So never believe any historical account is definitive. Histories always have an agenda or point of view of some kind.

Are there enough data?: Here we turn to some good old statistics. Always make sure there are enough data to make your study worthy. If you're doing a study about the US Depression and market reactions, the best you can do is an anecdotal analysis because there's just one instance with even remotely reliable data to study and that was from 70 years ago. That won't make for particularly rigorous or reliable conclusions.

Nothing's inevitable: Often when we look at history we get a sense things were "inevitable" or they were easy to see and that folks knew what would come next. Never! Things were always just as uncertain as today, always will be. Through history, investors only knew what was happening day to day, just like us.

Markets evolve: Markets are never the same from one era to the next—they evolve and grow. So most things aren't comparable the further back you go. Will America be the greatest empire on earth or just a footnote to history? It's impossible to say. Charlemagne's European empire looked as if it would last forever, and today it's something most folks don't even know existed. Today, there is little trace of the Roman Empire except artifacts. And that was only two thousand years ago—a blip in world history. Today's events seem very important to us, but as we live through them we cannot tell if they will turn out to be profound changes or mere passing trifles.

Be time period aware: I see headlines in the news like, "This is the worst trading day since 1997!" or similar all the time. Who cares? What about 1997 is significant? The answer is nothing— it's a false anchor for people to focus on and only creates inane biases. Investors often unwittingly use arbitrary time periods for studies. "From 1982 to 1996 inflation was only 3 percent."

Why is that important? What about that time period is meaningful? Nothing. The lesson: Always be cognizant of the time period used—it can create huge biases and misconceptions.

THEORY WARNING

I admit it: We can't live without theories. But it's important we understand what theories really are. Folks tend to consider theories as some kind of discovered "rules" about how the world works. Wrong. A theory is a way of describing something in terms we can understand—a guide, not a rule.

Semantics? Hardly. No theory is foolproof—there are always exceptions. One of the great problems of any scientific field is *moving from the particular to the universal*. This is the place where most theories explode. For reductive science, exceptions are very bad things. If there is an exception to a theory, that weakens it severely. The more exceptions, the worse the theory.

Theories are handy tools for the physical sciences, where matter behaves so consistently and uniformly, there are, for intents and purposes, "rules" about how things work. But this cannot be so for markets and economies (CEAS). Every theory will have many exceptions in the arena of complexity. There are no "rules," only attempts to describe how things tend to act—patterns. That is the function of theory for stock markets—to give us clues on how things tend to be, not how they will be.

There are essentially two ways to arrive at a theory:

1. **From principles**: Take a set of assumptions about the world and from them generate a theory about how something works. For instance, leaves will always change colors in autumn because they don't get as much sunlight as in spring and summer. The problem with this kind of theory-making, of course, is that it relies on the underlying principles. If the principles aren't right, then the theory isn't right.

2. **From statistics**: Look for statistical data patterns and predict they will continue. This presupposes a belief the past will repeat itself. Any seasoned investor knows the familiar dictum: "Past performance is no indication of future results." We know the past can never fully resemble the future, but it is true certain patterns do tend to repeat.

These two kinds of theory-making might look familiar. They're otherwise known as deduction and induction—the root types of formal logic (which we covered last chapter). In any case, the vast majority of "rules" for stock investing fall into one of these two categories. Neither of these methods will ever produce a foolproof forecasting system for stocks, but they can be helpful to us in trying to gain better context and understanding.

THREE BIG DRIVERS

Whether we're looking at economic fundamentals or scouring historical data for clues, there are three basic categories of patterns that can influence stock markets: *Economic, Political,* and *Sentiment.* Always think *extreme* with these. Most factors aren't saying much of anything about market direction most of the time. When analyzing with the three big drivers, look for big things that the market hasn't yet priced in.

ECONOMIC

Obvious but true: Big economic trends often have the power to flow through and broadly move stock market valuations. But often not exactly how we'd think. Many pore over economic data—reports, surveys, and the like—scores of hours, trying to find some useful, secret nugget. I have done so myself as a matter of fact. And after doing so for some years, here is what I've found: *Economic indicators are useful approximations of a situation and nothing more.*

Economic indicators are any data that claim to be descriptive of the macroeconomic environment. That is, GDP readings, unemployment numbers, personal incomes, and so on. Don't put full trust in them. Most of them are broken beyond repair—esoteric calculations based on shoddy surveys from politically biased think tanks or government bureaus with sloppy methods.

For instance, the basic formula for GDP seems simple enough:

$$\textbf{GDP} = \text{Consumption} + \text{Gross investment} + \text{Government spending} + (\text{Exports} - \text{Imports})$$

But in reality, it is incredibly complex—based on surveys and myriad assumptions. If you have some time, look up how GDP is calculated by the Bureau of Economic Analysis (you can do it online at www.bea.gov). You'll immediately see how contingent the data are upon huge conjecture, incomplete numbers, and strange calculations. It will be clear to you GDP is not worth ascribing much significance to as an exact calculation. It can only give us a general sense, at best, of what the economy did. This is one reason why the numbers are revised repeatedly.

Economic indicators help you see the forest for the trees. Far too many folks fret over whether quarterly GDP will come in at 2.0 percent or 1.9 percent. As if existence depended on that 0.1 percent! It doesn't. Things will be fine either way, and it isn't likely to make a material difference on the markets in the long run. Gross Domestic Product is too broad and abstract a concept to worry about minutiae and exactitude. What matters in this hypothetical case is the economy is growing at a relatively normal pace.

 Investors tend to erroneously believe a pattern of past behavior will always continue into the future—an assumption that is often wrong.

Note also that so-called economic indicators don't really "indicate" anything. They're descriptions of what's happened. Past tense. Investors tend to erroneously believe a pattern of past behavior will always continue into the future—an assumption that is often wrong. Another thing: There are far too many data for us to see. Daily, weekly, monthly, sometimes quarterly data are too short term to see a trend. It usually takes years to see an actual trend.

Instead of wasting your brainpower and time on such details, ask yourself what current forces are likely to drive economic growth throughout the world? Make it simpler for yourself: Is GDP going to accelerate, stagnate, or contract? What is the outlook for interest rates (up or down) and how would that impact things? What is the outlook for technology and infrastructure spending among countries? Focus on what has the potential to materially and broadly impact the companies whose stock you're considering buying. Form opinions on them and decide their implications for markets, then test to see if those have proven true in the past. Next, see if it matches up with current sentiment or if your views are different than current expectations.

Here's a sampling of hypothetical economic drivers that could impact market performance:

- US economic growth will be higher than consensus expectations.
- Long-term interest rates will move markedly higher this year.

- Mergers, acquisitions, and share buybacks will remain strong.
- Personal consumption will fall much further than most predict.

Economic indicators are among the most looked at and studied metrics in all stock market forecasting. So the truth is you're very unlikely to find many patterns here not already priced in.

Remember, *economies and markets aren't the same, nor do they necessarily always act the same, especially in the short term.* Stock markets are representative of public firms. Most business and commerce is actually done privately. So a stock market is first and foremost a representation of corporate earnings of companies that trade publicly. Of course, those are generally large enough to function as a proxy for the broader economy, but it won't be exact and sometimes will be materially different. It's absolutely possible to have positive GDP and shrinking corporate earnings, as seen in the second half of 2007 and the first half of 2008, when the Financials sector's losses took down corporate earnings but GDP remained positive.

POLITICAL

Politics also matter for stocks. Not only do politics influence sentiment, they also directly affect regulation, trade, and commerce. Politicians, for better or worse, direct the allocation of vast amounts of capital and resources.

Political drivers can be country-specific or affect interaction between regions (like trade policies). Categories to watch include taxation, government stability, fiscal policy, and political turnover.

Also ask yourself which countries are experiencing a change in government that could have a meaningful impact on their economies. Are new taxes on the docket? Where? Are countries generally undergoing pro-growth reforms or restrictive new regulations?

Investors often suffer from home country bias, where they put too much attention on the politics of their own country. Always keep in mind it's a big, interconnected world out there and geopolitical developments everywhere can have implications for everyone.

Here are some examples of political developments that can drive stocks up or down:

- Elections and political party changes
- Trade policy
- Fiscal policy
- Monetary policy
- Property rights and changes to legal system
- Protests, government coups, and general political instability

When it comes to investing, it's generally best to leave your ideology at the door. Ideology can usually only cause biases and blindness to reality. Be as callous and objective as you can in your judgments and don't assume any party or point of view is necessarily right. Test and see.

Free markets are wonderful things and deserve to be as unfettered as possible, but we need government. We need laws; we need a system of stable and clear property rights and protections from what we consider criminal activity. Governments are there to make and enforce those rules and protect rights. When rules change or things become more uncertain, politics can cause dislocation and fear—a bad thing for stock markets. Usually, the status quo is best. Often, governments do more harm than good and new policies inevitably have unintended consequences. Governments are command systems—by definition less agile and efficient than CEASs. Therefore, overreaching government initiatives attempting to regulate a CEAS by definition make things less efficient. That's generally bad for stocks.

SENTIMENT DRIVERS

Understanding investor sentiment is one of the largest and most important ways to find patterns in stock markets to help in forecasting. We already tackled this topic at length in Chapter 4. Flip back there if you need a refresher.

AN OPTIMISTIC NOTE ON FUTURE PATTERNS

Before we move on, a brief note about pattern seeking. It's easy to fall into despair about stock market patterns—how can we possibly find any new ones that aren't already priced into stocks? There are so many millions of people out there seeking patterns—some equipped with highly sophisticated technology and mathematical algorithms. Surely, all the patterns must be found by now!

Not a chance. Throughout civilization, many otherwise brilliant people have come to the conclusion "there is no more to know—we've discovered everything." Whether it's science, economics, ecology— anything—at one time or another we've had the audacity to believe we've learned it all. And every time that sentiment is proven absurd. This will prove especially true for capital markets and economies.

In truth, we're at the beginning. Capital markets are nascent and developing at an ever-accelerating speed, changing, growing, evolving. There are undoubtedly more techniques, ideas, and patterns out there yet to be discovered. I'd bet we haven't even scratched the surface.

That doesn't mean pattern seeking will be easy or any less rigorous. It just means opportunities are not so easily exhausted, and they are out there for those who seek them.

CHAPTER INSIGHTS

A second way to forecast stock markets is by pattern recognition. (The first way is via probability, described in the previous chapter.)

- Ultimately, using valuations, economic "drivers," or anything that uses the past to try and predict the future is about pattern recognition.
  - The best way to test and find reliable market patterns is via the scientific method.
- Pattern recognition is a common kind of analysis in many kinds of study, but has some important specifics in stock markets such as statistical significance of past data and problems with correlation and causation.

(Continued)

(Continued)

- Stock markets are full of random price movement, or noise, so the goal is to detect the patterns through the noise.
  - Often, real market patterns are widely known—which means they are already priced into stocks and thus have little value. Therefore, the job is even tougher because we must find patterns that are not only reliable through time, but also are not yet widely known about.
- Understanding how a pattern will affect the market is about relative expectations, not absolute results. It is about understanding if reality will turn out differently than what the public expects and has priced in.
- History is the "research lab" of studying and testing market patterns.
- Three big categories of patterns, or "market drivers," are:
  - Economic
  - Political
  - Sentiment

8

PRACTICAL PORTFOLIO MANAGEMENT

*My practicality consists in this, in the knowledge that if
you beat your head against the wall it is your head which breaks
and not the wall.*

—Antonio Gramsci

*Between falsehood and useless truth there is little difference. As
gold which he cannot spend will make no man rich, so knowledge
which he cannot apply will make no man wise.*

—Samuel Johnson

How does everything we've learned so far translate into portfolio management? This chapter won't be comprehensive—like the
bulk of this book. Here we're going to cover a few basics about how
to *think* about portfolio management using what we've learned so far.
What are the baseline assumptions and perspectives a long-term, successful portfolio strategy should employ?

For the nuts and bolts of portfolio construction, I recommend
any of the sector guides in the *Fisher Investments On* series, or Aaron

197

Anderson's excellent *Own the World*, a study on how to create a diversified portfolio of global stocks.

If there's one thing we've seen in our travails, it's that managing portfolios in a practical way requires keeping things as simple as possible. Oversimplification can be a bad thing, true, but we are too full of biases and blindnesses not to find some basic heuristics to make things easier on ourselves. Each piece of advice in this section in some form or another is traceable back to the lessons of previous chapters.

This chapter is geared toward investors who want to beat the stock markets over the long term—but do it with enough prudence and practicality so as not to put their long-term investment goals in peril. If you're someone who's satisfied with market returns minus a few transaction costs (index fund investing), then good for you, but this chapter won't do you much good. Also, if you're a high-flying, hit-the-ball-out-of-the-park, I-want-100-percent-returns-in-a-single-year kind of investor, this chapter likewise doesn't have much of anything to say to you other than best of luck and don't call me when you're broke.

THE VIRTUES OF HEURISTICS

This chapter is, at its core, about *heuristics*. Sometimes colloquially called a "rule of thumb," a heuristic is a method used to help solve a problem or facilitate learning. One of the most important features about heuristics is that they're "loose," which means they are not meant to be rigid rules but guidelines to point us in the right direction.

Sometimes colloquially called a "rule of thumb," a heuristic is a method used to help solve a problem or facilitate learning.

This is a very human idea—it's like a shortcut so we don't have to try to remember every single thing we've learned each time we are confronted with a problem to solve.

But we must exercise caution on two fronts with heuristics. One, we need to be careful about confusing heuristics with reductionism. Recall from Chapter 1, reduction is the process of taking a big problem and cutting into smaller, easily solved problems with the assumption that all the smaller solutions can be put back together again to solve the big problem. Our example was a car, where the motor can be taken out, fixed, and then put right back in and the system will work just fine. A good heuristic shouldn't seek to reduce a problem but instead allow it to be more freely and easily solved.

Second, always reserve the right to say a certain heuristic is not appropriate in a situation. That's the "loose" feature of heuristics, where we can decide it simply doesn't apply to the problem at hand. Disciplined investing is not the absence of heuristics—we need them. Rather, we should be mindfully blending rigor and rules of thumb to reflect substantial self-awareness and self-discipline in thinking.

George Polya's 1945 book, *How to Solve It: A New Aspect of Mathematical Method*, is considered a classic on heuristic thinking. The book was actually intended to be a treatise on solving math problems, but much of it can be applied to problem solving generally. Polya provides many general bits of wisdom like "look to the unknown" or "if the problem is abstract, try examining a concrete example." We'd do well to heed many of them. A few other examples of basic heuristics:

- **Variation of a problem**: Can you vary or change your problem to create a new problem whose solution will help you solve your original problem?
- **Generalization**: Is it possible to find a problem more general than your problem?
- **Problem relation**: Can you find a problem related to yours that's already been solved and use it?

Based on all we've learned so far, we're going to look at some heuristics on stock investing.

GOAL SETTING

The first—and possibly most important—step in practical portfolio management is following some heuristics about investing objectives.

In previous chapters, we saw how myopic and bogged down investors often get in short-term time periods and minutiae. It's funny and kind of sad that most folks fail to take this first and all-important step in goal setting. Your investing goals in large part will dictate the appropriate strategy. So the first thing we need to do is get practical and set goals.

NEVER HAVE ANOTHER BAD DAY . . . EVER!

I get a kick out of self-help gurus. I like to observe them and see how they operate. I think about self-help gurus a lot because their brand of salesmanship is often pretty close to how investment advice is sold. You know who I mean—those goofy folks on TV and in bookstores with their "programs for success," giving you the rules on how to achieve something. "Be rich and happy and attractive and never have another bad day . . . ever! Just like me! It's a simple 15-step program . . . all for $399.99!"

Sure, it's schlocky. But beneath all that garish overexcitement there is something truly interesting: Just about all self-help gurus talk in terms of setting and achieving goals. That's an idea worth exploring.

Think of it this way: There's virtually no way to achieve anything without a goal in mind. If there's nothing defined, then it's impossible to know if anything was achieved. For instance, say your portfolio grew 8 percent last year. Is that good? Bad? How would you know? It only makes sense if you have a certain goal in mind and a way to judge your performance.

I'll go a step further: Our minds and cultures are geared for goals—it's one of the primary ways we understand things. (If you don't believe me, check any investment sales and marketing collateral. Invariably they are about investment roads, paths, maps, journeys, and so on. It's all goal-based metaphors about travel and "getting somewhere." Advertising has always been a glimpse into the human psyche—marketers and branders know human minds as well as any group of professionals I can think of.) Let's flip it around for a moment—most folks aren't content simply "existing." A few are, but most feel they need to fulfill, accomplish, and achieve some kind of relative standing in the world. We want to learn; we give ourselves trophies when we "win"; we strive for the "finish line"; we want permanent stone markers in the ground after we die to prove we existed. And so on. Most of us have to train ourselves to "let go" if we just want to exist like a monk; it doesn't come naturally for the most part.

So, pursuit is human nature and it's also the most basic feature of good portfolio management. That's why it's such a shame most investors only have an opaque idea of their real goals—no amount of investment knowledge can help them until they figure it out.

So, pursuit is human nature and it's also the most basic feature of good portfolio management. That's why it's such a shame most investors only have an opaque idea of their real goals—no amount of investment knowledge can help them until they figure it out.

There are two kinds of goals worth discussing: *personal goals* and *portfolio goals*. Both must work with each other—yet it's imperative they are thought about in discrete ways.

PERSONAL GOALS

What do you want from your money? How should it work for you? A standard question most are asked by their investment adviser is if they want "Growth, Income, or Capital Preservation? Choose one." Huh? That question is pretty dumb. Why? Let's take "capital preservation" first. I've never known anyone who invests with the long-term idea of losing their capital. Never. So why would capital preservation be a primary goal? Seems pretty implicitly wrapped up in the idea of "investing" in the first place, doesn't it? Then there's "growth" or "income." I don't understand those, either. Why would those two necessarily be mutually exclusive as goals? Why couldn't you have income and also a goal of growth? Generic "growth" isn't a real goal, and a goal of "not losing money" is similarly abstract and won't work, either.

These basic questions—standard in investment advisory today—are not just insufficient; they come from an invalid point of view. Namely, that investing goals should have something to do with distinctions about income and perception of risk. I don't like these options—they don't say anything about *your* actual goals, what you really wish to achieve. A better way to consider goals is in terms of *terminal value.* Terminal value is a way to think about where you want things to be at the end. Figure out the end goal and then reverse engineer the plan from there. Here are a few reasonable ways to decide on your terminal value based on the type of goal you set:

- **Maximize terminal value**: To grow your assets as much as possible in whatever time frame you've designated for them.
- **Maintain purchasing power**: Structure your investments to keep up with the erosive effects of inflation so your money can always purchase the same relative amount of goods and services.
- **Maintain current value**: Similar to maintaining purchasing power, but also growing your assets enough to account for whatever cash distributions you may take over time.
- **Deplete portfolio over time**: Maybe you decide your kids are spoiled brats and so are your grandkids—no need to leave them anything. You just want to have fun in your life so you want to spend it all. Your goal is to splurge on fun stuff and have one dollar left in your account on the day you die. (Happens more often than you'd think, and it's a perfectly reasonable goal.)

Notice how different goals will likely require much different tactics. So figure out what your endgame is first! Someone looking just to combat inflation doesn't necessarily need to cope with the volatility of stocks (maybe they can just use inflation indexed bonds), but someone wanting to maximize terminal value or grow the portfolio for their heirs certainly will.

But that isn't all. We need to consider one more feature: *time horizon.* Time is usually the ultimate difference. Folks are so darned worried about return in, say, a calendar year, they forget about time.

I've got good news and bad news for you—you're probably going to live longer than you think. Good? Yeah! You get to live longer! Bad? Yeah! That's a long time your money has to last you.

How long? Put it this way: According to the most recent IRS census, a 55-year-old can expect to live another 30 years to be 85. That's the *average*. Half will live longer. Meaning if you're 55, you should plan for at least 40 years to be safe. There isn't any other way to slice it—that's a long time horizon. And remember—life expectancies are trending consistently higher. There's no reason not to believe that will end anytime soon. So in those 30 years to come, the average life expectancy will rise. Medical science marches on, often at an exponential pace.

Your expected time horizon will play a big role in what kinds of investments you choose. If you're really young—anything below, say, 50—that's a long time horizon and there's little point in even trying to determine your expected age. No matter how you slice it, you've got a long time ahead for your money to last you—at least 30 years and maybe more like 45 or 50.

The point: The time you need your investments to last is probably longer than you think, making time horizon a very important issue.

Table 8.1 shows all IRS data for life expectancy. Look yourself up and see where you're at.

And remember those are averages! Half will live longer. Now, do a couple calculations to personalize the average for yourself:

- **Heredity adjustment**: How long did your parents live? Their parents? Any trends? Add or subtract a few years from the average based on that.
- **Health adjustment**: Particularly vibrant? Something ailing you? Only you and your doctor will know for sure. Add or subtract a few years based on your judgment.
- **Medical advancement**: Medicine will advance. Consistently since the start of the twentieth century in the US, for every three to five years that pass, life expectancy goes up about a year. So you can tack a few years on there as well.

Now you've got a good hold on your goals, what the endgame is, and how long you have to get there. Now—and only now—can you start thinking about how your portfolio should look.

Table 8.1 IRS Life Expectancy

Age	Median Life Expectancy	Remainder of Life Expectancy
51	84.3	33.3
53	84.4	31.4
55	84.6	29.6
57	84.9	27.9
59	85.1	26.1
61	85.4	24.4
63	85.7	22.7
65	86	21
67	86.4	19.4
69	86.8	17.8
71	87.3	16.3
73	87.8	14.8
75	88.4	13.4
77	89.1	12.1
79	89.8	10.8
81	90.7	9.7
83	91.6	8.6
85	92.6	7.6
87	93.7	6.7
89	94.9	5.9

Source: IRS. 2007.

One last note before moving on: *Understand your ability to tolerate risk.* If you can't stand risk—if stock market volatility keeps you up at night, makes your belly quiver, and your bones tremble—you need to understand that about yourself. (We'll discuss risk in detail next chapter.) If you haven't yet thought much about self-understanding, go back and read Chapter 2 again.

If you can't stand risk—if stock market volatility keeps you up at night, makes your belly quiver, and your bones tremble—you need to understand that about yourself.

Be very honest with yourself and understand whether your emotions ultimately drive your decisions. I've talked to scores of clients who sell or buy at exactly the wrong times because they simply "can't stand" the rollercoaster of stock investing any longer. If that's you, be smart about it, know it about yourself, and act accordingly. In investing, there is no getting around the fact that risk and return are linked. Generally, the more return you seek, the more risk you take on.

True, stocks offer better long-term returns than any other highly liquid asset class. But they're also the most volatile. In my view, stocks are best suited for long-term investors. If you believe you're destined to be a stock investor, it means you're comfortable seeing your life savings sometimes dip 8 percent in a day (à la October 2008). If you can't take it, my advice is to stay out of the game and adjust your goals downward. Otherwise, you're going to blow yourself up very quickly by making moves based on emotion and not discipline.

THE LONG AND THE SHORT OF IT

There are two things investors should always remember: In the short term, stocks are volatile, but folks need their money to last a long time—that is, they have long time horizons.

Sadly, we too often forget this contrast. A lot of investors claiming to have a long time horizon still get tripped up by what I call a "trial period." Folks tend to revaluate their portfolios too often—like quarterly or even monthly. They make strategy adjustments based on those shorter periods. What nonsense! Their time horizon is long, not a few months! This is particularly true in bear markets, where folks begin questioning their long-term strategies after big paper losses.

Risk is understood in the financial industry as *volatility*. The antidote? Don't let arbitrary short-term periods derail your long-term plans. Stocks move every which way in the short term, but for most investors with the long run in mind, the short term doesn't much matter.

PORTFOLIO GOALS

Now that we have some idea about terminal value and time horizon in relation to personal goals, let's talk portfolio goals.

This is a key part of the discipline of investing—dividing your personal goals from market action. You need to make them work together but they are mutually exclusive.

This might sting a little, but you deserve the truth: *The market doesn't care about you.* It doesn't care what your goals are or if you win or lose or fall somewhere in between. It doesn't care if you're jubilant or afraid. It doesn't care about your situation and needs. The market's on its own schedule.

Stock markets don't care who you are or where you are in your time horizon—they're going to do what they do independent of your situation and needs.

Always remember that distinction. Stock markets don't care who you are or where you are in your time horizon—they're going to do what they do independent of your situation and needs. So you have to think about how the markets work independently of yourself. Therefore, don't let your personal situation color your outlook for the market. Be just as objective and callous in your appraisal of it as it is to you.

Successful long-term investors generally don't swing for the fences. Instead, they focus on a financial goal and remain disciplined toward that end. Important rule: *Stay focused.* Don't worry about what oth-

Important rule: *Stay focused.* Don't worry about what others are doing or what your neighbor says they're doing. Focus on achieving your goals.

ers are doing or what your neighbor says they're doing. Focus on achieving your goals. Whatever they do doesn't matter. Maybe Jim your brother-in-law got 30 percent last year investing in soybean futures. Good for Jim! But so what? You're not Jim. Stick with the strategies that make achieving *your* goals most likely. View market outcomes as independent of your personal needs. How to do it? Let's investigate a few ideas.

First Things First: Stocks Are the Best

A simple fact: Over 20-year rolling periods, stocks outperform bonds 98 percent of the time. Even better? Stocks blow bonds away by an average 4-to-1 margin in those epochs (930 percent for stocks versus 235 percent for bonds). So if your time horizon is 20 years or more, stocks are highly likely—as in 98 percent likely—to be the right choice (assuming those past measurement periods will generally resemble the future. See Chapter 7 for a refresher on patterns).

So, as a baseline to everything we think and do, understand that for long-term investors, stocks are generally the place to be. A few more points on the virtues of stocks:

- **Compounding returns**: I don't believe in magic, but I think the principle of compounding returns is a pretty wondrous thing. So much of investing is just about letting time work for you. Over long periods, returns compound, letting the market do the work for you as your assets grow. Of course, that should be true for any investment, not just stocks, but knowing long-term stocks deliver the best returns, compounding happens faster and bigger than most other investments if you stick with them.

- **No leverage!**: Many investments require leverage to get a sufficient return (as in, taking on debt). Real estate is an example. But higher leverage means higher risk. The really nice feature about stocks is you don't have to be leveraged to benefit from their superior returns. That may sound obvious and trivial, but boy is it nice! You can just own stocks free and clear without liability on the other side of your ledger.

- **Homemade dividends**: If you need regular income (most retired folks do), just selling stock—done the right way— can be as good as income from bonds or other forms of cash income (and sometimes even better for tax reasons).

- **Stocks are highly liquid**: Another one many take for granted. You can buy or sell your stocks just about any time you want. Compare that to some other asset class like real estate—good luck selling in and out of your home quickly without huge transaction costs and penalties.

- **Ownership**: When you buy a stock you own a share of something tangible. Most securities like bonds are contracts and obligations and don't feature ownership. Ownership is key because having a claim to the company's assets is what allows investors to get superior returns. In some ways, this is the most important feature of stocks—never forget that when you buy a share, it's not just a piece of paper. There are people and assets behind it.

Knowing all this, why do investors with long time horizons love bonds or other asset classes so much? Beats me. You'd have to ask them. It's true bonds are less volatile in the shorter run, so those with short time horizons may want the stability of bonds. Also, some just can't handle short-term stock market gyrations—also reasonable. Seeing the value of your assets fluctuate a lot day in and day out can be scary. But if you've got 20 years or more to grow your money, there is a very strong probability stocks won't be beaten by any other highly liquid asset class.

Know You Could Be Wrong—Or, Why We Diversify

I find the idea of "sleep well" investments silly. They're all the rage when markets are down, and then the reverse becomes true in big bull markets—folks start craving riskier assets. When times are tough, everyone wants to "sleep well" with their investments. Then, in good times, we want to juice it and go for it! Neither are good ideas. Why? Just the notion of "sleeping well" or "going for it" is a reflection of emotion and not discipline.

Diversification is a concept—it's the idea that blending negative or low correlated assets can reduce overall risk in a portfolio. The discovery of diversification is one of the true and lasting gifts from Modern Portfolio Theory.

For our purposes, there are essentially two kinds of diversification. The first is *diversifying across asset classes*. This is the one folks often get wrong. Standard advice is to always have some mix of stocks and bonds and cash (AKA, asset allocation). There is nothing fundamentally wrong with the idea—except we just saw a moment ago stocks outperform all asset classes over 20-year periods! So if you have a long time horizon, it doesn't make sense not to own all stocks. If you're 50 and own a lot of bonds, that's not diversification in my view—that's just missing out on a better return opportunity. In a situation like this, bonds and cash can be actually *riskier* than stocks because the lower returns lessen the chances of achieving your long-term goals (remember, we're always thinking in terms of goals).

One could argue it's necessary to diversify across asset classes to lessen the risk of stocks generally. I guess—but, again, the only way that makes sense is if you believe stock markets could one day head to zero or significantly underperform bonds and cash over long periods—we just saw how unlikely that is. Impossible? No, nothing is. But practically speaking, it is among the safest bets in investing.

The second way to diversify is *within the asset class*—in this case, stocks. Here is where the real value of diversification lies. Individual stock performance often features huge variance. Most of the time, an investor is looking to capture the benefits of stock markets, not necessarily just the individual company. So by diversifying properly, investors can enjoy the long-term benefits of stock ownership without carrying too much company-specific risk.

Perhaps the best way to achieve appropriate diversification is via benchmarking, which we'll discuss momentarily.

TRAIN YOURSELF TO SEE THE PORTFOLIO, NOT THE STOCKS

I've worked hard through my life not to care about individual stocks. Dumb thing for a stock analyst to say? No way! People always turn their noses up when I say this, but it's true and it works. If stocks are diversified properly in a portfolio, some will zig and zag—sometimes wildly. But if you're focused on your goals and not the minutiae, you know individual stocks aren't nearly as important as the overall portfolio performance.

Many will scoff, "How could you own that stock? It's down 50 percent this year! It's just stupid!"

I say, "What's the difference? That one stock might be down, but if my portfolio is up significantly in the period, then the goal was achieved. Why would I care about that one stock so much?" I certainly don't believe I have the foresight or knowledge to pick *only* "good" stocks. I expect some of them to fall. So should we all; that's why we diversify.

We tend to look at the parts more than the sum. In portfolio management, the sum of the parts—the portfolio itself—is all that matters. This is somewhat related to a classic behavioral quirk called *frequency bias*. This happens all the time in investing where folks tend to get more fixated on the frequency of something and ignore the magnitude of those things.

 We tend to look at the parts more than the sum. In portfolio management, the sum of the parts—the portfolio itself—is all that matters.

Often, the magnitude is more important. Unwittingly, most investors would prefer a portfolio that had every stock up but returned 10 percent overall instead of a portfolio that only had half the stocks up but returned 12 percent for the year. Perverse but true!

Train yourself to see the portfolio, not the stocks. It's a simple shift in perspective. The truth is you care a lot less about the stock that dropped a lot in your portfolio than you think you do. What you really care most about is portfolio performance.

THE TOP-DOWN PHILOSOPHY

We know that stock markets are CEAS (Chapter 5), and, therefore, the larger system must be observed for patterns instead of its constituent parts (individual stocks) to properly understand how things work. The practical way to exploit that idea is via the "Top-Down" investing philosophy. Here's a very brief crash course.

STOCKS ZIG AND ZAG TOGETHER

Much of this book has dealt with the importance of thinking about investing issues correctly so you don't waste time on less important things. To wit, amateur investors spend far too much time thinking about stocks and far too little thinking about the general market direction and their overall portfolios.

In portfolio management, the most important thing is forecasting the general market direction correctly. Not industries or sectors, and not individual stocks—the market itself. A number of studies have proven, over time, 70 percent of stock returns are derived from the decision between stocks or some alternative like cash or bonds; 20 percent of returns from which countries, sectors, and styles are chosen; and 10 percent from stock selection. *Only 10 percent from stock selection!*

Stocks are mostly directionally correlated—that is, stocks tend to move in the same direction of the market and the differences between them are usually an issue of magnitude more than actual direction. You might pick the greatest companies in the world, but if the market is headed downward, there's an overwhelmingly likely chance those stocks will head down along with it. This isn't true for the just US; it's true for stocks all over the world. It's pretty rare for a single major country to zig while others are zagging. Globally, stocks tend to zig and zag together.

Thus, good investors will spend the bulk of their time thinking about market direction and less time on comparatively trivial factors like stock selection. Figure 8.1 shows this concept graphically.

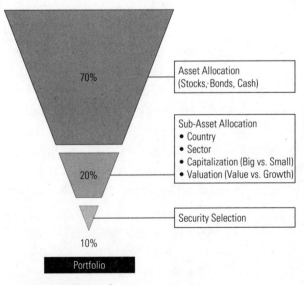

Figure 8.1   70/20/10 Funnel

It works like a funnel. First, you decide on market direction. If you think stocks are going up, then you invest in them. If down, then maybe you sit in cash or bonds for a while.

If you believe stocks are headed up, then decide on things like sectors, countries, and styles. There are usually significant correlations at each level. That is, choosing an Energy stock to invest in should have more to do with the fact that you believe Energy stocks as a category will do well because Energy stocks tend to be positively correlated with each other. Only after all that do you start thinking about actual stocks, picking the best from the funneling process mentioned previously.

The top-down approach makes intuitive sense in relationship to what we've learned so far about CEASs and how to forecast them (Chapters 5 through 7). Top-down portfolio management takes account of the larger system first, helping construct a portfolio of individual stocks based on the features and patterns of the system, not the constituent parts. That should be the correct way to forecast in a complex system. The very fact there are such strong directional correlations between stocks at the market, country, and sector level is a kind of corroboration of our hypothesis that stock markets are indeed CEASs—there are patterns of the system that are not detectable or explainable by just looking at the individual parts.

Top-down portfolio management takes account of the larger system first, helping construct a portfolio of individual stocks based on the features and patterns of the system, not the constituent parts.

A bottom-up process (picking the stocks first and worrying about the macro factors later) should ultimately have much more difficulty delivering value based on the perspective that stock markets are CEASs. Bottom-up can only capture the micro behavior, which we know isn't necessarily representative of how the larger whole moves.

Here are the four pillars of top-down portfolio management.

1. **Select an appropriate benchmark**: Managing a portfolio against a benchmark creates the connective tissue between your portfolio and the broader market and gives you a metric for judging your performance.

2. **Analyze the benchmark's components and assign expected risk and return**: AKA, assign a probability to the outcome to understand the potential returns relative to the risks. _allocation_

3. **Blend non-correlated or negatively correlated securities to mitigate risk relative to expected return**: Or, diversify.

4. **Always remember you could be wrong, so don't stray from the first three rules**: The heart of dealing with CEASs, which shift and change and sometimes create unpredictable outcomes. When this happens (and it will), a properly constructed portfolio will keep you from ruining your long-term goals.

The Joys of Benchmarking, or Why I Hate Stamp Collectors

I've seen a lot of portfolios in my day. Most of them look like collections, as if a portfolio of stocks were akin to collecting stamps or baseball cards. "Ooh! I just picked up the new stamp of Elvis at Graceland! Now my collection is complete!" Similarly: "Ooh! I just picked up that new hot biotech stock! Now my collection is complete!"

Too many folks hold stocks with little rhyme or reason other than they just think they're holding good companies. This is a very old way of thinking about investing. Today we know it's not just about the stocks you own, it's also about how those stocks relate to each other that matters.

Instead of the stamp collector model, use a _benchmark_. This is an important part of the top-down method.

What is a benchmark? It's an index that tracks the performance of a particular asset class. You've probably heard of the Dow Jones Industrial Average or the S&P 500. Well, those are stock indexes that track the performance of US stocks. So if you invest mostly in US stocks, those are potential benchmarks.

There are other types of indexes, too—bond indexes tracking the performance of bond markets; real estate indexes tracking the real estate market; commodity indexes tracking the price of everything from gold to corn. And so on. All benchmarks.

Benchmarking is about two things: *context* and *risk control.* Both are indispensible roadmaps for structuring a portfolio, monitoring risk, and judging performance over time. The context part means you have a way to judge your success. This is much better than picking some random goal out of a hat. If your benchmark returned, say, 10 percent this year, how did your portfolio do relative to that? Did it beat the benchmark or underperform it? This is key because it links you to stocks' long-term excellent returns. That's a great baseline to judge yourself by.

There are good benchmarks and bad benchmarks. Good ones are typically broad-based groupings of securities that are market-capitalization weighted (like the S&P 500 or the MSCI World Index, for example). Bad ones are the opposite—narrow, price-weighted indexes like the Dow Jones Industrials (just 30 stocks in this benchmark!) or the Nikkei 225.

I particularly favor the MSCI World Index because it's the broadest, most diverse measure of global stocks among developed nations available. Another good one is MSCI's All Country World Index (ACWI). (Check them out for yourself at www.mscibarra.com.) But, depending on your goals and needs, some other benchmark might be better for you.

Whichever benchmark you choose, choose wisely because that will dictate a great deal of your long-term performance and volatility experienced along the way.

What do you do with a benchmark? Analyze it—see what it's made of and structure your portfolio around that. For instance, let's say the S&P 500 is your benchmark. And in the S&P 500, 15 percent is Energy stocks. Many folks think a neutral position to Energy stocks is 0 percent. Nope! Neutral is 15 percent. If you're going to be neutral to Energy in the S&P 500, you'd need to carry 15 percent Energy stocks in your portfolio. If you want to be overweight, you'd hold more than 15 percent Energy; underweight would be less than 15 percent; and so on for each sector and style.

Tactically, a portfolio should be structured to maximize the probability of consistently trying to beat your chosen benchmark. This is inherently different than trying to "maximize" returns. Unlike aiming to achieve some fixed rate of return each year (which will cause disappointment when capital markets are very strong and is potentially unrealistic when the capital markets are very weak), a properly benchmarked portfolio provides a realistic guide for dealing with uncertain market conditions.

THE BIGGEST RISK

When managing money (yours or someone else's), you should never try to maximize returns. Surely that sounds strange! Who wouldn't want to make as much as they can? What other reasonable goal is there? But folks who think that way are setting themselves up for heartbreak. As always, risk and return are linked. So risk control is equally important in achieving your goals as the returns you're seeking. Look to maximize the likelihood of achieving your investment goals by beating an appropriate benchmark.

Please sear this into your brain: If you're a long-term investor with a goal of growing your portfolio over time, the riskiest thing you can do is hold cash. That sounds perverse and weird, I know. And that's the reason it's so important to understand.

One thing we know is stocks go up most of the time. Bull markets are much bigger and longer than bear markets. Sure, bears come around once every three to four years or so, but all the other years are bull markets. When you hold cash, you're essentially posturing yourself against stocks. That's rarely good because there's little sense in positioning yourself against something that goes up most of the time.

At an absolute minimum, you want to achieve market-like returns. Just think of what happens if you're wrong and the market goes up and you miss out—it becomes almost impossible to catch up and achieve a market-like result from there. It's especially important because your long-term goals will likely be tied to the expected long-term return on stocks. If you get in and out unduly, you also incur transaction costs and pay taxes. I've seen too many investors harm themselves in turbulent times because cash feels safe and they wait for "clarity" or "things to settle down." Bad move. Stocks are almost always safest for those with long time horizons.

Say it over and again like "Om"; mutter it in your sleep; write it 100 times on the chalkboard. I don't care how you do it, but get it in your head: *The biggest risk to most long-term growth investing goals is cash.*

Say it over and again like "Om"; mutter it in your sleep; write it 100 times on the chalkboard. I don't care how you do it, but get it in your head: *The biggest risk to most long-term growth investing goals is holding cash.*

Passive, Active, and Being Offensive

An interesting feature about all life: It moves. Cells move, blood moves, hearts beat, things run and grow. Anything in stasis is usually dead. Even trees are moving (just slowly). Life is all about dynamic movement. But then again, a lot of life is also pretty chaotic.

A key toward the market goal of beating a benchmark over time lies in being *dynamic*—never adhering for all time to a single investment idea. In other words, you cannot adhere to a single set of "rules" and hope to outperform markets over time. Being dynamic means switching in and out of stocks when it's time to be defensive—switching out of styles and sectors, countries, and so on.

Top-down investing is inherently dynamic. Starting out with an all-stock portfolio doesn't mean you have to be perpetually invested in stocks. Even though stocks are almost always your best bet over the long term, stocks do experience significant periods of decline, and it's good to have a strategy to deal with those periods.

Passive portfolio management is generally understood as buying and holding an index fund and doing nothing. Some investors are well served with this strategy. A passive investor knows so long as your time horizon is long enough you can get well in excess of 10 percent nominal returns from the market if you just buy shares and go to sleep.

Market timing is any attempt to allocate a sizeable portion of a portfolio to cash or other defensive securities to avoid a stock market downdraft and participate in the updraft. It gets a bad name. I've read

I HATE PERMA-BEARS

I just don't like perma-bears. Of course, they're always right at some point. As the old saying goes, "Even a broken clock is right twice a day." But the timing is everything. Famous bears are bearish forever. I've never known or heard of a wildly rich perma-bear with a consistent track record of beating the market over time without getting lucky somehow. Take a look at the Forbes 400 richest folks—not a single one was a perma-bear. All of them were ultimately optimistic and believed in the long-term growth of the economy and made their fortunes off that in some way or another. Since we know stocks go up about 68 percent of the years since 1926, a perma-bear by definition has little chance of beating the market. That means, if you're going to be anything, be a perma-bull and not a perma-bear. (But try not to be either if you can help it.) And anyway, perpetual pessimism can't be good for one's long-term health.

countless experts admonishing investors not to try and "time" the market. The truth is any active strategy is by definition a market-timing strategy. You can't turn bearish or bullish without timing.

Here's an example of how important market timing can be: Recall that former Fed Chief Alan Greenspan said the market was "irrationally exuberant" in 1996. Had you gotten out too soon, you'd have missed the big bull market of the late 1990s that was just getting revved up—it had at least three more years to run before succumbing. It wasn't until just about everyone jumped in—from taxi drivers to hair stylists to spiritual gurus to ballet dancers—that stocks headed down in 2000.

In fact, it's worth withstanding small losses in the short term in order to make sure your portfolio captures all the gains. But let's get something straight: There are good kinds of timing and bad kinds. Many investors jump in and out of positions far too often. Folks who try to time the market daily, monthly, even quarterly, are doing themselves harm. Markets are too risky and chaotic in the very short term. On balance, less is more when it comes to portfolio changes.

All active management is about market timing, but it isn't about perfect timing. This is part of the myth of exactitude in investing.

Investing is sometimes a messy business. Because markets are CEASs, there is no way to time things at the exact peak or trough. You should instead aim to get it mostly right and to make sure you're always exposed to equities when they are heading upward. In fact, trying to time an exact bottom or top is not only impossible, it can actually hurt you. Imprecision can be a good thing. If you can identify a bear and knock off, say, 20 or 30 percent out of a 40 percent bear market, you're far ahead of the game, and over time, that benefit will compound to big returns over the benchmark.

THE FOUR MARKET SCENARIOS

In Chapters 6 and 7, we discussed the thinking behind how market forecasting might work. Now here's a practical way to implement those thoughts.

There is no in-between a bear and a bull market. It's one or the other. Yes or no. In the practical portfolio management sense, there's no such thing as a flattish or stagnant period. Cute terms like mini-bears, bear cubs, and the like only muddle the issue. There are "counter-trend rallies" or "corrections" in bears and bulls, respectively, but those are different critters altogether. Those are fleeting and fast moving—don't try to time them. Just leave them be. Trying to time short swings in the market amid a larger bull or bear is perilous, treacherous, and foolish. Bears and bulls are the real beasts that matter for long-term portfolio performance. Those are all you should try to forecast. This little heuristic makes your decision much easier—all you need to do is decide which one you're in and plan accordingly.

As we saw in Chapter 5, in the short term, markets wiggle a lot. They feature disorderly, messy patterns. We know the global market averages about 10 percent yearly over long time periods, but we also know that returns rarely come out that way in a single year. Annual returns look much different than the average. Only a few times have stocks actually returned around 10 percent. Instead, most years gyrate wildly. Up a lot, down a lot, and everything in between. This is true globally.

Such disorder can cause a lot of chaos in your brain. Finding a simpler heuristic to think about annual market returns is important here. Despite all the variability, markets can only do four things: Go up-a-lot, up-a-little, down-a-little, or down-a-lot, as shown in Figure 8.2.

Go ahead, I dare you to find a single year when the market doesn't fall into one of those four categories. You can't! These four conditions simplify possible outcomes and help you see more clearly and make more disciplined decisions. They also provide a way for you to assert some self-control over your behavior. Your brain will try to tell you the market could do any number of things, but it can really only do one of those four. Why is this so effective? Because the important part of stock market forecasting is getting the general direction of the market right, not the exact magnitude. Precision isn't worth much in this game.

Notice the four market scenarios are about *looking ahead.* They're for making statements about the future. The four scenarios fit nicely into our forecasting goal of creating probabilities and generalizations for where the market is headed. We only need to assign a probable outcome to a limited number of situations.

But wait! We can make it even simpler. Only one of those four quadrants really matters: down a lot. Down a lot is the only time you should ever change your portfolio from stocks to some other category like cash. In the cases of up-a-little and up-a-lot, that should be obvious.

Up-a-Little Forecast (0% to +20%)	Up-a-Lot Forecast (+20% or more)
Down-a-Little Forecast (0% to −20%)	Down-a-Lot Forecast (−20% or more)

Figure 8.2   Four Market Scenarios

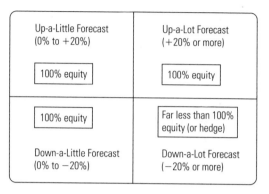

Figure 8.3   Four Market Scenarios with Portfolio Action

You think stocks will go up, so you should be in stocks. These four options are shown in Figure 8.3.

But why hold stocks in the down-a-little category? Because trying to avoid a little downside can really hurt you. Unless you know something big that others don't, you're too likely to be wrong—stocks go up and you miss out on the gains. Remember, the opportunity cost of missing out on stock rallies is the most dangerous of all things in the long-term investing game.

The difference between up a little and down a little can be a month's worth of psychological sentiment swing. It's too small and fast to try and predict. And what if you do get it right and the market drops 5 percent? Was it really worth the transaction costs of getting out and then back in later? Probably not unless you timed it exactly perfectly. Instead, in those down-a-little times, grit your teeth, take your lumps, and stay the course.

THAT GOOD-OLD HOME COUNTRY BIAS

Hey, I've got nothing against patriotism. Big fan of it, in fact. But when it comes to investments, I'm something of a fair-weather patriot. I like to spread my investments liberally around the globe according to my benchmark. Most investors don't do this, however. They tend to heavily weight their portfolios with what's familiar—their home

Table 8.2   US as Percentage of World GDP

	2007 GDP ($) Trillions	% of Total
US	13.8	25.3
Developed World Ex-US	23.7	43.4
Rest of the World	17.2	31.4
Entire Globe	54.7	100

Source: International Monetary Fund; as of October 2008.

country. Look at most US investor portfolios, and I can just about guarantee you the vast majority of holdings will be US-based. If it's a Brit, they'll have mostly UK stocks. And so on. It's called the *home country bias.*

Home country bias reminds me of rabid sports fans and their undying allegiance to their teams. Ever noticed with sports fans, it's always "we" and not "them"? As a fan of the Los Angeles Dodgers (the finest franchise in baseball), I would say, "We have a game versus the Giants today." As if I were somehow a part of the Dodgers. The same is true for home country bias. We think of ourselves as Americans and the rest of the world as "them." That's classic home country bias stuff. Work to take the "we" out of it and get as objective as you can when it comes to investments.

Table 8.2 shows some shocking stats—the US' relative size in the world. The US comprises only a quarter! Perhaps more shocking, emerging markets are a whopping third of global GDP. It's true for economic output and also more or less true for percentage share of the stock market, as shown in Table 8.3.

This tells us two important things:

1. If something is true about America, it's probably true about the rest of the world, too. This is especially apt knowing that global stock markets are highly directionally correlated. In fact, global trends are likely to be more powerful than the US. It's true that in the past, the US dictated the action in much of the world economy and markets, even today it is perceived as

Table 8.3   US as Percentage of MSCI World

	% of Total GDP
US	50
UK	10
Japan	10
France	5
Germany	4
Canada	5
Other Europe	12
Other Asia-Pacific	4

Source: Thomson Datastream as of September 30, 2008.

the world financial leader. But the fact is the US is likely to be dragged along with the broader world's trends today, not the other way around. It simply isn't economically big enough anymore.

2. You're doing your portfolio a disservice if you're not properly diversified on the global scene—only exposing yourself to a quarter of the available market.

A Quick Word on Emerging Markets . . .   Many think about emerging markets as something "other" than a traditional stock investment. And for decades, that would be right. But that is changing quickly or has already changed. Once upon a time, emerging markets were unstable countries with little infrastructure (financial or physical) and usually had an elite rich class and a vastly larger poor class, with small or no middle class. The old emerging market country would make products for cheaper than we could and then sell them to us.

All of that is still true to some extent. But it's a much different world today. At 31 percent of world GDP, emerging markets are building infrastructure quickly, have near-developed financial markets in many spots, and are generating internal demand via growing middle classes. Countries like Brazil, Russia, India, and China (the

"BRIC" countries)—but many others, too—are coming online as economic forces to be reckoned with.

The natural reaction to this? Panic and fear, of course. Outsourcing! Competition for resources like oil and steel! Yikes! It's just about all wrong. Real believers in capitalism know that emerging market countries are joining the world, trading freely, and making it a more efficient, interconnected place. It's expanding the world's ability to create wealth for all. Some of the changes may be dislocating in the short term, true, but in the long run it's very likely a good thing.

Emerging markets are here to stay and are a big part of the world's economy. It's well worth allocating a portion of any well-diversified global portfolio of stocks to it.

MISCELLANEOUS HEURISTICS

Here are a few extra miscellaneous investing heuristics, in no particular order . . . .

FEES ARE EXPENSIVE—INACTIVE IS GOOD

Let's say you're contemplating selling your stocks. You think stocks are headed down 10 percent in the next few months. Selling your portfolio probably costs 1 to 2 percent in transactions and commissions; getting back in will cost you another 1 to 2 percent. So right away, you're giving up a minimum of 2 percent of your money just to make the move. Fees and commissions add up!

So, of that 10 percent down forecast you made, you can only see 8 percent benefit. But that's if you time it perfectly! (No one ever does.) In that case, your benefit dwindles to a few percent . . . if any.

And what if you're wrong and stocks charge ahead!? (They're prone to do that in the short term by the way.) In that case, you're sacrificing fees and the opportunity cost of stocks' upward move. Doubly damaging!

Two lessons come from this example: First, don't trade very often, and do so only when you're dead certain it's the right thing to do. Holding steady is often the better move. Portfolio activity is usually anathema to investing success. Second, when it comes to market gyration, don't trade on anything other than what you perceive as big moves—20 percent or more in either direction. Small market moves are too difficult to dance around.

Don't Fire Your Bad Employees, or When to Buy and Sell Stocks

I've heard this logic a number of times: *"When I have a bad employee, I fire them. When I have a poorly performing stock, I sell it. Same thing."* That makes intuitive sense, but portfolio management doesn't work that way. Remember, the short term is full of noise and random price movements.

Never sell a stock just because it's down—sell it if the fundamental reasons you bought it have changed. If not, don't do anything. Often the short-term worst performers will rebound the hardest—in the medium to long term, the fundamentals will eventually be reflected in the price.

Many investors have a "target price" mentality when thinking about portfolio performance. Usually, a target price acts more as a self-imposed ceiling on gains than a logical portfolio tactic. If it's going up, let it run! Only sell if the reasons you held it in the first place have changed.

Give your investing ideas and individual stocks time—it often takes the markets months or years to fully appreciate the correct fundamentals. Don't abandon your strategies after a few weeks.

Conversely, know when you're wrong and let it go. The old "even broken clocks are right twice a day" saying is not something you want to follow, either. How will you know when to hang on or when to give in? It will vary on the situation but still comes back to the same issue of fundamentals. Keep checking back in with them. If those have changed or never panned out like you thought they would, then perhaps it's time to give up the ghost in pursuit of a better opportunity. But if they haven't and you still see great value others aren't, hang tough.

DON'T BE A CONTRARIAN

In Chapter 3 we talked about being the layer on top of the layer—not just watching market and economic action, but also watching the folks who watch those things to see what they do. Since what the market believes is already priced in (our Golden Rule), we should rarely if ever act in accord with the consensus. Often such a practice is called being a "contrarian."

Since what the market believes is already priced in (our Golden Rule), we should rarely if ever act in accord with the consensus.

Wrong! Contrarians do the opposite of what the consensus does. It could be the case that investors are bullish, but not bullish enough; or maybe they're bearish, but not nearly enough. You don't necessarily have to do the opposite of the herd. Heck, it's even possible the crowd is bearish for the wrong reasons, but you see completely different reasons to be bearish that aren't yet priced in and so are bearish with the crowd. Could happen! The discipline part is knowing the difference between using unique information or simply succumbing to the crowd.

BE ALONG FOR THE RIDE

I've never much cared for the mindset of trying to "beat" the market. It implies adversarial competitiveness and is a bad metaphor for investing. If you're a long-term investor looking to start a "war" with the market, you're going to lose decisively. Even Agamemnon couldn't keep it up for that long.

The market doesn't have to be an enemy to you. A better mindset is to be along for the ride. Successful long-term investing is not about victory over an enemy so much as it is about establishing the right conditions for success in the environment. No one will ever "master" the market. There will be randomness, there will be exceptions, there will be errors. There will be manias, pessimism, booms, busts, and you'll never get them all right. The idea is to do the right things generally to maximize the chances of achieving what you want. If you think too competitively about it, my guess is you'll end up taking chances you don't need to take.

SECULAR IS BLASPHEMY

You shouldn't forecast more than 12 to 18 months into the future. Ignore anyone trying to sell you a forecast that goes any further out than that, and especially beware of experts touting "secular" market cycles.

Let's say it's 1998, the bull market is in full gear, and you want to make your forecast for the next 10 years. You'd have had to call the tech implosion, September 11th, a war with Iraq, a credit crisis, rising oil and commodity prices, two Bush victories for the White House, and about 100 other significant events that affected stocks. Seems pretty unlikely anyone could do that.

So here we are today. Ready to make that 10-year forecast? Personally, I don't think you've got that kind of clairvoyance, and neither do I. If you call a 10-year "secular" bear market, you'd better hope to all that's holy you're right. Because if you're wrong, and you stay bearish for 10 years while the market doesn't cooperate (and remember, we've already shown most years the market goes up), you've essentially jettisoned any chance of reaching your long-term goals or even performing remotely as well as the market over time.

As we'll see, real bear markets usually don't last that long, and they last less than half the duration of bull markets. Anyway, it's unlikely markets price in much of anything longer than a few years into the future, so there's really no reason you should, either.

It doesn't matter if secular bear or bull markets exist or not. If you tried to actually manage your money with such a system you could never, ever accomplish your financial goals. God forbid you're wrong! A 10-year mistake would probably derail your investment goals for good.

It's impossible to forecast the long run with any accuracy. Anyone selling you a decade-long forecast is telling you more about what they don't know than what they do. Ultimately, stock prices are determined by supply and demand (Chapter 6). But no one can successfully forecast supply or demand more than a couple years ahead, at best.

It's impossible to forecast the long run with any accuracy. Anyone selling you a decade-long forecast is telling you more about what they don't know than what they do.

Demand for stocks can be extremely fickle and change on a dime—in a matter of a day, even. Supply is relatively unchanging in the short term but quite elastic in the long term. Again, no way to predict any of that looking ahead 10 or even 5 years, so it's best not to try.

So, again, think about what markets are likely to do 12 to 18 months in advance. So not daily or monthly or quarterly, but about a year or so into the future. This is a generalization to be sure, but one designed to deal with the fact brains weren't made to see the future well—they were made to fulfill immediate needs. True experts have a heck of a time just trying to forecast monthly or quarterly numbers. The world moves too quickly and evolves too rapidly (and the rate of market evolution is accelerating, too) for forecasters to have any confidence in a market outlook more than a year or so into the future. You're better off using your horoscope to make investments than you are to heed someone selling a 10-year forecast.

CHAPTER INSIGHTS

Of all the investing perspectives we've seen in previous chapters, most all of them point to making investing choices as simple and disciplined as possible for yourself.

- Using *heuristics*, or rules of thumb, is important for investing success, but they must be flexible, changeable, and appropriate to the situation.
- Goal setting and determining time horizon are musts before an investor can determine an appropriate strategy.
  - Personal investing needs and market behavior are different. Therefore, always make portfolio decisions independent of personal needs.
  - Personal goal setting requires:
    - Knowing the desired terminal value for your assets.
    - Determining the time horizon for your assets.
    - Most investors have longer-term goals, but often waste time and effort worrying about short-term issues.
- Over 20-year periods (long time horizons), stocks have overwhelmingly beat bonds throughout history—and by wide margins.

(Continued)

(Continued)

- Diversification is an important feature of portfolio management, but is often overdone.
  - Use diversification to blend non-correlated stocks to mitigate portfolio risk but still capture the superior returns stocks offer.
  - Do not use diversification to "balance" a portfolio between other asset classes just for the sake of doing so.
- The top-down investing philosophy jibes well with CEASs—complex, emerging, adaptive systems.
  - Stocks are usually directionally correlated, meaning they tend to move in the same direction. It is only magnitude that varies greatly.
  - An easy way to diversify properly and capture stock-like returns is via bench-marking to an appropriate index.
- Many fail to realize it, but the biggest risk to long-term investing goals is NOT being invested.
  - Stocks tend to rise over time; not fully capturing their gains makes it more difficult to achieve long-term goals.
- "Market timing" gets a bad name. Any strategy that is not "passive" is a "dynamic" asset allocation. No investing style dominates for all time, so it is important to be versatile and change allocation when necessary.
- A way to keep investing decisions simple is via the "four market scenarios."
  - Only in the "down a lot" forecast should a stock investor lessen his/her exposure to stocks.
- Think globally when stock investing. The US is a mere fraction of the global markets and GDP today. If you're not globally diversified, you're exposed to a tremendous amount of country-specific risk.
- Successful long-term managers usually have very low portfolio turnover. Inactivity can be an active decision and usually serves investors well. Move only when warranted—not on emotion or short-term gyrations.
  - Don't sell a stock just because it's down. Only buy or sell if the fundamentals have changed.
  - Don't be a contrarian—sometimes the consensus is wrong only in magnitude, not in market direction.
  - Even if such a thing as a "secular" market cycle exists (it likely does not), it's wrong to base a portfolio strategy on it because doing so imperils long-term investing goals.

9

THE NATURE OF RISK AND NAVIGATING MARKETS IN TROUBLED TIMES

If you wait to do everything until you're sure it's right,
you'll probably never do much of anything.
                                        —Win Borden

If fear alters behavior, you're already defeated.
                                        —Brenda Hammond

Risk is a way of describing an emotion. Search around on Wikipedia for "risk" and you'll find something interesting: There is no universal definition of risk. For each corner of the world that needs to account for risk, there's a different methodology and perspective.

But fear is a human universal. Of all the emotions, fear is one of the most powerful because in the wild, eons ago, we needed that emotional kick in the pants to motivate us to get out of harm's way to survive.

In today's world, this manifests itself in strange ways. The innate mechanism of fear has been overlaid in sometimes perverse ways in our daily dealings as "risk." We mask it by dispassionately calling it volatility or, sometimes, probability. But no calculation can quantify fear. Any amount of "risk" calculated by a spreadsheet ultimately has to be executed in the real world. By you.

But no calculation can quantify fear. Any amount of "risk" calculated by a spreadsheet ultimately has to be executed in the real world. By you.

There, risk suddenly becomes a question of guts. Can you keep your gumption on days of big market slides when your whole retirement is on the line just because your risk model says your strategy is foolproof? If not, no amount of math is going to help you sleep. Real risk goes directly back to *metaxis*—your ability to live with ambiguity and make a rational judgment without certainty. It's different in everyone. The ability to think clearly in the midst of danger varies widely among us. So a number telling you about risk isn't actually worth all that much. Risk calculations only work if you're cool enough to use them right—and even then they contain huge pitfalls.

Psychologically, humans perceive risk in weird ways. Daniel Kahneman and Amos Tversky won the Nobel Prize for *Prospect Theory*, which found that we humans hate losses 2.5 times more than we like an equal-sized gain. Often, risk has its most powerful effects after the fact. That's shown by the principle of *regret shunning*, where past losses clearly have an influence on future decisions. How we perceive an event matters for perception of risk—for some people, stocks might be a very risky investment (say, if the person has a short time horizon), but bonds might be riskier for others (say, those with long time horizons needing to reach a certain annualized rate of return). Thus, risk is often a relative thing and can be perceived differently depending on the person and perspective.

This chapter will deal with risk in a few forms—from its emotional impact on investors, to the hard calculations of finance, to what happens when everything goes haywire in markets (like the financial crisis of 2008).

RISK AND UNCERTAINTY

Some experts like to make a distinction between uncertainty and risk. Frank Knight, in his book, *Risk, Uncertainty and Profit*, described the distinction thusly:

> . . . Uncertainty must be taken in a sense radically distinct from the familiar notion of Risk, from which it has never been properly separated. The term "risk," as loosely used in everyday speech and in economic discussion . . . are categorically different . . . The essential fact is that "risk" means in some cases a quantity susceptible of measurement, while at other times it is something distinctly not of this character; and there are far-reaching and crucial differences in the bearings of the phenomenon depending on which of the two is really present and operating . . . It will appear that a measurable uncertainty, or "risk" proper, as we shall use the term, is so far different from an unmeasurable one that it is not in effect an uncertainty at all. We . . . accordingly restrict the term "uncertainty" to cases of the non-quantitive type.

The lesson? Never underestimate an academic's ability to describe a concept in as complicated a way as possible! Outside that, what Mr. Knight is saying is "risk" should be thought of as something truly known and quantifiable. If you flip a coin and bet on heads, there is a 50 percent risk it will come up tails. In other words, risk is a verifiable and known probability of an outcome. Uncertainty, on the other hand, is not having a way to credibly quantify probability—a truly unknown or unaccountable factor.

That's an important distinction for investors—it's good to know if you really understand a risk or not. Are the parameters and possibilities of the situation really known, or are things really more "uncertain" and unpredictable than they appear? In many cases, we fool ourselves with fancy calculations into believing we know the risk, when we're really just masking uncertainty.

In many cases, we fool ourselves with fancy calculations into believing we know the risk, when we're really just masking uncertainty.

Uncertainty isn't calculable—it is, as a statistician would say, "un-computable." Trying to assign a value to the unquantifiable only leads to heartache, but it's attempted all the time in investing. Investors should think about risk as a judgment about *uniqueness and uncertainty*— we know the future will never repeat the past exactly and there are clearly many unknowable things about what's ahead, but based on history, we can make some tacit assumptions about what is likely to happen.

I make it a rule never to trust risk calculations any more than any other kind of valuation: They are great descriptors to get context about a situation, and that's about it.

I make it a rule never to trust risk calculations any more than any other kind of valuation: They are great descriptors to get context about a situation, and that's about it. Financial calculations about risk generally use history to determine a future possibility. That isn't entirely useless, but it brings with it significant limitations.

There are essentially two ways to calculate risk. The first is via past data. These are things like standard deviation and beta (more on these in a moment). The second is risk assessment based on principles. An example: Stocks are riskier than bonds because the ownership feature of stocks makes shareholders more susceptible to losses since, in the event of bankruptcy, bondholders usually get paid first.

What do you notice about both of the following: Risk based on past data and risk based on principles? They're very similar to the two types of forecasts we covered in Chapters 6 and 7—risks based on probability and risks based on patterns. That means trying to determine financial risk is a variation of forecasting methodology. Why? Because both are statements about the future—about expected return. Thus, the same problems that apply to forecasts generally apply to assessments of risk in financial assets.

As mentioned in Chapter 1, when it comes to investing, math is most useful in helping to understand and describe abstract concepts and to help explain relationships between things, not to make exact calculations. To wit, my favorite definition of risk is simple and abstract:

Risk = (probability of an event occurring) × (impact of the event)

I think this is all you need to know about risk: the expected probability of something happening and its magnitude. Essentially, it's another way to say "expected return" (Chapter 6). There's little need for exact numbers because they cannot be obtained reliably anyway.

FINANCIAL RISK, OR WHAT HAPPENS WHEN YOU ASSUME

Risk is universal for investment—no exceptions. No risk, no return. Investment risk only varies by degree. I say this because there are still folks out there who believe otherwise. Many think of the yield on US Treasury bonds as a "risk-free" rate, which is a misnomer usually originating from the capital asset pricing model (CAPM). Even the "risk-free" rate is risky . . . it's just the least so. No matter if it's US Treasury bonds, CDs, or money market funds—they all bear some degree of risk; don't let anyone tell you otherwise. It's just that the risk of those instruments is very low—which in turn is why their yield is so low. Even the good-old US of A could default on its bonds one day—it's not impossible, just highly unlikely.

Financial analysts think about risk in myriad ways. We won't cover them all—just a few salient ones to challenge some textbook definitions of financial risk and uncover how limiting and often wrong they can be.

But we won't spend much time on calculation. Like we saw in Chapter 1, when it comes to understanding stock markets, math is best used as a way to describe and understand—not to seek precision in numbers. *The crux of risk is to understand it as a concept. It's usually the attempt to calculate risk that causes trouble.*

Most believe in the linear view of risk and return—the higher the risk, the higher the potential reward—that there should be a straight correlation between the two. In many cases there is, but there can often be anomalies (as described in Chapter 6 on probability). So we can't even take that relationship as ironclad. Later, we'll discuss *asymmetric risks*, where risk and return don't necessarily match up as they should.

Standard Deviation

In modern portfolio theory, risk is understood as the *standard deviation* of return. What's standard deviation? It's a measure of the dispersion among a collection of values or data. It is, essentially, taking a set of data and seeing what the norms are and how often a data point goes outside that norm and by how much.

So, on October 13th, 2008, when the S&P 500 jumped 11 percent, that was a "5 standard deviation event," which simply means stocks moved much more than usual in a single day. Most days, the market moves a few tenths of a percent in either direction. Those "normal" days would be very low standard deviation days because they are so similar to regular daily stock movements.

Systemic Risks

From standard deviation follows the idea of *systemic risk* and *non-systemic risk*. Systemic risk is about the system itself. It is any risk directly associated with the larger whole, like the stock market. Non-systemic means risk not directly associated with the larger system. Think of a specific company that may, for example, have a pending lawsuit against it. The lawsuit has to do with the company only and not the broader market. So the lawsuit is a non-systemic risk.

Systemic (market) risks are the ones investors should be most worried about because we know the vast majority of investing returns are a result of market direction. (Recall our discussion on the top-down investing philosophy last chapter.) Systemic risks are the ones that can move the whole market. Typical systemic risks are "the US budget deficit will sink the whole US economy" or "inflation will erode all asset prices." The nice part is most systemic risks are

Systemic (market) risks are the ones investors should be most worried about because we know the vast majority of investing returns are a result of market direction.

widely discussed, making them already priced in to stocks—our Golden Rule again! That means you don't need to worry about them in the same way the rest of the market does—you just need to decide if the market is over- or under-estimating that risk.

One of the main reasons to diversify a portfolio is to mitigate exposure to non-systemic, or company-specific, risks. This is very important when investing versus a benchmark.

BETA TO THE MAX

Next is *beta*—a measurement comparing the risk of a single security versus the risk of the market by using variance and co-variance. Beta can be calculated for a stock relative to the portfolio it's in, or even a whole portfolio relative to the broader market. (Figure 9.1 shows the calculation for beta.) If a stock has a beta of 1.0, that means it tracks the market perfectly—step for step. A beta less than 1 means it's less volatile than the market, and a beta above 1 means it's more volatile than the market. Theoretically, high-beta stocks are riskier but should provide higher returns than low-beta stocks.

This seems simple enough, but something quite sneaky has just happened—the introduction of beta as a standard measurement of risk has changed the game of risk perception. How? Our original notion of risk was defined as the probability of an event happening and its magnitude. Beta is something different. Beta is a *relative* measurement—risk based on something else. Beta for stocks is not stand alone, but dependent on the whole category of stocks. *Beta is context dependent on the stock market itself.*

This is stunning! Our search for an accurate and appropriate way to measure stock market risk has led us to a very circular way of thinking—assessing the risk of a stock based on the universe of stocks it is a part of!

This places huge importance—more than ever—on understanding market direction. Why? Because a stock with a beta of 1.0 would seem hugely benign and "riskless," but all it really means is it mimicked the market perfectly. Well, what if the market was down 30 percent that year? I'd hardly call that riskless!

$$\beta_\alpha = \frac{\mathrm{Cov}\,(r_\alpha,\, r_p)}{\mathrm{Var}\,(r_p)}$$

Figure 9.1 Beta Calculation

It's also worth noting this definition of risk is completely based on the past. It assumes the past behavior of both the market and the stock itself will be similar in the future. Big assumption!

THE SHARPE RATIO

The Sharpe ratio is a way to measure return versus variance. Put another way, "How much return did I actually get for the risk I took on?" It's kind of the next evolutionary step after beta. Sharpe ratios measure return versus a "unit" of risk. Have a look in Figure 9.2.

The Sharpe ratio measures risk adjusted return. It measures return on an asset (like a stock) in relationship to a benchmark asset (like the risk-free rate of return), all divided by standard deviation. It's sort of putting all the concepts we just described into one big pot and stirring. The results are thought by some to be able to ascertain an "expected" value for future return as well.

Some believe this is a better way to judge risk—institutions seem to love it as their risk metric of choice. But there are still big problems. First, notice "expected value" jumped into the equation. Yipes! Expected value is, by definition, an *assumption about the future*. Expected value in this example is essentially an arbitrary value—and worse, it's a *circular* arbitrary value because it's being ascertained relative to the market. What a jumbled mess that is! To me, that's a very poor way to conceptualize and understand reality.

Why can't we get out of this circular mess and find some absolute measurement of risk? From the beginning of this chapter, we said risk is a *concept*, not a thing. Concepts (as with most things we call "knowledge") can generally only be understood in context and relative to other things. There cannot be a stand alone measure of financial risk because, without something to compare it to, risk is essentially meaningless.

$$S = \frac{E\,(R - R_f)}{\sigma} = \frac{E\,(R - R_f)}{\sqrt{\mathrm{Var}\,(R - R_f)}}$$

Figure 9.2   Sharpe Ratio

Comparing asset classes to each other (when possible) is just as important—it's better to know if stocks generally will outperform bonds. But that is often very problematic because when comparing bonds and stocks, for instance, it's tough to find good apples-to-apples comparisons since they are different types of assets. That's why we're so often locked into the circular logic of comparing like assets to themselves to judge risk.

The moral of these examples? Be wary of what others say is risk, and judge it for yourself. These metrics can be very helpful, no doubt. They're good for understanding diversification within a similar asset class and help us understand the risk we are taking within a portfolio. The Sharpe ratio is a good step forward because it is able to at least compare returns to something like a T-bill or similar. But it still clearly has many shortcomings.

Value at Risk (VaR)

Here's a real-world example of the failure of math-based risk metrics.

Many believe the 2008 financial crisis can, in large part, be traced back to a bad mathematical equation. Throughout history, many financial collapses have been at least partly caused by undue faith in math or by balance sheet trickery.

In the 1990s, accountants and statisticians developed a financial metric "value at risk," or VaR. VaR uses history to calculate variances and covariances to calculate risk for a security. VaR claimed it could generate a 99 percent probability that an investment could not lose more than a certain amount over a certain time period. Figure 9.3 shows what the equation looks like. In some ways, it is not so far from the Monte Carlo simulations we studied in Chapter 6, as it uses past relationships to generate probabilities about the future.

VaR is used widely in finance for risk management and measurement. It's even applied often to non-financial risk assessments. In short, VaR is a measure of risk that takes into account a specific

$$VaR_\alpha = \inf\,[l \in \mathfrak{R}: P(L > l) \leqslant 1 - \alpha] = \inf\,[l \in \mathfrak{R}: F_L(l) \geqslant \alpha]$$

Figure 9.3   Value at Risk Formula

portfolio's assets, the probability of an event (usually the failure of the asset), and time horizon. Essentially, it's a way to calculate the risk of a rare or exogenous event—if an asset's value will go bad or not.

Banks used the VaR for years to compute the risk of holding debt securities like collateralized debt obligations (CDOs). Supposedly, VaR would take the "worst case" and see if a bank has the ability to cover losses and maintain capital requirements. Over the years, VaR became an industry standard and executives put huge faith in its validity.

But there's a big problem with VaR, and with any mathematic calculation of risk, for that matter: *It can't account for extreme or unprecedented events.* It is classic number-jiggering to achieve a desired outcome, not a reflection of reality. It's impossible to assign a reasonable probability to an "exogenous" event, and always has been. *Exogenous* means something that originates outside of the local environment or is extraneous in origin. It is an event outside the model. Frankly, financial mathematics today doesn't know how to deal with the exogenous. It's sort of like asking, "What is the afterlife like?" There's no way to know because it's outside our ability to perceive or measure. So exogenous is, by definition, non-predictable.

That accountants and executives ignored this fact represents huge hubris: They fell into the trap of believing a math calculation could provide safety in a hugely complex system like credit markets. They trusted they were safe because "the data said so."

Of course, reality said otherwise. Debt and CDOs generally imploded in 2008—differently and beyond anything any math could predict or even rationalize. Some might argue that it wasn't the math's fault; it was the human's fault for trusting it or using math in ways it shouldn't be used. It matters little either way. If VaR is right, it is only right in theory. In reality, it failed its job.

This section on financial risk metrics is called "What Happens When You Assume." We all know the joke. Apparently, statisticians and financial executives don't, though. In the quest for more "sophisticated" risk metrics, all that ended up happening was increased circularity, ambiguity, and greater assumptions.

TAKE YOUR EMOTION OUT OF IT

On any decision you make, try to take your feelings out of it.

I admit that's tough to do. Actually, it's impossible. One of the greatest and longest held myths about how humans think is the notion that "reason" and "emotion" can be separated. They can't—they're one and the same.

If you do an fMRI scan on anyone's brain, you'll quickly learn there is no exclusively reason- or emotion-based thought. True, a lot of cognitive emotion is found in the so-called limbic and reptilian parts of the brain, and of course reason mostly exists in the neocortex—but all thoughts use various portions of the brain, not just one. You can't be purely "objective"—you simply don't have it in you. We are always and everywhere trapped inside our bodies—we can never really have a point of view except our own.

Emotions have a pejorative context when it comes to investing and science. "Don't be emotional! Take your emotions out of it!" That's a silly way to think about emotion, which provides the texture and meaning of life. You darn well wouldn't want life without emotions—to simply be a computing machine. Moreover, emotions are what provide us motivation, a key ingredient in any decision we'll ever make.

But it is also true they can get your investments into trouble. The best way to get objective is to find ways to go outside yourself. That's what science is for—a controlled way to take subjectivity out of the equation. I've never—ever—heard of or known about a long-term successful investor who acted consistently on intuition and emotion (though I've known many who've lost a lot of money that way).

Use the rigors of the scientific method as often as possible to help you, and always ask yourself: Is this how I *feel*, or is this what I *know*?

IN TROUBLED TIMES

We think of risk most often when markets tank. Troubled times, like the financial panic of 2008, are unfortunate and quite unusual but not totally without precedent. Bear markets happen, and when they do, our reactions tend to be similar. This section outlines a few observations about what to do when the sky feels like it's falling.

FOR EVERY BEAR, A BULL

It's eternally informative to behold folks—time and again—abandon tried and true investing wisdom in favor of panic and fear when times get tough. We so easily forget and eschew principles in the face of fear. But this much has always been true: *Every bear market is followed by a bull market.*

We so easily forget and eschew principles in the face of fear. But this much has always been true: *Every bear market is followed by a bull market.*

Long term, when is risk highest? When folks are happy, complacent, and fearless—that's usually when stocks are most apt to plunge. When is risk lowest? When folks are grumpy, actively selling, and fearful—usually shortly after stocks jump higher.

It's always and forever been this way, yet we throw it out the window on a whim when times start looking bleak. That this happens in virtually every bear market is a stunning statement about the emotional component of risk and the archetypal power of human behavior. It's near universal that investors lose their cool in bear markets. Just the existence of bear markets proves that many long-term investors suddenly (and irrationally) become short-term investors for a period.

The simplest, oldest wisdom in investing is to buy low and sell high. Get in when there's "blood on the streets," and so on. Instead, in just about every bear market in history—especially near the end—investors will proclaim the "death" of equities. In this new and dreadful world, stock prices cannot rise highly ever again—we have entered a "new paradigm" where cash and bonds are kings. Happens every time!

When fear begins to overtake reason, investors fall prey to the "do something" reflex. Our Stone Age minds were made to react to fear—any sign of threat and our bodies get ready for action. That's great for living in the wild with a saber-toothed tiger on your heels, but it makes for horrible investing decisions.

When fear begins to overtake reason, investors fall prey to the "do something" reflex. Our Stone Age minds were made to react to fear—any sign of threat and our bodies get ready for action. That's great for living in the wild with a saber-toothed tiger on your heels, but it makes for horrible investing decisions.

In fearful times our minds get warped. It feels like implosive market dives have lasted forever when, in truth, it's only been a few months—fleeting in the scheme of things. Perversely, a recovery also seems distant or impossible. A total time warp—no end and no beginning! How? Regularly, market action has a certain place in your life when times are normal. But in "crisis" times, worry takes energy and sops up a lot of conscious thought. That increased conscious effort changes our perspective and makes it seem as if more time has passed than really has. (Bad days are always the longest, good days seem to just whiz by, no?) An excellent study of our (mis)perception of time is James Gleick's *Faster: The Acceleration of Just About Everything.*

What is the financial definition of risk and fear? Movement! Toward the end of bear markets, volatility tends to spike—freaking folks out good. A tranquil market is a less risky, less scary place. The best thing to do through such turbulence—always—is just sit tight. It will pass. Trying to navigate through a volatile market usually only gets you whipsawed. When things get their craziest, sit tight and know a bull market is not far behind. That bulls follow bears is one of those observations that's so obvious, we often miss it or forget it.

Legendary investor John Templeton said, "The four most dangerous words in the English language are 'It's different this time.'" With stocks, it always feels different this time, yet never is. Every bear market in some sense is unique—the world changes and causalities from downturns can be similar but never exactly the same. Yet human reaction to bears is similar and near archetypal. Bear market doomsday talk is the trickster market out to get you. It wants you to believe this time is different and stocks will never recover. If you're going to believe anything, believe that bulls always follow bears.

KEEP THE STRATEGY, CHANGE YOUR MIND

After a spate of selling, you can always find a bevy of reporters gleefully asking, "Is it time for a new strategy?" The argument goes that, since stocks have been down awhile, maybe it's time to start asking whether the old tried and true methods of stock market investing should be abandoned.

This is absurd. It's associated with the idea that "it's different this time." Tried and true investing strategies are designed to deal with turbulent times. Bear markets aren't unprecedented events—they happen a couple times every decade on average.

A sound strategy should not change—if it's a good one, it will carry you safely out the other side. It's your attitude that needs an adjustment. Often, an investor will shun regret for making a bad decision and blame the strategy rather than him/herself. *Sometimes a perfectly good strategy will be wrong.* The fact is, no strategy will always be right—that's foundational to managing based on probability.

Sometimes a perfectly good strategy will be wrong. But the fact is, no strategy will always be right—that's foundational to managing based on probability.

Navigating bear markets requires guts to get the glory. It's directly linked to discipline as self-knowledge. The vast majority of bear market folly is emotion based, not fundamental. An emotion-based error is always your fault.

The best investors will usually have a proven track record of beating the market over time. *But not every time.* Trying to be right all the time in investing is like trying to hit 1.000 in baseball—no one's ever done it and no one ever will. Instead, look to have a great batting average. In investing, if you can get two-thirds of your calls right over the long haul, you're a super-duper mega-star. One of the best of the best. The vital thing is to situate yourself in an investing framework that accounts for those human foibles of yours and mine.

It also means you've got a full third of the time to be wrong. That's the part where folks are most uncomfortable and tend to abandon their longer-term strategy. In fact, the best investors stick to their guns even when wrong, knowing their emotions will fail them in tough times, but their disciplined strategy will work over the long term.

When the best investors are wrong, they don't shun regret—they objectively try to understand where they went wrong and learn from it.

When the best investors are wrong, they don't shun regret—they objectively try to understand where they went wrong and learn from it. If you're counting on a strategy that promises to avoid every market downturn, you're in for one heck of a rude awakening.

Sidestepping the Bear

If you want to beat the stock market over the long term, identifying and sidestepping a bear could be the most important thing you can do. Why? Remember back to our discovery that nearly 70 percent of portfolio returns over time will come simply from getting the market direction right. So knowing if it's a bear or bull is the key decision.

To call a bear, you usually have to be of a different opinion than the consensus. That might sound fine and good on paper, but when you're really faced with that decision, it takes chutzpah to make the right call. I have empathy for most investors. When your retirement is on the line—when the future of you and your family is right there in your hands and you see stocks dropping 5 or 8 percent in a day—it's not easy to approach the situation without emotion.

We take comfort in being with the pack and get anxious when we stand alone. Humans are communal animals. Couple that with the pressure of seeing your life savings sink, and it's near impossible for most folks to make rational decisions in bear markets. Hence, emotion-based reactions commonly happen.

Again, we return to the discipline of investing and the importance of self-knowledge. To really beat the market you need to be comfortable being alone—having your neighbor tell you you're insane, reading headline after headline that's contrary to your view. It's a lonely, lonely road and will usually feel very uncomfortable as it happens.

Here are a few tips to sidestep bears.

Bears Are Rare!   Obvious but true: Stocks go up most of the time. Bears are rare! That may sound strange or contradictory—just a few pages ago I said bear markets generally happen a couple times a decade! But a different way to look at it is stocks go down less than 33 percent of years. True, a calendar year's results do not determine a bear market. But that's vital information for anyone who hunts bears. It tells you most of the time you need to be fully invested and only worry about big downdrafts on limited occasions. If you miss calling a bear market, there is a right way to be wrong and a wrong way to be wrong. Actually, there are two right ways.

The first right way to be wrong has to do with time horizon. If you've got anything like a decade or more left in your time horizon, and you're not sure which way the market might head in the immediate future, *the right way to be wrong is being fully invested.* Why? As a baseline, you want to always ensure you get a market-like return over the long run. The only way to do that is by being invested. Remember: Long-term stock market returns are inclusive of all the bear markets in history. Even if you sit through a big bear fully invested, eventually you will reap gains in stocks if your time horizon is long.

The worst thing to do is to be out of the market when it goes up. Since we know stocks go up far more often than down (in magnitude and duration), the best thing to do is be in. Only get out when you're absolutely sure it's the right thing. Not holding stocks is the only possible way you can fail to achieve long-run stock market returns.

If you don't call a bear upfront, ride it out. You can't call a bear market after it's already happened, yet folks have a nasty habit of sell-

 If you don't call a bear upfront, ride it out. You can't call a bear market after it's already happened, yet folks have a nasty habit of selling at the end instead of the beginning of a bear.

ing at the end instead of the beginning of a bear. No good is done in selling at the end of a bear. Folks get "whipsawed," selling at lows and locking in losses, only to see the markets shoot upward as the new bull begins. Double whammy! Getting whipsawed is perhaps the greatest and most costly of all investing mistakes.

Just as bad: Investors who choose to stay out after the bull market recovery has already started so they can wait "for things to become clearer." Stock markets will usually recover long before economic data. Why? Since we know markets discount known information and look to the future, current negative headlines are less relevant than what happens in the near future. Since economies are spiral and recoveries follow declines, a future recovery will be priced into the markets before the actual economic data reflect it.

The second way to be right about being wrong is trade activity. When in doubt, do nothing. The more trading you do, the more likely you are to make mistakes. Volatility is uncomfortable, and that's why people often blow their portfolios to smithereens. No matter how bad things are in the markets, you have the power to make things worse by acting rashly. It's an active decision to sit tight, particularly when others are panicking around you.

This principle is illustrated in the war of the sexes: Women are, by far, better investors than men, and ostensibly for one main reason. A study by Brad Barber and Terry Odean demonstrated that men trade 45 percent more than women do and annually do about 1.4 percent worse because of that increased activity.

Why? Men are generally more over-confident than women and believe they can do better, so they trade more. Hence, they do worse. The lesson: Only make a move when you're absolutely sure of it. Most of the time, we have no good justification for trading other than emotion.

The lesson: Only make a move when you're absolutely sure of it. Most of the time, we have no good justification for trading other than emotion.

The only times to trade are when you know something the consensus isn't fully appreciating or if the reasons you once held a stock have fundamentally changed—that is, when you have unique information. That should be darn rare. Do you really know more than the person on the other side of the trade? Why presume you can make a smarter move off the same information everyone else has? Are you so much smarter or just overconfident? Overconfident types are the market's greatest prey.

FORMULA FOR A BEAR

The causes of most bear markets can be distilled into one sentence: *A negative fundamental event that will take most investors by surprise.* That means:

- The negative event has to be big enough to move the whole market. It can't be something small.
- It has to take the consensus by surprise. That is, it can't be widely discussed because if it is, it will already be reflected in stock prices (the Golden Rule).

The causes of every bear market are different, yet there are archetypal, or common, elements consistent in most. Calling bears requires both knowledge of history and a correct appraisal of the current environment. That means there are no silver bullets to calling a bear, but there are common elements we can look to for help. Mastering the common elements—and how they can differ or even diverge from the norm—is a key to forecasting most bears.

But not all of them! Remember from Chapter 5, since economies and markets are complex and emergent systems, unpredictable events often occur. So calling a bear market correctly is important, *but just as important is doing the right things when you fail to call one.*

Most bear markets throughout history fit the following formula.

Unforeseen Negative Fundamentals   ⟶   Monetary Policy Error

                                   Fiscal Policy Error

            +   Trade Policy Error

                                     Geopolitical Instability

                                     Changes in Regulation and
                                             Government Involvement

Euphoric or Complacent Sentiment
_____

= Bear Market!

Not only must we get a negative unforeseen event, but it must be widely unappreciated. The fact is most worries aren't worthy of a bear market. It takes the biggest, baddest, and most unforeseen events to cause one. Most worries get priced in and bull markets move up the wall of worry.

As of this writing, we're still knee-deep in the bear market that started in 2008. Time will tell, but already some of these elements are culprits.

Bears and Recessions. It is true that most bear markets are paired with economic downturns. But bear markets will start before economic data turn south, and stocks will recover before economic data turn positive. Similarly, positive outlooks and media headlines will persist long after the bear's already started, and negative outlooks will continue well after a new bull market begins.

Why? The Golden Rule. Stock markets price in the future—they look ahead. Therefore, they'll begin moving long before any headline or economic report can. Economic data are a reflection of the past. It may be well and good to intend to sell your stocks before a recession comes, but economists have never been able to forecast that very well. So it's very difficult to do. We only know a recession definitively in hindsight. By the time one is recognized, the big market drops have already happened.

Also, it's worth noting there is no useful difference between a recession and a depression. Recently, I read financial articles saying, "Economists are wondering if the current data could spell recession or even depression ahead." There is no information in that statement. Depression is not a technical term—it's just an adjective for a severe recession. There is no good investing reason to spend time wondering if something is technically a depression or not. Labeling an epoch a "depression" doesn't trigger some kind of magic rule about how stocks will behave. Instead, focus on the future and position yourself for when the bear will end.

Bubbles and Panics Are the Same.   Believe it or not, bubbles and panics are basically the same. My favorite definition of a bubble is when folks are too scared NOT to dive in for fear of being left behind. Tech stocks in 2000 and the US housing market circa 2005 are great examples. Conversely, a panic is when folks are too scared to own anything at all. True panics are rare, but the second half of 2008 is about as good an example as it gets, as many investors were willing to take a negative return on US T-Bills—literally pay the government for the right to own a short-term bond—because it seemed to be the safest place for cash at the time. This is simply not rational.

Both these situations are resultant of unrealistic expectations—heaven and hell. Fundamentals take a backseat and sentiment rules. The normally heterogeneous marketplace of diverse opinions becomes a homogeneous tide of polar opinion. Fear can be just as powerful as greed—sometimes more so—but they are both emotions and non-rational and never last forever.

The Panic of 2008: The Simplest Choice.   In times of panic, investing choices get simpler. That doesn't mean they will feel any easier, but the normally vast complexity of the investing landscape dwindles down to a mere two options—to be or not to be (in stocks).

In May 1932, shortly after stocks had shed 86 percent from the 1929 highs, stockbroker Dean Witter wrote a note to his clients: "There are only two premises which are tenable as the future. Either we are going to have chaos or else recovery. The former theory is foolish." Mr. Witter was absolutely right in both forecast and logic. This will always be true when times seem darkest.

Most often, investors must be deliberate and weigh many factors about the economy, politics, sentiment, and so on before deciding to be invested or not. Will the economy keep growing? If so, by how much? What about interest rates? Inflation? Taxes?

But when sentiment takes over, that's all out the window. When stocks go into freefall, only two options matter:

1. The world is ending and markets are headed to zero.
2. Eventually, stocks recover.

The second half of 2008 and into 2009 saw a true global market panic—the kind one can usually only fathom or learn about in history books. One thing we know about manias and panics alike is that in the short term, they can be irrational on the upside and downside. Rarely are they of the proportion and magnitude of 2008, but an overshot is an overshot. Long term, markets right themselves to reflect reality.

I wouldn't describe 2008's investor sentiment as "worried." Fear isn't really the right word, either. In that time, I noted a shift from fear and uncertainty in 2007 to staid overconfidence and surety we were doomed later in 2008. That kind of calcified, homogeneous sentiment points to irrational market behavior.

Times like these are no-brainers and present simple choices: It's either doomsday or we're near a new beginning. Nothing else! If you believe we one day will recover, such times are super to buy and hold stocks. In irrational times, forget all the subtle gradations and considerations about government actions and economic results. Save those for some other day. To believe stocks are going to zero is against all history and says you truly believe "it's different this time." I wouldn't bet on that, no matter how bad it might feel at the moment.

Crucibles. I find it interesting that human sacrifice has always existed in mankind—we've just gotten a bit more refined and sophisticated about it over the years. Anytime something goes bad, we need to blame someone and burden them with the crucible of failure. It was not our fault—it was theirs.

In tough times, CEOs (often heroes in boom times and gracing the covers of business magazines) become villains and subject to witch hunts. Make no mistake—there are wrongdoers out there, always will be. And when we find them, they should be punished. But in times of crises, people often get blamed unduly for investing losses. It's a simple fact.

Note that most regulatory policies are *responses*. That's because capitalism works faster to weed out weakness than any system of central command. By definition, then, a response to a problem is punitive to those who were already following the law to begin with! There is seldom much point in this. The responses of a central command system (the government) are rarely as good as free-market responses—which are frequently quick and brutal enough as it is.

I can't speak for everyone, but I've never really seen the government do anything well when it comes to financial intervention. I find it perverse and tragic the public looks to them for stability and answers in times of financial crisis. Their involvement is usually a foreboding signal.

Government involvement can sometimes work, but clumsily and at the great cost of future dynamism and innovation in the economy. To see this, just observe Europe over the last decades. Growth? Yes, but slower than the rest of the world and even less quick to adapt to the changing economy.

One can argue reasonably either way whether the government "saved" the financial system in 2008. Some moves were appropriate, others probably exacerbated the situation on balance, it's intervention probably did more harm than good. It's worth noting, however, that the central banking systems of the world are highly developed, agile, and almost undoubtedly a positive stabilizing force in the financial system today.

In any case, it's impossible for the government to predict a "crisis." The best minds in the world all thought the global credit situation was fine when 2007 began. I'm not sure why or how we'd think the government could monitor it more successfully than the world's leading financial thinkers. Heck, former Treasury Secretary Henry Paulson brought in outside financial minds to run the government rescue program!

In some form, much new regulation goes back to regret shunning. Most folks are angry when risks don't go their way and they lose money. They'd love the government to step in and recoup their losses. We all want guaranteed returns. But the more governments move to "guarantee" assets and stem risk, the less return we will all be able to get in the future.

I certainly don't know what happens next in the world. I do know there will be another boom and a bust to follow—probably many! Wars! Terrorism! It will happen. But if the past is any indication, from all that also comes greater prosperity. Two steps forward, one back. On and on.

The future will be shaped by billions of players in an infinitely complex global economy, each acting in their own self-interest, and locally to form a system more intelligent and versatile than any single person. We will discover and mass produce innovations heretofore never thought of, and on a scale none of us can imagine just yet. And in the midst, our system will correct itself—so long as we are wise enough to let it do so, painful as it may seem in the moment.

The Amazing (and Destructive) Adaptability of Capitalism. We learned in Chapter 5 that capitalism works so well because it is, essentially, a recognition of the power of emergent systems independent of central command.

When inefficiency or excess is recognized, capitalism is swift to squelch it—usually long before any entity like government gets a whiff of it.

An important feature to remember, however, is capitalism has a brutal and decisive destructive side to it: *adaption.* When inefficiency or excess is recognized, capitalism is swift to squelch it—usually long before any entity like government gets a whiff of it. This is somewhat analogous to Joseph Schumpeter's idea of *creative destruction.* In the end, this seemingly vicious process of fat trimming is a wonderful thing for society at large—it paves the way for better systems and efficiency, greater innovation, greater wealth creation, and broadly higher standards of living.

So, in some perverse sense, we ought to cheer the times capitalism steps in and wipes out inefficient or wrong practices. I stress "perverse" because in reality, the process isn't pleasant. The Tech bust beginning in 2000 and the wiping out of Wall Street in 2008 are not exactly things to get jubilant about. Recessions and job losses aren't what we wish for.

But in the end, we're much the better for allowing capitalism to correct itself. Recall what we saw in Chapter 7 about cycles: They're generally bad metaphors. The capitalistic world doesn't chase its tail forever in a circle; it moves up in a *spiral*—two steps forward, one step back. An important feature of the spiral metaphor is that capitalism creates wealth—it doesn't just divvy it up.

A common investor error is to get "anchored" to one part of GDP. In the early 2000s, many saw residential housing growth as the driver of economic growth and got anchored to it. As if, for all time forward, housing would be the economy's saving grace. But when housing began dropping precipitously in the middle of this decade, we found that other things like consumer spending, commercial real estate, and a boom in exports picked up the slack and GDP continued its growth despite a housing recession for some years. How? Capitalism adapted and found ways to grow without the housing boom. We tend to underestimate just how fast capitalist economies and markets can correct themselves independently. In times of crisis, the world's citizens don't just sit there and allow events to beat them about the head—they respond and adapt.

In tough times, folks always have trouble envisioning a brighter future. But the fact is, envisioning the future accurately is tough no matter the environment. Today's vibrant kings of the finance jungle will be tomorrow's dinosaurs—extinct and replaced by new life, new species. Yes, the independent Wall Street investment banks are extinct, but that only means the path is clear for a new breed. It does not mean financial life ends.

Remember, the US has moved from an agrarian economy to a manufacturing-dominated one, to a service-dominated economy all within 150 years or so. That is incredibly fast! One might think such sweeping changes would cause huge dislocation and pain. Yet throughout that time (most of it, anyway), the populace enjoyed rising standards of living and high rates of employment. Capitalism at work.

CHAPTER INSIGHTS

Risk is an abstract concept we often fail to quantify properly.

- There is a difference between risk and uncertainty: A risk is a quantifiable or known variable. Uncertainty can't be quantified.
- Standard measures of risk like beta and Sharpe ratios can only measure risk relative to other stocks, which means they do a poor job of taking into account the risk of the system itself.
  - Comparing risk between asset classes like stocks and bonds is difficult and often not quantifiable.

In troubled times, like severe bear markets, risk seems to be different than normal circumstances. But risk is no different than any other epoch. Fear-driven behavior is prevalent in these times, but the best thing to do is not to change strategy.

- Every bear market is followed by a bull.
- A good investing strategy is sometimes wrong. Don't abandon it just because it failed once.
- Bear markets are rarer than bulls.
  - The right way to be wrong in a bear market is to stay in the market and not panic sell if the downdraft has already happened.
  - To get a true bear market, there must be a negative fundamental event that will take the market by surprise. That is, not priced in.
  - Bubbles and panics are polar ends of the same homogeneous, irrational psychology.
  - During or shortly after every bear market, CEOs and other business executives become scapegoats for investors shunning regret from their investment losses.
- Capitalism is amazingly adaptive. Bear markets and market cycles generally represent an important part of capitalism's work of creating efficiency and stronger economies and markets over time.

PARTING THOUGHTS

Renowned businessman and statistician Roger W. Babson published the first edition of *Business Barometers Used in the Management of Business and Investment of Money: A Textbook on the Applied Economics of Merchants, Bankers, and Investors* in 1909. (What a title!)

The book had many editions throughout his life, and in the version updated December 1929 (shortly after the market crash), Babson wrote a new preface. He begins with the disclaimer, "Fundamental Principles which readers of this book should always keep in mind." Babson contends anyone can successfully forecast the stock market if they have two things:

1. "One must develop self-control, both to refrain from attempting to profit by the monthly fluctuations, which 95 percent of the people endeavor to follow, and to act quickly and take advantage of the major movements, which 95 percent of the people fail to profit by, either because they are infatuated with prosperity or scared by panic or depression."
2. "One must develop patience, and remember that it takes years to build up a fortune in this way, and that it is an especially slow process at first . . . ."

Those two small quotes tell the tale of *20/20 Money* perfectly. It is amazing and appropriate the lessons of this book were known so long ago—merely in different words. Absent the fancy lingo and theories in this book, Babson understood intuitively the power of self-control and utilizing the right way to view the world—which too often is contrary to how "95 percent of the people" will act, in his words.

Like we saw throughout this book, the best wisdom about investing and markets is repeated over and over again in new ways—updated and restated for new generations. But no matter the words, the wisdom remains the same.

Later in the preface, Babson writes, "We who study fundamental conditions and act in accordance with what they teach, will both perform a distinct service to our country and slowly but surely create for our institutions and ourselves huge fortunes."

I believe that is true and well worth the endeavor.

Through all this talk about brains, psychology, math, science, complex systems, and more, it ultimately comes down to self-knowledge and patience. We often find the deepest intellectual journeys lead us back to the simplest truths; that the further we explore, the more we come back to the same common wisdom. Much of this book has been that way, and I believe there is great value in that. It's through the travails of learning and thinking that we get those basic lessons into our bones and are able to really adhere to them with discipline.

I hope this book has offered you a few new ways to see your own investments, and I wish you luck in the journey.

NOTES

CHAPTER 1: INVESTING IS A SCIENCE

1. Daniel Kahneman, "Two Big Things Happening in Psychology Today," *Edge Editions*, no. 262 (October 2008).
2. Francis Bacon, *Novum Organum* (Open Court Publishing Company, 1994).
3. Ken Fisher, *The Only Three Questions That Count* (Hoboken: John Wiley & Sons, 2007), 16.
4. Charles S. Peirce, *The Essential Peirce: Selected Philosophical Writings 1893–1913* (Indiana University Press, 1998), CP 5.9.
5. George Lakoff and Rafael Nunez, *Where Mathematics Comes From: How the Embodied Mind Brings Mathematics Into Being* (Basic Books, 2001), XI.

CHAPTER 2: INVESTING IS A DISCIPLINE

1. According to Standard & Poor's Indices versus Active Funds Scorecard (SPVIA). The SPIVA Scorecard shows that for the five-year period through June 30, 2008, the S&P 500 outperformed 68.6 percent of actively managed large-cap funds, the S&P MidCap 400 outperformed 75.9 percent of actively managed mid-cap funds, and the S&P SmallCap 600 outperformed 77.8 percent of actively managed small-cap funds. Results were similar within the international arena. Among global equity funds, five-year results show the S&P Global 1200 outperforming 70.1 percent of global equity funds, the S&P International 700 outperforming 86.5 percent of international equity funds, and S&P IFCI Composite outperforming 73.9 percent of emerging-market funds. Source: Reuters, 11/13/2008, http://www.reuters.com/article/pressRelease/idUS183834+13-Nov-2008+PRN20081113.
2. Andrew Newberg and Mark Waldman, *Why We Believe What We Believe: Uncovering Our Biological Need for Meaning, Spirituality, and Truth* (Free Press, 2006), 253.

3. David Chalmers, *The Conscious Mind: In Search of a Fundamental Theory* (Oxford University Press, 1997).
4. Steven Pinker, *How the Mind Works* (W.W. Norton & Company, 1999), 295.
5. Ibid.
6. See Note 3, 55.
7. Steven Pinker, *The Language Instinct: How the Mind Creates Language* (Harper Perennial Modern Classics, 2007), 257.

CHAPTER 3: HUMAN BEHAVIOR

1. Steven Pinker, *How the Mind Works* (W.W. Norton & Company, 1999), 424.
2. Marvin Minsky, *The Emotion Machine: Commonsense Thinking, Artificial Intelligence, and the Future of the Human Mind* (Simon & Schuster, 2007), 6.
3. From the Quantitative Analysis of Investor Behavior study, originally conducted by Dalbar, Inc. in April 1994, using data from Ibbotson Associates, Inc. Investors' decision making is quantified by analyzing cash flows in and out of mutual funds, tracks the nature and timing of investor behavior, and calculates their respective returns. The study measures average investors' success in self-directed investment performance and shows the average investor falls far short of fund returns, attempting to time the market.
4. Marco Iacoboni, *Mirroring People: The New Science of How We Connect with Others* (Farrar, Straus, and Giroux, 2008), 152.
5. Eric Kandel, *In Search of Memory: The Emergence of a New Science of Mind* (W.W. Norton, 2007), 316.
6. Marcel Proust, *Remembrance of Things Past* (Wordsworth Editions Ltd, 2006), 214.
7. Andrew Newberg and Mark Waldman, *Why We Believe What We Believe: Uncovering Our Biological Need for Meaning, Spirituality, and Truth* (Free Press, 2006), 255.
8. Ken Fisher, *The Only Three Questions That Count* (Hoboken: John Wiley & Sons, 2007), 15.

CHAPTER 4: SENTIMENT AND THE MEDIA

1. George Lakoff and Mark Johnson, *Metaphors We Live By* (University of Chicago Press, 1980), 90.

2. Ibid., 34.
3. Ibid., 257.

CHAPTER 5: HOW STOCK MARKETS REALLY WORK

1. Adam Smith and Alan Krueger, *The Wealth of Nations* (Bantam Classics, 2003), 477.
2. Joseph Schumpeter, *Capitalism, Socialism, and Democracy* (Allen & Unwin, 1952), 83.
3. F. A. Hayek, *The Counter-Revolution of Science* (Liberty Fund Inc, 1980), 113.
4. Milton Friedman, *Capitalism and Freedom* (University of Chicago Press, 2002), 15.
5. Technically, these are examples of complex, adaptive systems that display emergent behavior, but for the sake of clarity I have wrapped into one more useful acronym to describe markets and economies.
6. Elena Argentesi, Helmut Lukepohl, and Massimo Motta, "Acquisition of Information and Share Prices: An Empirical Investigation of Cognitive Dissonance," (March 23, 2005), http://www.iue.it/Personal/Motta/Papers/informationstock1Sep2006.pdf (accessed December 16, 2008). Additionally, a succinct summary of the study and its findings can be found in the January 5, 2007 article from CXO Advisory Group, "More Information is Better, Isn't It?" http://www.cxoadvisory.com/blog/external/blog1-05-07.
7. Ken Fisher and Meir Statman, "Sentiment, Value, and Market-Timing," *Financial Analysts Journal* (Fall 2004).

CHAPTER 6: FORECASTING, PART 1—THE PRINCIPLE OF PROBABILITY

1. "Commentary: Buffett's Career a Battle of Greed vs. Principles," *CNN.com* (October 20, 2008), http://www.cnn.com/2008/POLITICS/10/17/schroeder.buffett/index.html (accessed December 16, 2008).

CHAPTER 7: FORECASTING, PART 2—RECOGNIZING PATTERNS

1. Ken Fisher, *The Only Three Questions That Count* (Hoboken: John Wiley & Sons), 23.

SELECTED BIBLIOGRAPHY
AND FURTHER READING

For your perusal, a (rather lengthy) selected bibliography that also may serve as a guide for further reading. *20/20 Money* has a decidedly interdisciplinary approach—it's psychology, mathematics, systems theory, science, to name a few. So the list is long and various—more like a chronicle of influential books I have come across and that inform the views of this book. Some books will have apparently little to do with investing and markets; some deal with it directly. Some are esoteric, turgid research papers, others accessible, lighthearted discourses. However, anything directly referenced in the book can be found here.

Part of the intended lesson of *20/20 Money* is to break conventional categories and see things differently. Thus, these books are not categorized by topic but merely organized alphabetically. I invite you to make the associations. A book on neuroscience might directly follow a study on the method of weather forecasting, or a book about narrative composition might be juxtaposed with a philosophical discourse on logic. And so on. The point is to not only study the topics that can make you a better investor, but also conjure new connections and associations we otherwise wouldn't think of.

Diane Ackerman, *An Alchemy of Mind: The Marvel and Mystery of the Brain* (New York: Scribner Press, 2004).

Nancy Andreasen, *The Creative Brain* (New York: Penguin Press, 2005).

Karen Armstrong, *A History of God* (New York: Gramercy Books, 1993).

Rudolf Arnheim, *Visual Thinking* (Berkeley: University of California Press, 1969).

Erich Auerbach, *Mimesis: The Representation of Reality in Western Literature* (Princeton: Princeton UP, 1953).

Roger Babson, *Business Barometers for Anticipating Conditions* (New York: Cosimo Classics, 2006).

Francis Bacon, *New Organum* (New York: New World Library, 1996).

Eric D. Beinhocker, *The Origin of Wealth: Evolution, Complexity, and the Radical Remaking of Economics* (Harvard Press, 2007).

Simon Blackburn, *Being Good* (Oxford: Oxford UP, 2001).

—, *Think* (Oxford: Oxford UP, 1996).

Susan Blackmore, *Consciousness: An Introduction* (Oxford: Oxford UP, 2004).

David Bohm, *On Creativity* (London: Routlage Classic, 1996).

—, *On Dialogue* (London: Routlage Classics, 1996).

Susan Bordo, *The Flight to Objectivity: Essays on Cartesianism and Culture* (New York: State University of New York Press, 1987).

Donald Brown, *Human Universals* (Boston: McGraw Hill, 1991).

David J. Buller, *Adapting Minds* (Cambridge: MIT Press, 2006).

F. Capra, *The Web of Life: A New Scientific Understanding of Living Systems* (New York: Anchor Books, 1996).

—, *The Hidden Connections* (New York: Anchor Books, 2002).

Joseph Campbell, *The Hero with a Thousand Faces* (Princeton: Princeton UP, 1949).

David Chalmers, *The Conscious Mind* (New York: Oxford UP, 1996).

Noam Chomsky, *On Nature and Language* (Cambridge: Cambridge UP, 1996).

Henry J. Coleman, Jr., "What Enables Self-Organizing Behavior in Business?" *Emergence* 1, no. 1 (1999), 33–48.

Joseph Coppin and Elizabeth Nelson, *The Art of Inquiry* (Putnam: Spring Publications, 2005).

A. Cowles, "Can Stock Market Forecasters forecast?" *Econometrica* 12 (1933), 206–14.

Francis Crick, *The Astonishing Hypothesis* (New York: Simon and Schuster, 1994).

Antonio Damasio, *Looking for Spinoza: Joy, Sorrow, and the Feeling Brain* (Orlando: Harvest Books, 2003).

Morton D. Davis, *Game Theory: A Nontechnical Introduction* (New York: Dover Publications, 1983).

Richard Dawkins, *The Ancestor's Tale* (New York: Houghton Mifflin, 1994).

—, *The Extended Phenotype: The Long Reach of the Gene* (New York and Oxford: Oxford University Press, 1982).

—, *The Selfish Gene* (Oxford: Oxford UP, 1976).

Miguel De Landa, *A Thousand Years of Nonlinear History* (New York: Zone Books, Swerve Editions, 1997).

Daniel Dennett, *Brainchildren: Essays on Designing Minds* (Cambridge: MIT Press, 1998).

—, *Consciousness Explained* (New York: Time Warner Books, 1991).

Guy Deutscher, *The Unfolding of Language* (New York: Henry Holt and Co., 2005).

Elroy Dimson, Paul Marsh, and Mike Staunton, *Triumph of the Optimists: 101 Years of Global Investment Returns* (Princeton, Princeton UP: 2002).

Norman Doidge, *The Brain that Changes Itself* (New York: Viking Press, 2007).

George B. Dyson, *Darwin Among the Machines: The Evolution of Global Intelligence* (New York and Menlo Park: Addison Wesley, 1997).

Gerald Edelman and Giulio Tononi, *A Universe of Consciousness: How Matter Becomes Imagination* (New York: Basic Books, 2000).

Barbara Ehrenreich, *Blood Rites: Origins and History of the Passions of War* (New York: Henry Holt and Company, 1997).

—, *Dancing in the Streets: A History of Collective Joy* (New York: Henry Holt and Company, 2006).

Albert Einstein, *The World As I See It* (Filiquarian Publishing, LLC, 2007).

—, *Ideas and Opinions* (Three Rivers Press, 1995).

James Fallows, *Breaking the News: How the Media Undermine American Democracy* (New York: Vintage, 1997).

E.F. Fama, *Random Walks in Stock Market Prices: Selected Papers* (Chicago: University of Chicago Press, 1965).

Les Fehmi and Jim Robbins, *The Open Focus Brain* (Boston: Trumpeter, 2007).

Ken Fisher. *The Only Three Questions That Count: Investing By Knowing What Others Don't* (New York: John Wiley & Sons, 2007).

Milton Friedman, *Capitalism and Freedom: Fortieth Anniversary Edition* (Chicago: University of Chicago Press, 2002).

David Galeson, *Old Masters and Young Geniuses: The Two Life Cycles of Artistic Creativity* (Princeton, Princeton UP, 2006).

Howard Gardner, *Intelligence Reframed* (New York: Basic Books, 1999).

Murray Gellman, *The Quark and the Jaguar: Adventures in the Simple and the Complex* (New York: W.H. Freeman and Co., 1994).

James Gleick, *Chaos: The Making of a New Science* (New York: Penguin Books, 1987).

Eugene Goblet d'Alviella, *Symbols: Their Migration and Universality* (Mineola: Dover Publications, 2000).

Daniel Goleman, *Emotional Intelligence* (New York: Bantam Books, 1995).

—, *Social Intelligence* (New York: Bantam Books, 2006).

Deborah Gordon. *Ants at Work: How an Insect Society Is Organized* (New York: Free Press, 1999).

Jonathan Gottschall and David Sloan Wilson, Ed., *The Literary Animal: Evolution and the Nature of Narrative* (Evanston: Northwestern UP, 2005).

Stephen Jay Gould, *Full House: The Spread of Excellence from Plato to Darwin* (New York, Harmony Books, 1996).

—, *The Hedgehog, the Fox, and the Magister's Pox: Mending the Gap Between Science and the Humanities* (New York: Three Rivers Press, 2004).

Stanley Greenspan and Stuart Shanker, *The First Idea: How Symbols, Language, and Intelligence Evolved From Our Primate Ancestors to Modern Humans* (New York: Da Capo Press, 2004).

Benjamin Graham, *The Intelligent Investor* (New York: Harper Business, 1973).

Stephen Halliwell, *Aristotle's Poetics* (Chicago: University of Chicago Press, 1998).

Friedrich Hayek, *Individualism and Economic Order* (Chicago: University of Chicago Press, 1996).

—, *The Counter-Revolution of Science* (New York: The Liberty Fund, 1980).

P. Halpern, *The Pursuit of Destiny: A History of Prediction* (Cambridge: Perseus Press, 2000).

David Herman, Ed., *Narrative Theory and the Cognitive Sciences* (Palo Alto: CSLI Publications, 2003).

Richard Heuer, Jr., The *Psychology of Intelligence Analysis* (New York: Novinka Books, 2006).

James Hillman, *Archetypal Psychology* (Putnam: Spring Publications, 2004).

Eric Hoffer, *The True Believer* (New York: Perennial, 1951).

Douglas Hofstadter, *I Am a Strange Loop* (New York: Basic Books, 2007).

Douglas Hofstadter and Daniel Dennett, *The Mind's I* (New York: Basic Books, 1981).

John H. Holland, *Emergence: From Chaos to Order* (Reading: Helix, 1998).

Lewis Hyde, *Trickster Makes This World* (New York: North Point Press, 1999).

Marco Iacoboni, *Mirroring People: The New Science of How We Connect with Others* (New York: Farrar, Straus, and Giroux, 2008).

William James, *The Varieties of Religious Experience* (New York: Barnes and Noble Classics, 2004).

Julian Jaynes, *The Origin of Consciousness in the Breakdown of the Bicameral Mind* (Boston: Mariner Books, 2000).

Steven Johnson, Emergence: *The Connected Lives of Ants, Brains, Cities, and Software* (New York: Scribner, 2002).

—, *Interface Culture: How Technology Transforms the Way We Create and Communicate* (San Francisco: Harper Edge, 1997).

C.G. Jung, *Man and His Symbols* (New York: Dell Publishing, 1964).

Eric Kandel, *In Search of Memory: The Emergence of a New Science of Mind* (New York: W.W. Norton, 2005).

Michael and Ellen Kaplan, *Chances Are . . . Adventures in Probability* (New York: Viking Press, 2006).

Kasparov, Garry, *How Life Imitates Chess: Making the Right Moves, from the Board to the Boardroom* (New York: Bloomsbury USA, 2008).

Stuart Kauffman, *At Home in the Universe: The Search for the Laws of Self-Organization and Complexity* (New York and Oxford: Oxford UP, 1995).

J.A. Scott Kelso, *Dynamic Patterns: The Self-Organization of Brain and Behavior* (London and Cambridge: MIT Press, 1999).

J.M. Keynes, "The General Theory of Employment," *Quarterly Journal of Economics* 51 (1937), 209–23.

Paul Krugman, *The Self-Organizing Economy* (Oxford: Blackwell Publishers, 1996).

Thomas Kuhn, *The Structure of Scientific Revolutions* (Chicago: The University of Chicago Press, 1962).

Ray Kurzweil, *The Singularity Is Near: When Humans Transcend Biology* (New York: Penguin Books, 2006).

George Lakoff and Mark Johnson, *Metaphors We Live By* (Chicago: University of Chicago Press, 1980).

—, *Philosophy in the Flesh: The Embodied Mind and its Challenge to Western Thought* (New York: Basic Books, 1999).

—, Rafael Nunez, *Where Mathematics Comes From: How the Embodied Mind Brings Mathematics into Being* (New York: Basic Books, 2000).

—, Mark Turner, *More Than Cool Reason: A Field Guide to Poetic Metaphor* (Chicago: University of Chicago Press, 1989).

Jonah Lehrer, *Proust Was a Neuroscientist* (Boston: Houghton Mifflin, 2007).

Thomas Lewis, *Fari Amini and Richard Lannon, A General Theory of Love* (New York: Random House, 2000).

G.C. Loomes, "Probabilities versus Money: A Test of Some Fundamental Assumptions About Rational Decision Making," *Economic Journal* 108 (1998), 477–89.

T. Lux and M. Marchesi, "Scaling and Criticality in a Stochastic Multi-Agent Model of a Financial Market," *Nature* 397, 498–500.

B. Malkiel, *A Random Walk Down Wall Street* (New York: W. W. Norton Company, 1999).

J. Magolis, *A Brief History of Tomorrow* (London: Bloomsbury, 1997).

B. Mandelbrot and R.L. Hudson, *The (Mis)behavior of Markets: A Fractal View of Risk, Ruin and Reward* (New York: Basic Books, 2004).

J.L. McCauley, *Dynamics of Markets: Econophysics and Finance* (Cambridge: Cambridge UP, 2004).

James McConkey, Ed., *The Anatomy of Memory: An Anthology* (New York: Oxford UP, 1996).

Robert McKee, *Story* (New York: HarperCollins, 1997).

R.R. McKitrick, "The Econometric Critique of Applied General Equilibrium Modeling: The Role of Functional Forms," *Economic Modeling* 15, 543–73.

M. Midgley, *Evolution As a Religion: Strange Hopes and Stranger Fears* (London: Methuen, 1985).

Marvin Minsky, *The Emotion Machine* (New York: Simon and Schuster, 2006).

—, *The Society of Mind* (New York: Simon and Schuster, 1985).

Read Montague, *Why Choose This Book? How We Make Decisions* (New York: Penguin Books, 2006).

Jacob Needleman, *Why Can't We Be Good?* (New York: Penguin Books, 2007).

Erich Neumann and F.C. Hull, Trans., *The Origins and History of Consciousness* (Princeton: Princeton UP, 1993).

Andrew Newberg and Mark Waldman, *Why We Believe What We Believe: Uncovering Our Biological Need for Meaning, Spirituality, and Truth* (New York: Simon and Schuster, 2006).

P. Ormerod, *The Death of Economics* (New York: John Wiley & Sons, 1997).

David Orrell, *The Future of Everything: The Science of Prediction, From Wealth and Weather to Chaos and Complexity* (New York: Thunder's Mouth Press, 2007).

Charles S. Peirce and Christian J. W. Kloesel, Eds., *The Essential Peirce: Selected Philosophical Writings* (1867–1893) (Bloomington, IN: Indiana University Press, 1992).

Stephen Pinker, *The Language Instinct* (New York: Harper Collins, 1994).

—, *How the Mind Works* (New York: W.W. Norton Company, 1997).

—, *The Blank Slate: The Modern Denial of Human Nature* (New York: Penguin, 2002).

—, *Words and Rules: The Ingredients of Language* (New York: Perennial, 1999).

Christopher Gill and Desmond Lee, Trans., *The Symposium* (New York: Penguin Books, 2006).

—, Christopher Gill Plato and G.M. Grube, Trans., *The Trial of Socrates* (Indianapolis: Hackett Publishing Co., 2000).

K.R. Popper, *The Poverty of Historicism* (Boston: Beacon Press, 1957).

Ilya Prigogine and G. Nicolis, *Exploring Complexity* (New York: W.H. Freeman, 1989).

Marcel Proust, *Remembrance of Things Past* (New York: Modern Library, 2001).

Paul Radin, *The Trickster* (New York: Schocken Books, 1956).

Tristine Rainer, *Your Life As Story* (New York: Penguin Books, 1997).

Richard Rorty, *Philosophy and the Mirror of Nature* (Princeton: Princeton UP, 1981).

Douglas Rushkoff, *Media Virus! Hidden Agendas in Popular Culture* (New York: Ballantine Books, 1974).

Carl Sagan, *The Varieties of Scientific Experience* (New York: Penguin Press, 2006).

Joseph Schumpeter, *Capitalism, Socialism, and Democracy* (New York: Harper and Brothers, 1942).

Jeffrey Schwartz and Sharon Begley, *The Mind and the Brain: Neuroplasticity and the Power of Mental Force* (New York: HarperCollins, 2002).

Andrew L. Shapiro, *The Control Revolution: How the Internet Is Putting Individuals in Charge and Changing the World We Know* (New York: Century Foundation Books, 1999).

Leonard Shlan, *The Alphabet Versus the Goddess: The Conflict Between Word and Image* (New York: Penguin Press, 1998).

Adam Smith, *An Inquiry into the Nature and Causes of the Wealth of Nations: A Selected Edition* (Oxford: Oxford University Press, 2008).

Claude Steiner, *Scripts People Live* (New York: Grove Press, 1974).

Mark Turner, *The Literary Mind: The Origins of Thought and Language* (Oxford: Oxford UP, 1996).

Josh Waitzkin, *The Art of Learning* (New York: Free Press, 2007).

Mitchell M. Waldrop, *Complexity: The Emerging Science at the Edge of Order and Chaos* (New York and London: Simon and Schuster, 1992).

Alan Wallace, *The Attention Revolution: Unlocking the Power of the Focused Mind* (Somerville: Wisdom Books, 2004).

Chip Walter, *Thumbs, Toes, Tears and Other Traits that Make Us Human* (New York: Walter and Company, 2006).

Jude Wanniski, *The Way the World Works* (Gateway Editions, 1998).

Edward Wilson, *Concilience: The Unity of Knowledge* (New York: Random House, 1998).

M. Wood, *The Road to Delphi* (New York: Ferrar, Straus, and Giroux, 2003).

Adam Zeman, *Consciousness: A User's Guide* (New Haven: Yale UP, 2002).

Philip Zimbardo, *The Lucifer Effect: Understanding How Good People Turn Evil* (New York: Random House, 2007).

—, John Boyd, *The Time Paradox: The New Psychology of Time that Will Change Your Life* (New York: Free Press, 2008).

Lisa Zunshine, *Why We Read Fiction: Theory of Mind and the Novel* (Columbus: Ohio State UP, 2006).

ABOUT THE AUTHOR

Michael J. Hanson (San Francisco, California) has been an investment banker, a stock analyst, and a lecturer at the University of California, Berkeley on topics in Money Management. He is also currently a senior editor and columnist at Fisher Investments' MarketMinder.com. Michael wrote his first book at age 20, and his essays and interviews have appeared in numerous publications since. This is his fourth book. He speaks regularly throughout the country on a variety of topics including capital markets, behavioral finance, psychology, and mythology. Michael completed undergraduate coursework in Economics with a minor in Leadership at Claremont McKenna College and holds a masters degree in Mythological Studies with an emphasis in Depth Psychology at Pacifica Graduate Institute. He is currently a doctoral candidate in the same field at Pacifica and lives in San Francisco.

INDEX